Y0-BTB-723

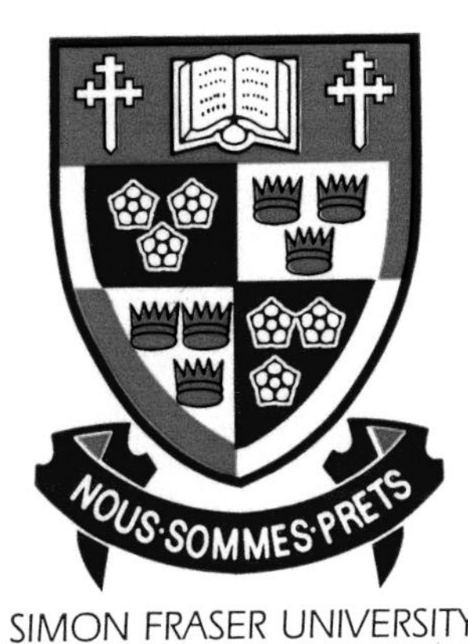
NOUS·SOMMES·PRETS

Regional Security Structures in Asia

This book argues that explanations of international relations in Asia in the post-Second World War period have relied too much on the Cold War as a key explanatory factor, and have not given enough emphasis to the useful concepts of 'regional power formation', 'conflict formation' and 'conflict resolution'. The author outlines these concepts and goes on to elaborate them, and to apply them to three key Asian regions – North East, South East and South Asia – discussing practical strategic issues in a historical perspective and arguing that the concepts, and other concepts which he discusses, are extremely helpful in making sense of the complex pattern of international relations in Asia.

Ashok Kapur discusses the work of a wide range of scholars, considers factors including economic interdependence, competitive nationalism and sub-nationalism, national states and the impact of their domestic agendas, and links to global superpowers. He explores a wide variety of concepts, including, besides those mentioned above, 'balance of power', 'bipolarity' and 'multipolarity', and 'global hegemony' and 'regional hegemony', to establish a coherent system of international relations which explains developments in Asia.

Ashok Kapur is Professor and Chair of Political Science at the University of Waterloo, Ontario. He is the author of several books on South Asian nuclear policies, South Asian international relations, most recently, *Pokhran and Beyond: Indian Nuclear Behavior* (2001) and *India and the United States in a Changing World* (co-editor, 2002).

Regional Security Structures in Asia

Ashok Kapur

LONDON AND NEW YORK

First published 2003 by RoutledgeCurzon
11 New Fetter Lane, London EC4P 4EE

Simultaneously published in the USA and Canada
by RoutledgeCurzon
29 West 35th Street, New York, NY 10001

RoutledgeCurzon is an imprint of the Taylor & Francis Group

Typeset in Times by M Rules
Printed and bound in Great Britain by
Antony Rowe Ltd, Chippenham, Wiltshire

British Library Cataloguing in Publication Data
A catalogue record for this book is available from the British Library

Library of Congress Cataloging in Publication Data
A catalog record for this book has been requested

ISBN 0-7007-1616-5

Contents

Figures

Maps

Tables

Acknowledgements

This study was made possible by the support of the Social Sciences and Humanities Research Council of Canada. This award enabled me to do the fieldwork in different sites in Asia–Pacific.

A number of individuals and organizations facilitated the preparation of this work. The Canadian Department of Foreign Affairs was most helpful in organizing my interviews with academic and official practitioners in Tokyo, Seoul, Taipei and Singapore, and officials in the Ottawa headquarters shared their time and expertise on a variety of policy questions. In Canberra, Mrs Tonia Shand, then Chief of Protocol, Department of Foreign Affairs, and Professor Rick Shand, Australian National University were gracious hosts and opened many doors to high level experts in the Department. In New Delhi, Professor M.L. Sondhi, was most helpful in arranging meetings with knowledgeable experts, and as always, the members of the Indian Ministry of External Affairs provided valuable background information. These individuals and organizations carry no responsibility for the contents of this book. That is solely mine.

Three individuals helped me with the timely completion of this book. Michael Alandu was a most capable research assistant, and Joan Hatton cheerfully and effectively deciphered my handwritten notes and prepared the various drafts of this work under considerable pressure of time. Marta Nestaiko skilfully prepared the maps.

Finally, I thank Peter Sowden, commissioning editor at RoutledgeCurzon, for encouraging me to write on Asia–Pacific. I am grateful also to the anonymous reviewer for the helpful comments and suggestions.

1 Introduction

This book argues that explanations of international relations in Asia in the post-Second World War period have relied too much on the Cold War and bipolarity as key explanatory factors and have not given enough emphasis to the useful concepts of 'regional power formation', 'conflict formation' and 'conflict resolution'. The book outlines these concepts, which were originally formulated by Vayrynen and goes on to elaborate them, and to apply them to three key Asian regions – North East, South East and South Asia – arguing that the concepts are extremely helpful in making sense of the complex pattern of international relations in Asia. I discuss the work of a wide range of scholars, consider factors including economic globalization, competitive nationalism and sub-nationalism, national states and the impact of their domestic agendas, and links to global superpowers, and explore a wide variety of concepts, including 'balance of power', 'bipolarity' and 'multipolarity', and 'global hegemony' and 'regional hegemony', to establish a coherent system of international relations which explains developments in Asia.

With a few exceptions, North American studies of South Asian (1947–present) and North Asian (1945–present) international relations are inaccurate and misleading. They do not explain the pattern of change that shows 'regional power formation', 'conflict formation' and 'conflict resolution' – powerful concepts, in international relations in these regions – in a historical perspective. A major reason for the errors of commission and omission in scholarly work lies in the negative influence of the Cold War on scholarship. Gunnar Myrdal, a world-renowned scholar in developmental economics and international politics makes the point that the scholarly profession has made an accommodation with 'political realism' and the narrow strategic interests of a state or a bloc of states. To quote him:

> the most perceptible political influence on the research approach in Western countries to the problems of South Asian countries is the predominant role given to considerations of national power and international power relations. In a world full of perils to national security and survival, this tendency is understandable; it is often asserted to be a more realistic direction of social research. The implication is, however,

> that studies of the problems of underdeveloped countries are now undertaken, not with a view to the universal and timeless values that are our legacy from the Enlightenment, but with a view to the fortuitous and narrow political or, narrower still, military-strategic interests of one state or bloc of states. All sorts of studies are now justified by, or focussed on, their contribution to the 'security' of Western countries. This officious accommodation by the scholarly profession to a new political 'realism' in research often borders on the ridiculous.[1]

Myrdal cites the American novelist Robert Wright as follows:

> I state that emotion here precedes the idea, that attitudes select the kind of ideas in question . . . We are human; we are the slaves of our assumptions, of time and circumstances, we are the victims of our passions and illusions, and . . . our critics can ask of us . . . Have you taken your passions, your illusions, your time, and your circumstances into account? This is what I am attempting to do.
>
> A social scientist should not be less humble and assume that he is purely 'factual and objective'. He cannot, in any case, escape valuations, as he needs explicit, or implicit, value premises even to ascertain the facts.[2]

From Myrdal and Wright, I propose to argue that (i) American scholarship in particular, is biased by US national 'interests' and national security considerations; (ii) due diligence is needed on our part in making scholarly biases transparent; and finally (iii) the search for theory requires the following research procedure.

Emotions ➔	Definition of ➔ Research Questions	Search and ➔ Organization of Empirical Materials or Data	Explanation(s)

The work relies on R. Vayrynen's theory of 'regional conflict formation' and then it extends it.[3] Vayrynen argues that shifts in distribution of international power create new centres of growth and conflict in regions. Two processes are at work: fragmentation and order. Thus, we have regional power formation as well as conflict formation: and regional powers create boundaries/barriers in the flow of economic and military power from the international powers (e.g. USA) to the regions, and secondly, the interactions within the regions increase parallel to the decrease in the flow of international power. In my judgement these changes lead to conflict formation (CF) and are the basis of conflict resolution (CR). The notion of CR is known in the literature (e.g. there is a *Journal of Conflict Resolution*). However, the factors and processes that explain the shifts from 'chaos' to 'conflict formation' and 'regional power formation', and from 'conflict formation' to 'conflict resolution' are not well understood. My task is to do so in the three conflict zones and to create a foundation for further comparative work (i.e. Middle East, Ukraine and Central Europe). Note that Vayrynen does not assess the factors and processes underlying these shifts, but he lays this foundation for such an understanding.

This project is meant to be innovative in approach in outlining the pattern of change and structure of the three regions in a historical way. But the project is not history. The approach is conceptual and analytical using data in a historical perspective with a view to explaining current realities. It is expected to advance Asian studies and to sharpen the value of studying regional structures in a multipolar world. The work also has social value as it enables us to think about strategies to shift from conflict formation to resolution.

Since 1945, the distribution of power has shifted in the world. The international and regional structures are in one way crystallizing, but in another way they are fragmenting. Instead of thinking of the world as a continuity where power travels from one or more international centres or blocs throughout the international system, it makes sense to study the discontinuities in the flow of power from the Major Powers (who have dominated the international system in the past) to the regions or sub-regions in Asia–Pacific (i.e. from the 'Dominant' to the 'subordinate' spheres[4]); to examine the discontinuities between regions, and finally examine the continuities or linkages in the organization of 'pattern of power' or pattern of alignments[5] within regions (sub-regions) in Asia–Pacific, and between neighbouring regions in these areas. In other words, our bias is to search out the continuity or durability of relationships (conflictual and/or friendly), within regions. This project critiques and then builds on major works. The task is to explain the characteristics of three important regions in Asia–Pacific and in world politics: North Asia, South and South East Asia and the major geo-political pivots which dominate the Asian strategic landscape.

The project seeks to broaden and deepen our understanding of inter-state conflict and its management in three high-risk conflict zones where the cold wars are not over. The issues are complex and controversial, the policy and academic audiences are diverse and difficult, with highly charged policy and academic agendas, and great analytical skill is needed to explain the patterns and trends of the three regions in a historical and a comparative way.

Generally, North American studies take a 'top–down' approach, looking at regions in the context of the structure of the international system and Western policies that were shaped by a view that world politics or international relations was primarily or entirely a story that was shaped by the Cold War and bipolar experiences and attitudes. I propose a 'bottoms–up' approach that stresses regional and domestic dynamics and multipolarity in the distribution of power/influence at both levels; and of course, consider the international influences in regional affairs. Understanding the historical dynamics of shifts towards conflict resolution in these regions will build a bridge between security and area specialists, between academic and policy studies and between strategic and peace studies. These regions have many interesting cases to test the shifts: e.g. US–North Korea, China–India, India–Pakistan, USA–Japan; PRC–Japan; North and South Korea. 'Security' here does not have a narrow military meaning; it entails consideration of military, economic and cultural/ideological issues in the context of several regional security complexes.[6]

The book evaluates the characteristics and the contexts (international, regional and domestic) as well as the strategies and processes which create conflict formation and conflict resolution in the regions.

Appendix A lists the attributes to be searched in defining the characteristics of the regional power/security structures. During the Cold War, the South Asian region referred to the international relations of India, Pakistan, the smaller South Asian states and the great powers. Today, South Asia has a broadened geographical and strategic focus. It refers to the policies and relationships of India and Pakistan as well as countries in the neighbourhood, i.e. China, Iran, Myanmar and the USA. New strategic and economic issues and relationships (e.g. India–Iran–Central Asian relationships; China–Myanmar–Bay of Bengal relationships, efforts to create a Bay of Bengal economic community that involves Thailand, Myanmar, India, Bangladesh and Sri Lanka (but excludes Pakistan) have eroded the traditional systemic boundaries. The role and influence of the superpowers has declined significantly in Asian regions (sub-regions). With Soviet Russia's changed status and with America's internal preoccupations and weaknesses, there is no external power that can continually confront and dominate China in Asia. Furthermore, local and regional (e.g. Sino-Indian, Sino-Japanese, inter-Korean and Taiwan–PRC) rivalries are more evident and less restrained by Cold War alignments. The China factor looms large in Asia–Pacific strategic and economic affairs. The flow of Chinese power, albeit in a circumscribed way, to different Asia–Pacific areas (especially North Korea, and the Korean peninsula, South China Seas, South East Asia, as a wedge between the Indian subcontinent and South East Asia through China's special relationship with Myanmar and, through its special relationship with Pakistan, to the Indian Ocean and the Persian Gulf/Central Asian region) provides an enhanced Chinese overlay to Asia–Pacific international relations. Of course, American naval and military power is strong in Asia, but doubts persist about the quality of American leadership in Asia despite its forceful action in Afghanistan in 2001. My study therefore, is based on the belief that Chinese and American power provides the overlay in Asian strategic affairs, but Russia, Japan and India are also players. In this context, multipolar power/security structures have formed in our regions, with varying degree of volatility and stability. What are the characteristics and case histories of regional structures? What sort of factors and circumstances led to shifts from chaos to conflict formation and conflict resolution in both regions? What are the causes and strategies that produce security/insecurity and stability/instability in regional international relations, and what are the lessons to be learnt from a study of regional actors' perspectives and behaviour?

In summary, my objectives are: (1) review and critique the intellectual orientations of Western literature on regional international politics; (2) demonstrate the utility of Vayrynen's and Buzan's work (with substantial modifications) by examples from three areas; (3) establish the characteristics of regional structures of Asian regions today and the dynamics and the causes of shifts from chaos to conflict formation to resolution in the three regions; (4) show the value of studying the regional sub-systems within the international system. By a systematic social science type analysis of regional norms and behaviour in these high-risk conflict regions, a huge gap in the literature will be filled by an in-depth historical and comparative study of conflict formation and conflict resolution in the regions.

Context: the orientation of the literature

There is a large body of literature dealing with Asian affairs, but there are no American or Canadian scholarly book-length studies that offer an integrated, historical and comparative analysis of the relationship between conflict formation and conflict resolution in these conflict zones; and regional structures that function in the context of global and regional multipolarity, and competitive inner-state and domestic policy constituencies are not usually studied.

The dominant intellectual orientation of Western regional security and international studies, especially the works by Cantori and Spiegel (dominant–subordinate relations and international politics of regions), Michael Haas and Michael Brecher (international sub-system definition), E. Haas (regime decay), S.M. Walt (regional alliance formation), W.R. Thompson (development and transformation of sub-systems), Barry Buzan (regional security complexes), Martin Wight (regional great powers and middle powers), and E. Haas (regional integration), were crafted in the context of the Cold War situation and superpower bipolarity. This body of literature projected the premise of great power dominance and small state subordination. (Martin Wight took the middle powers concept seriously but he did not develop it in his work.) The studies overestimated the importance of superpower influences in regional affairs and discounted regional power influences. The superpowers provided the overlay, so the overestimate was understandable although it was not farsighted. These studies are also vulnerable to Gunnar Myrdal's criticism that many Western scholars allowed the Western policy agenda(s) to affect their work.

This intellectual orientation requires a sustained critique to clear the background. Today, the international system and regions with acute social and military conflict are multipolar; regional powers have emerged and they are autonomous entities. Even small states and pariah regimes have access to modern arms and, given diplomatic skill, they can bargain with the superpowers (e.g. North Korea–USA). Although some specialists (e.g. Jonathan Pollack of Rand Corporation) speaks of USA's 'linchpin role' in Asia–Pacific, the emergent consensus among Western and Asian specialists suggests otherwise. A Chinese view argues that multipolarity existed during the Cold War; bipolarity led to mutual weakening of the superpowers; the US has lost its erstwhile superiority and 'division and realignment are continuing [and] the composition of the poles [of power] is unstable'.[7] The IISS Annual Survey (1994-5) and Paul Dibb, a senior specialist at the Australian National University doubt USA's linchpin role and project China's pivotal role in a post-hegemonic world. Soviet Russia's collapse shows how quickly the international structure of power can change. This has particular relevance for Asia–Pacific because the US-Soviet and Sino-Soviet rivalries of the Cold War have been replaced by the Sino-US competition and regional powers as well as small powers have gained bargaining opportunities.

Another dominant Western scholarly tradition is preoccupied with the development of an international and regional regime to control weapons of mass destruction and to gain regional security through unilateral and/or negotiated arms control, confidence-building and transparency between enemies. With the end of the Cold War, this tradition has gained ground; for instance, the Stockholm International Peace Research Institute and several major Western institutes are investing heavily in this policy agenda. This scholarly tradition is driven by US policy concerns in an area deemed vital for US security. Recently, the US Central Intelligence Agency established a unit 'The Weapons Intelligence, Non-Proliferation and Arms Control Center' that involves, according to press reports, about 500 analysts, scientists and support personnel to deal with these issues. The US government also announced plans to recruit intelligence agents from within the proliferating states in response to USA's intelligence failure with respect to India's 1974 and 1998 nuclear tests.[8] A clear convergence exists here between the US policy agenda and the non-proliferation work of many Western arms control specialists.

While the goals of peace, security and stability are laudable, the problem is that the policy agenda is driving the academic research agenda. By focusing on narrow, verified arms control and global regime enhancement measures, the academy loses sight of the characteristics of regional power and security structures in Asia that respond to local, parochial, informal arrangements and understandings and behaviour patterns rather than Western-style legal formalism and moralism that is inherent in any arms control agreement. Regional security architectures are built around regional histories and memories of conflict and in the context of domestic and international vetoes. Where are the vetoes, and who are the potential negotiating partners from among the domestic and external enemies of the key players? The arms controllers fail because they lack regional area expertise to discover the veto points and the limited but hidden cracks that contain the negotiating opportunities. The shifts from chaos to conflict formation and eventual resolution require orchestration of domestic bargains before these become inter-state bargains in regions of acute conflict. Likewise, domestic and inter-state bargaining or wiggle space opportunities must be assessed before deadly quarrels can be converted into ritual confrontations, and methods to manage and settle conflicts are developed and institutionalized. Arms controllers have neither the training nor the inclination to probe these connections. My task is to show the interdependency between domestic politics and inter-state relations in Asia. I call this 'systemic interdependency'. This differs from 'particular and changeable alignment(s), relationships of conflict or amity between states involved in regional affairs, which are durable, but not necessarily inevitable or permanent'. The latter is the focus of Buzan's work, while I stress the necessity of studying both.

I intend, however, to build on two Western scholarly traditions, and to modify and enlarge them substantially. Buzan's work on regional security complexes is pertinent but it has its defects. It was crafted when the superpowers and China provided the external overlay to regional affairs; today the structure and nature of the overlay is radically different. His regional systemic and geographical boundaries require redefinition: in the case of South Asia it requires inclusion of Iran, Central Asia and Myanmar/Bay of Bengal/eastern Indian Ocean; in the case of North Asia it requires inclusion of South China Seas and a greater emphasis on the link between Chinese policies in the South China Sea and Taiwan. Buzan is dismissive of multipolarity in South Asia. He prefers Indo-Pakistani bipolarity whereas the pattern of alignments, now and in the past, show military asymmetry since 1971 within the region, and a pentagonal set of alignments in the region and the neighbourhood; the end of the Cold War has enhanced the latter. Lastly Buzan employs the concept of 'security interdependency' but he fails to capture the total population of every such 'interdependency' in regional affairs. Despite these defects, I intend to push Buzan's notion of 'security interdependency(ies)' (defined as alignments) along with the distribution of power, to capture the variety and the history of such alignments in Asian regions, and to assess their influence in shaping multipolar regional structures. Care must be taken to interpret 'interdependency' as a situation where geographical neighbours or major and minor powers are tied together by interests and issues; i.e. they cannot be detached from, or indifferent to, the actions of others. For Martin Wight, an 'interdependency' such as between USA and Canada implies the absence of a rivalry (as distinct from a trade dispute) and the existence of a political settlement. Countries, however, are tied together by rivalries and competing interests, and here the pattern of behaviour may reflect a changing pattern of alignments – given the absence of a political settlement. Thus, the difference between Martin Wight and Barry Buzan definitions of 'interdependency' must be noted.

R. Vayrynen's work on 'regional conflict formation' and regional powers and structures is especially of use to me. He argues that shifts in the distribution of international power create new centres of growth and conflict. Fragmentation and order are both at work. The first produces discontinuities in international relations; the second creates boundaries among regions, produces sub-system formation, and lets regional power centres emerge. Of course, regions are affected by the global capitalist economy and by great power influences, but the issue concerns the nature, extent and limits in the flow of power/influence from the international system to the regional centres. If the external powers can manage regional conflict continuously, then the peripheries are integrated into the great power-dominated international system; otherwise, regional power centres and regional structures gain ground. The dominant Western scholarly tradition values and predicts regional outcomes in the first way; following Vayrynen's lead, I expect to explore the second outcome.

The book provides a new research direction by going beyond the following intellectual orientations. (1) The global economic interdependence paradigm emphasizes less status, reduced military and more multilateralist dimensions in international relations; here economic and political liberalization supposedly restrains armed conflict and power politics, or makes both redundant. (2) On the other hand the national power/security approach highlights statism, military force and power struggles and competitive nationalism (or sub-nationalism). (3) Finally, the post-hegemony (American, Japanese and Chinese in Asia–Pacific in the 20th century) approach requires and predicts the emergence of an Asia-wide balance of power. The first and the second paradigm emerged during the Cold War; the third comes from influential Australian scholarship. In a stimulating monograph Dibb[9] visualizes an equilibrium among five Asian powers (China, Japan, India, Russia and USA). He theorizes an Asian balance that will check the regional hegemonies. He also asserts the absence of Asian arms control and alliance activity (other than with the US) and sees a shift in the centre of gravity of power to North Asia. These contentions are examined in this work. 'Equilibrium' implies harmony or absence of friction among major and minor powers in Asia. My work assumes continuing rivalries and friction among the major and minor powers in Asia and balance of power activity is predicted on a situation either of 'manageable instability' or 'unmanageable instability' in Asia. Equilibrium requires a durable political settlement so that contentious issues involving vital interests and national prestige have been settled. Will Asian states move to the stage of equilibrium and conflict resolution or are they likely to remain in a situation of contention, friction, stable conflict formation and conflict management?

My framework differs significantly from current scholarship and yet it will build on it in an important way. The work is expected to inject realism about several scholarly traditions that have been outlined earlier. At the same time, we will learn more about the characteristics of three important regions (sub-regions) in the world.

The growth of the global economy and the value of multilateralism are undeniable but their implications are unclear. Armed conflict is restrained not simply by economic and political liberalization but often by developing a stable asymmetry in distribution of power and by development of policies which are calculated to use carrots and sticks to organize the relationships among major and minor powers. My work takes the minor powers (regional great powers, middle powers and small or local powers) seriously. Here the debt is to the work of Martin Wight. The emphasis on the role, policies, influences and strategies of minor powers in a regional and a multilateral context indicates value in the existence of a stability-oriented or a benign regional hegemony, a point which is unexplored in modern scholarship. Here I emphasize the ability of a regional hegemon to inflict punishment on a regional and an international rival, to cause a change in the distribution of power as well as the pattern of relationships by its ability to act alone, and to develop a process to achieve consent and restraint among rivals within a region. US practitioners are paranoid about 'regional hegemons' – US declassified foreign policy and strategy documents make this clear. The US Department of Defence took a negative view of 'regional hegemony'. To quote:

> Asia is an area of significant potential power – political, economic and military. The development in this region of stable and independent countries friendly to the United States and seeking to direct their potential power into constructive channels would enhance the security of Asia and strengthen the world position of the United States. Conversely, the domination of Asia by a nation or coalition of nations capable of exploiting the region for purposes of self-aggrandizement would threaten the security of Asia and of the United States. Recognition of these principles has been implicit in our traditional policies toward Asia: We have consistently favoured a system of independent states and opposed aggrandizement of any powers that threatened eventual domination of the region. (For the purposes of this report 'Asia' is defined as that part of the continent of Asia south of the USSR and east of Iran together with the major off-shore islands – Japan, Formosa, the Philippines, Indonesia and Ceylon.) . . . we must concurrently oppose the domination of Asia by any single country or coalition. It is conceivable that in the course of time a threat of domination may come from such nations as Japan, China, or India, or from an Asiatic bloc. But now and for the foreseeable future it is the USSR which threatens to dominate Asia through the complementary instruments of communist conspiracy and diplomatic pressure supported by military strength.[10]

Here the desirability of an Asian regional hegemon is questioned; the idea of a benign regional hegemony is rejected without just cause or public debate. American scholarship also reveals a blind spot about this issue: the possibility of the existence of a benign Asian hegemon is denied by an attitude of scholarly indifference.

My project presumes durability of competitive nationalism (sub-nationalism) and then introduces the central position of dyadic security linkages (defined as tied together by competing interests and rivalries) as nodal points of control of conflict within the regional structures. For example, the security linkages in South Asia are: US–Pakistan, US–India, India–Pakistan, China–Pakistan, China–India, India–Iran, China–Myanmar, India–Myanmar, Pakistan–Iran and Pakistan–Afghanistan. In North Asia they are US–Japan, US–Taiwan, US–PRC, PRC–Japan, Japan–two Koreas, US–two Koreas, PRC–Taiwan-South China Seas and PRC-two Koreas. In South East Asia, they involve ASEAN states. These linkages are the channels of strategic and economic discourse in the regions and they form a basis of the security architecture or structure of the regions. A regional hegemon(s) is present in each security cluster: India in the subcontinent and its neighbourhood; Vietnam and Indonesia in SE Asia; and China and Japan in North Asia. To the extent that they are a mature, outward-looking international force, and they seek negotiated restraint based on mutual interest and consent, the regional hegemons are benign. But if they are territorially expansionistic, they are malignant. Japan and India are benign hegemons. China is not and is widely believed by Asians to harbor expansionistic ambitions. However, China can function as a benign hegemon if it truly practises the principles of peaceful co-existence or if its use of coercive bargaining aims at a negotiated political settlement with its rivals.

These bilateral and associated linkages, if studied historically, are driven by parochial and regional considerations; they evolved without the stimulus of global interdependence. The linkages are both centres of conflict (moving from chaos to conflict-formation) and centres of conflict resolution where international inputs may help but not necessarily so. Each such locked-in region (sub-region) has evidence of regional power formation and regional conflict formation. My work examines the issue of stability in the context of regional structures and regional hegemons, in the absence of a great powers'–dominated Asian balance of power, and in the absence of integration of the regions into the global economy. I see regional hegemons pursuing two combined strategies: developing an asymmetrical distribution of military and economic power in relation to other essential players in the regional structure, and secondly, developing diplomatic linkages with rivals through formal and informal diplomatic, military and economic arrangements and issue-driven alliance activity. In other words, a necessary mix of both hegemonism and friction, and conflict management politics are at work in the development of regional structures. This is accomplished by limiting the agenda and the influence of the global hegemon(s). The context is post-US hegemony. The USA has a major role in Asia in the coming decade but it will need a combination of knowledge, power, conviction and consent of its allies to maintain a leadership position in Asia–Pacific.

Asia–Pacific, 1945–2000: bipolarity or multipolarity and a new paradigm

The dominant view of US practitioners and scholars highlighted the central importance of the bipolar structure of the Cold War international system in the formation and development of strategic relationships in the world in general including the sub-regions in Asia–Pacific. This section summarily outlines the view of several prominent Western scholars on Asia. The review is not comprehensive: it is meant to suggest a need to challenge and to revise orthodox scholarship.

Zagoria and Goodwin

Following USSR's collapse, the new orthodoxy highlights USA's position as the sole superpower. In this context, Donald Zagoria (among others) lays out the US formula for Asian security. He makes a number of points that require a critical reappraisal. (1) USA is still a pre-eminent power in Asia–Pacific. No one can replace US power. USA plays a 'balancing role in Asia'. (2) US power and influence is used to prevent the rise of 'hegemonic power' of others in Eurasia; that is, no regional hegemon will be allowed to emerge to threaten vital US interests. (3) A 'stable equilibrium of power' in Asia is desirable and do-able because Russia is not a hegemonic threat now. China and Japan could become hegemonic threats in future but this is not likely in the next decade. (4) Regional cooperation (economic, diplomatic, military?) is emerging but it is fragile; it is 'soft regionalism'. (This is Robert Scalapino's term.) Regional cooperation is desirable, and regional arms control or crisis prevention regime building is likely to dampen regional hot spots.[11]

The Zagoria paradigm finds support in Goodwin's reading of Chinese strategic analysis. Before the USSR's collapse, the US–USSR–PRC strategic/diplomatic triangle produced a 'multipolar' global distribution of power. In early 1990s, the balance of power was tending towards US unipolarity rather than multipolarity in Beijing's perceptions, according to Goodwin. The US was free from the responsibility and cost of containing the USSR, and

> it is now the pre-eminent military and economic power. According to the Chinese views, the absence of superpowers' competition permitted local conflicts to arise which earlier were suppressed by the dominant pattern of East-West conflict during the Cold war. This creates a danger of regional power vacuum after USSR's collapse (will Japan fill this? Beijing asks)[12]

In Zagoria's paradigm, it is unclear if the US is concerned about regional *hegemons who threaten regional neighbours*, or whether the concern is about *threats from regional and middle powers to US global and regional authority.* Territorially satisfied regional hegemons are not necessarily a threat to their neighbours. Indeed, to be a regional leader, a regional hegemon must negotiate with its smaller neighbours and secure their consent about their policies. However, a regional hegemon can be territorially satisfied at the regional level, but diplomatically dissatisfied and ambitious at the international level. Such a regional hegemon may be a threat to the political and moral leadership of the USA. In the international system, as Wight says, great powers seek to 'monopolize the right to create international conflict'.[13] Today, they do so either directly, or under UN cover, or through the NATO alliance, or by an international coalition. A regional hegemon is a threat to the US or another great power to the extent that it seeks to reduce the great powers' monopoly in terms of the *right and the ability* to fight to enforce the peace, or to keep the status quo, or to revise it in pursuit of great powers' interests. Regional hegemons can shrink the great powers' monopoly to initiate and manage conflict as India and Vietnam have shown.

Therefore, in our judgement a benign view of a regional hegemon is worthy of consideration in the context of Asia–Pacific today. If a regional hegemon is not expansionist territorially, if it seeks mutual accommodation with neighbours despite asymmetry in the distribution of military and economic power, and if it functions as a good traffic cop in a congested region, such a hegemon could introduce universal norms or values of international society into regional politics; and it may do so gently and subtly. As well it could function as a shock absorber who insulates the region against interventionary impulses from outside the region. If it only engages in the first activity, it is likely to be labeled a foreign collaborator who sold out to its international patron. A combination of both roles however, gives its legitimacy, and the region is likely to gain stability (or manageable instability) and predictability. This way a regional hegemon can participate in enriching and continuously coupling the regional sub-system and the international systems; and 'soft regionalism' can be institutionalized and developed into tight, safe regional multipolarity.

There are flaws in the Zagoria paradigm and in Chinese assessments as reported by Goodwin. (1) The issue is not that the US has more military and economic power than others. It does. The issue is not whether others can replace US power. They cannot. The issue is whether the US can act alone or if it needs outside help in pursuit of its interests, and if it must bargain with them as Lattimore urged and predicted. Zagoria is wrong to assert that US power or the US–Japan alliance has contained USSR/PRC communist expansion throughout the region. For example, communist insurgencies in South East Asia were defeated by the British in Malaysia, by the US–Indonesian military combination in Indonesia, by the Burmese military in Burma, and by the Indian government vis-à-vis Indian communists. Vietnamese communism remained undefeated despite asymmetry in the distribution of military and economic power between the USA and

Vietnam. In the context of world history, the pre-eminence of Western powers has declined. From 1600 to the early 1900s, Western powers dominated the globe. The Bolshevik, Chinese and Vietnamese revolutions cut off major parts of the world from Western domination and created new centres of independent strategic and political thought and centres of power, albeit minor ones compared to US military power. Today, China has strategic and political influence in Iran, Pakistan, Myanmar, South China Seas, the two Koreas, Hong Kong, and generally in North East Asian, South and South East Asian affairs. Chinese Communist influence has increased between 1949 and the present. Vietnam's influence has grown (1940s to the present) because it defeated superior US military power, it intervened in Cambodia, and now it is a part of ASEAN. North Korea, a 'pariah' state, has influence because of it ability to lock the US, the strongest military power on earth today, into a negotiating stance concerning its nuclear and missile program and the future of the Korean peninsula. So we must not generalize from the Soviet experience. The test of pre-eminence lies in an ability to continually dominate and change the domestic politics and foreign policy of other countries by the exertion of one's power and prestige. The test requires 'present power', not past achievements. The USA cannot act alone or in concert with like-minded Western countries and prevail in the Asia–Pacific regional or regional sub-systems. (2) The second point in the Zagoria paradigm of US policy has two aspects: (a) that US seeks to prevent the emergence of a regional hegemon, and (b) it seeks to divide and balance power within regions, e.g. between North and South Korea, between China–ASEAN and USSR–Vietnam, between Vietnam and Indonesia and is able to set itself up as the external guarantor or balancer in each region.

My view is that regional powers (or regional hegemon: expansionist? leaders?) in Asia–Pacific are here to stay. (Many of them also function as middle powers in the international system.) Regional hegemons should be taken seriously as a matter of practical necessity and efficiency (if they are leaders), or as a danger to regional stability (if they are expansionist). In the first sense, they act as traffic cops in regions with a dense population of players, competing/conflicting threat perceptions, complex web of competitive and/or cooperative alignments, a set of competitive state/national interests, culturally and emotionally loaded strategic core values or concepts, and a dynamic distribution of military and economic power. The existence of regional hegemons (leaders) precludes the possibility of regional power vacuums or instability. By their public and secret actions, such regional hegemons lubricate the regional systems and make them reasonably efficient and organized; they can and do shape the regional policy and research agendas. These are the qualities of benign regional hegemons. They differ from the malign ones – the expansionists. Unfortunately, US government pronouncements and scholarship fails to make the distinction.

Michael Yahuda too overplays the role of bipolarity and the Cold War international system and underplays the emergence of autonomous and interdependent regional (or sub-regional) systems in Asia–Pacific. *With a 'top–down' view he asserts that the end of the Cold War decoupled the international system from regional conflicts.*[14]

This is a mistaken view. As long as real or potential regional hegemons (leaders as well as expansionists) exist, they create an *automatic* and *durable coupling* with the stronger member(s) of international system. This coupling has little to do with the Cold War or its end, or with a bipolarity. This coupling has to do with the existence of real or potential regional hegemons or regional great powers. There are two different ways to pursue this point, and I will present them in the form of a hypothesis in two connected parts. Both parts assume that the US is opposed to the emergence of regional hegemons and is interested in maintaining its international pre-eminence; that is, it does not take a benign view of regional hegemons which it cannot control through its preferred alliance and economic arrangements.

Hypothesis I(a)

If X is a regional hegemon, then its policies are connected with the policies of the stronger members of the international system (Y) because Y will either seek to balance or constrain the regional hegemon's power and influence by *balancing* activity, by coercive diplomacy that includes military, economic and diplomatic pressures – either bilaterally or multilaterally; or Y will seek to co-opt it (*bandwagonning*) if coercive diplomacy fails. Leaving it alone is not an option for outside powers. This is why the USA is not likely to be able to leave India, China, Japan, Indonesia, Iran (to name a few regional hegemons) alone.

Hypothesis I (b)

If X is not a regional hegemon but it is widely seen as a potential one (i.e. it possesses ambition and the means to become one), then to prevent its emergence as a hegemon, international pressures by the outside powers (Y) will be used to retard/constrain its development as an autonomous centre of political and strategic thought and power/influence. Here as in hypothesis I(a), the potential regional hegemon (X) is connected with the international system (Y) because others will not leave it alone, and they cannot leave (X) alone as a matter of self-interest. The expectation is that the window of opportunity to apply pressure and to constrain/retard the emergence of a potential regional hegemon is limited. Here coupling exists between the potential upwardly mobile regional hegemon's activities and ambitions and the international (great power) efforts to constrain a potential regional hegemon through external intervention. The aim of the latter is to alter the domestic politics and foreign policy of the potential hegemon *before* it becomes a hegemon.

In summary, *great powers have a security dilemma vis-à-vis other powers as well as with regional (hegemonic or potentially hegemonic) powers.* As Wight points out, '*Great Powers can not cry for a halt to technological innovation*' and to an arms build-up.[15] In international history, a halt can be achieved temporarily by defeating a challenger by war (e.g. Germany and Japan after 1945), or through a comprehensive political settlement through negotiations. In other words, the great power cannot maintain technological superiority in the military sphere by seeking the disarmament of their rivals. The interactions between international politics and the arms race is two-dimensional; it concerns the distribution of power and the pattern of relationships among recognized great powers. Secondly, it concerns the distribution of power, and the pattern of relationships between the great powers and the emerging regional great powers. Consequently, the coupling between the international system and the regional system(s) is constant as a consequence of the relationship between politics and arms in the attitudes and behaviour of great and regional powers. The coupling between the international system (where the great powers are located) and the regional system (where a regional hegemon is located) is constant; it is not likely to change with a transitory development such as the rise and fall of the US–USSR Cold War and bipolarity. *As long as there are great and regional great powers, absent a profound political settlement or a major war that produces a permanent set of winners and losers, the coupling is embedded in the existence of states and their power politics.*

Conceptual considerations

My approach has several conceptual underpinnings.

1. The Cold War boundaries (1947–90) or traditional regional boundaries make no sense

Along with geo-politics and economics, today Asian international relations are driven by the politics of oil, religion, drugs and arms trade as well as ethnic, irredentist security fights, be they ritual confrontations or deadly quarrels in regions of conflict. The conflicts have two consequences. They reveal tension between considerations of global norms (e.g. human rights, arms control) and national security (e.g. military, trade and prestige related issues). Furthermore, the Cold War regional boundaries have lost their salience. Instead, the interactions and preoccupations of the players reveal connections between Central Asia, Persian Gulf, the Indian subcontinent (to take one extremity of Asia–Pacific), and between China–Myanmar–Bay of Bengal and the sea lanes from the South China Seas to the Indian Ocean (to take the middle zone), and between the Korean peninsula–Japan–Russia–Taiwan–USA–PRC (to take the other extremity of Asia–Pacific). The boundaries of Asia–Pacific have enlarged, and sub-regional nexus or centres of gravity have emerged. In the latter, clusters of players, issues and pattern(s) of interactions have emerged and they have a system-changing potential. Each cluster represents a regional or sub-regional pathway. Each pathway has a process and a pattern of engagement and each offers movement in terms of ideology, and economic and military power. In other words, the boundaries or the limits of interaction and influence are no longer the traditional Cold War boundaries of 'South Asia', or 'South East Asia' or 'East Asia'. Now *political ideas*, (e.g. militant Islam, secularism, human rights, democracy), *economic exchange* (e.g. official or unofficial trade, oil and drug traffic, economic reconstruction policy) and *military movement* (e.g. nuclear and missile trade, development of military communications) occur entirely within regions (or sub-regions) as well as between regions. 'Geo-strategy', i.e. the *organization of movement* and the *development of a system in a defined geographical sphere* is in full play in the major pathways in Asia–Pacific.

2. The traditional meanings of balance of power have limited relevance in Asia

The late Professor Martin Wight listed different meanings of balance of power. It could mean the *existing* distribution of power, an *equal* distribution of power, an *unequal* distribution of power in favour of the status quo power; and a major external power that can function as a balancer.[16]

In Asia–Pacific today, 'balance of power' means the existing distribution of power. The other meanings are not relevant because of the fluidity in the Asia–Pacific strategic environment. For instance, the US possesses more power than other Asian states, but it cannot function as a 'balancer'. Many uncertainties affect its policies and choices. It is now negotiating in Asia – with the North Koreans, Chinese, Japanese, Indians and Pakistanis on security issues. However, 'existing distribution of power' does not explain or predict much because it is subject to change through events like the Indo-Pakistani nuclear tests. Still, balance of power in Asia–Pacific is being taken seriously in modern scholarship. To quote Paul Dibb:

> There needs to be a new approach to regional security, which anticipates the growth of major Asian powers and a declining reliance on bilateral military alliances. For the first time in centuries, the future security of Asia will be shaped more by the large Asian powers than by external powers or foreign domination.[17]

Table 1.1 shows the existing distribution of power among the major powers in Asia.

3. The balance of power in Asia is evolving

Asian multipolarity lies primarily in the growth of sub-regional security structures and centres of gravity of action in Asia–Pacific today. Whether they are loose and unstable or tightly interdependent and stable is debatable. Not at issue however is the emergence of sub-regional structures that organize the movement of political ideologies, economic goods and military power (the three essentials of power politics or geo-politics). With each sub-region and between sub-regions, they have spatial and systemic definitions and characteristics. (1) They are centres of gravity of action and contention and they reveal the presence of multipolar alignments in sub-regional relationships. Disputes of special public importance exist that involve regional and extra-regional powers. The issues or politics concern activities to organize 'balance', or 'security' or 'stability'. The players have strategies to exercise power.

With each security structure in Asia–Pacific, there is an interdependent population of major and minor powers, a pattern of alignments, varied threat perceptions, élite or national interests, competitive core values and a dynamic distribution of military and economic power. Physical as well as systemic boundaries/discontinuities exist which reveal (a) durable interactions within each sub-regional (sub-Asia–Pacific) security structure, and (b) the boundaries where the interactions cease, fade or lack a critical mass. There is an expectation that the nature of the inter-state relationships will shift from 'loose' (conflict-prone) to 'tight, safe' (cooperative) multipolarity. (The characteristics of 'tight, safe' multipolarity are discussed later.)

Each region (sub-region) possesses actual, potential or undistributed power, although the pattern of distribution of military and economic power varies between regions in Asia–Pacific, and it is dynamic. Each structure fulfils the basic requirement of a region's security complex as defined by Barry Buzan, namely, the existence of geographical connectedness, the presence of a critical mass of continuous and durable interactions or relationships of conflict and/or cooperation, the existence of system and geographical boundaries and, finally, the players within a region are continuously attentive to the actions and consequences of other members of the region.[18]

This approach enables us to locate each regional (sub-regional) security structure in the context of a linear scheme that moves from (A) Chaos (unstructured conflict, i.e. civil war, mass migration of refugees), to (B) *Regional power formation* (war, arms racing, economic and psychological warfare, absence of economic liberalization or positive interdependence between rivals), to (C) *Stable conflict formation* (that reveals the existence of tight and stable multipolarity at the regional level). Here the major and minor powers are locked into a two-track mode. The 'conflict' track exists but it has well defined parameters that limit its escalatory potential; hence our characterization of this 'conflict' track as 'stable conflict formation'. The second track seeks negotiation – to extend existing ceasefires, to secure confidence-building arrangements, and eventually to work towards a political settlement.

Table 1.1 Present standings of China, India, Japan, USA and Russia

Population	*China*	*India*	*Japan*	*USA*	*Russia*
1993 estimation	1.196.3m[a]	901.5m[a]	120m[e]	258m[g]	147m[b]
HDI 1993			83 women 77	79.6 women	72.7 women
life expectancy at birth	68.6 years[1]	60.7 years[1]	men (1996)[5]	73.4 men (1995)[2]	60.4 men (1995)[2]
adult literacy	80%[1]	50.6%[1]	100%[5]		
real GDP per capital	2,330[1]	1,240[1]			
death rate per 1000			7.46[6] (1996)	8.8 (1993)[2]	12.2 (1992)[2]
birth rate per 1000			10.66[6] (1006)		
Infant mortality per 1000 live births	53[e] (1993)	79[e] (1994)	4.3[e] (1995)	9[h]	22[h]
National Income Accounts	1993	1993	1993	1993	1993
GDP	$425.6b[a]	$225.4b[a]	$479,071,9b[b]	$6,259,900b[b]	$172,893b[b]?
Economic Performance	1993	1993	1994		
GDP	$577.5b[a]	$263b[a]	$100.8b[b]		
Defence Expenditure 1995 Total	$31,731m[a]	$8,289m[a]	0.96% of GDP[f]	$278.9b[i]	$25.7b[i]
Military Manpower					
armed forces 1995	2,930,000[a]	1,145,000[a]			
soldiers per square mile 1997	0.31[c]		0.62[c]		
Science and Technology	(1993)	(1990)	(1992)	(1993)	(1993)
people doing research	642,500[b]	224,773[b]	813,360[b]	962,700[b]	778,800[b]
money spent on research	$19,600,000[b] (1993)	$41,864,300[b] (1990)	$13,771,524[b] (1991)	$171,000,000[b] (1995)	£131,557,000[b] (1995)

Foreign Trade					
imports	$71.8b[e] (1992)§	$25.5b[e] (1993)	$274.3b[e] (1994)	$689214.9[j] (1994)	$50518 (1994)
exports	$78.2b[e] (1992)	$19.8b[e] (1993)	$395.5b[e] (1994)	$512626.9[j] (1994)	$67642 (1994)[j]
Defence Budget	1997 $9.7b[c]	1995 $7.4b[d]	1997 $42.9b[c]	1997 $270.3b[k]	1997 R83,000b

Notes

a *Survival: The IISS Quarterly*, 40/2 (Summer 1998), 55.

b *United Nations Statistics Yearbook*, 42nd issue, United Nations Press.

c *RUSI Journal*, 143/1 (February) 1998), 64.

d *Asian Survey*, 25/5 (May 1995), 441.

e *Grolier Multimedia Encyclopedia* (1998), Windows 95/Windows 3.1, OEM Version 10.

f *International Organization*, 51/3 (Summer 1997), 389.

g US Bureau of Census, *Statistical Abstract of the United States*, 118th edition, (Washington DC, 1998), 8.

h *1993 Demographic Yearbook* (New York: United Nations, 1997).

i *SIPRI Yearbook 2000* (Oxford University Press), 236.

j *1996 International Trade Statistics Yearbook*, vol. 1 (New York: United Nations, 1997).

k *The Military Balance 2000/2001 International Institute for Strategic Studies* (Oxford University Press, p. 116.

The strategy here is to convert deadly quarrels into ritual confrontations, to convert general war(s) into limited conflict(s) – limited in terms of issue(s), geographical space and time frame – and eventually to enlarge the negotiation envelope and to reduce the conflict track. Finally, (D) *Conflict resolution* seeks a point of equilibrium rather than stalemate among the players. Our premise is that none of the nodal points in Asia–Pacific today are at (A); all can be usefully studied in terms of (B) and (C); and none enjoy the fruits of (D). The scheme is conceptually rich and challenging because (B) requires a detailed examination of the process, and (C) requires a detailed examination of the structure.

These sub-regional structures have emerged in the context of Lattimore's assessment of Asian international relations in the aftermath of the Second World War and the end of colonial empires in Asia. He made three points.

First, Asia is out of control; it cannot be dominated militarily or coerced economically by outside powers. The great powers cannot lay down the law. Second, the US and the USSR must negotiate with Asians. Third, there is much 'unredistributed power in Asia' which is outside the control of USA and USSR and which the Asian powers can be expected to acquire.[19]

4. Is Asian regional (sub-regional) multipolarity likely to be loose and unstable or tightly linked and stable?

Seyom Brown's views about tight/loose multipolarity help our discussion:

> The most dangerous international systems tend to be those characterized by either loose bipolarity or loose multipolarity. They are dangerous in two respects: the likelihood of war and the likelihood that war anywhere in the system will draw in the major powers. War is likelier because the ambiguity of mutual security commitments in the loose coalitions leads to opportunities for miscalculation and bluffing. These characteristics also provide temptations for great-power intervention in local conflict and the need for smaller powers to invoke coalition ties, however loose, to deter their adversaries from ganging up.

The safest international system presented in the model is tight multipolarity in the multipolar configuration: the world is divided into a number of international sub-systems, each a largely self-contained commercial and security community. Conflict is managed within these communities, with little likelihood of intervention in their affairs. Brown sees three problems with the hypothetical model of a 'safe tight multipolar' system. (1) Regional sub-systems like regional empires of the past cannot be expected to be 'content with what they have and refrain from balance of power games against each other'. There is a 'profound jealousy and suspicion' against *regional hegemons*. (2) There are no longer 'universally acceptable definitions of *which peoples constitute what regions*'. (3) Finally, *if multipolar regional subsystems do temporarily emerge*, the ever-present prospect of the disintegration will present outside powers with temptation to cultivate local *clients* and, in the event of actual disintegration, to intervene competitively.[20]

These ideas were expressed in 1987 but they are arguably wrong. In Asia–Pacific 'loose bipolarity' prevailed in US–USSR relations. During the Cold War, US–USSR rivalry compelled the two powers to participate actively in regional politics in the Korean peninsula, Africa, Middle East, South and South East Asia. However, with loose bipolarity, the superpowers only took calculated risks with each other. They recognised the dangers of direct military confrontation with each other. They engaged in military and ideological confrontation combined with a policy of restraint and a commitment to a limited war. Truman and Stalin established a pattern of restraint in the Korean War despite the harsh rhetoric on both sides. Having encouraged North Korea to take the South by force, Stalin feared US retaliation and was content to let North Korea and PRC fight the USA and the Republic of Korea.[21] In the Vietnam War, USSR and PRC avoided direct confrontation with USA. This war also had the characteristics of 'loose bipolarity' as noted above. The Cold Warriors were frightened of a general war because of the presence of nuclear weapons and/or because no compelling national interests required a general war. Despite the ideological differences, rationality prevailed. And yet they were able to maintain a process of military and diplomatic engagement with each other by limited (potential risk-taking) proxy warfare and by diplomatic negotiation. The Cold Warriors adopted the principles and practices of classical statecraft.[22] In international history, the great powers relied on compromise and compensation when intervention failed. They sought to co-opt a rival power if coercive diplomacy failed to produce the desired results. Later, the US relied on these principles by coopting its enemies either through war (Germany and Japan) or by diplomacy (USSR and PRC).

Seyom Brown's view that 'loose bipolarity' is dangerous is false. The US–USSR Cold War in Asia does not support his analysis. Other case histories of limited wars and crises after 1945 reveal that third parties were not able to manipulate the great powers to go to war unless they wished to do so for their own reasons; and the great powers deliberately kept wars limited in geographical scope, in the war aims and the scale of violence. Furthermore after 1953, the sites of armed conflicts and points of US–USSR confrontation (Angola, Central America, Afghanistan) were removed from the primary centres of US–USSR interest such as Europe and North East Asia. Thus US–USSR competition remained manageable and controlled in a setting of 'loose bipolarity'.

Brown's concerns about his hypothetical 'safe tight multipolarity' are also wrong at the regional level. Consider this. Regional sub-systems started to take shape after 1945 when the international system was allegedly dominated by the Cold War and the US-USSR central strategic balance. In 1945–90, Asia–Pacific saw two parallel developments that helped the process.

The first concerned the formation and stabilization of three major Cold Wars in Asia–Pacific (US–USSR; US–PRC; Sino-Soviet) during 1945–90. The second was to the origination of incipient regionalism in Asia during this period. Both developments prevented the emergence of tight, rigid, highly polarized and dangerous bipolarity or unstable multipolarity. These developments also contributed to the growth of loose multipolarity. The extension of the US–USSR competition into zones of conflict in Asia–Pacific was accompanied by the rise of independent centres of political and strategic thought in Asia–Pacific (e.g. North Korea, Vietnam, Indonesia, India, Burma, Iran). These were also centres of Asian nationalism. They were Lattimore's areas of 'unredistibuted Asian power' which the US and the USSR had failed to capture. The growth of regionalism is recognized in the literature[23] but Brown does not acknowledge the importance of Asian regionalism and the three Cold Wars in Asia (1950–90) as a sign of extensive 'loose multipolarity' in the Asia–Pacific.

Brown fails to appreciate that a regional sub-system or a regional hegemony – 'good' or 'bad' (e.g. China's) – in the Asia–Pacific inhibited the extension of 'great' US–USSR military power into regional politics; and it raised the costs of pursuing US–USSR bipolar and Cold War policies. Brown's mindset is cast in terms of 'great powers' and 'clients'. A client according to the dictionary means 'one who is at the call of his patron; a plebeian under the protection of a patrician in this relation is called a patron. One who is under the protection or patronage of another, a dependant. One who employs the services of a legal adviser; he whose cause an advocate pleads.' When such a term is applied to Asia–Pacific, it trivializes the possibility of independent thought and action by weaker states or by minor powers. My expectation is that regional (sub-regional) multipolarity in Asia–Pacific today is likely to be tight and safe, and it is poised to move from stable conflict formation to conflict resolution.

5. Global economic interdependence theory has a set of expectations and methodology which differs substantially from our view of regional (sub-regional) security linkages in Asia–Pacific

Interdependence theory expects the growth of a seamless web of international network of communication and exchange and the growth of a convergent or a universal corporate culture of markets and profits. Contemporary American works predict the dampening of armed conflict as a consequence of interdependence. And democracy will follow the growth of capitalism. With interdependence and democracy, the autonomy of the state declines and that of the marketplace increases. With democracy, the state is also less able to insulate domestic politics from external influences. Of course, interdependency theory has its critics but on balance, interdependency theory is popular and trendy, and more so following the end of the US-USSR Cold War.[24]

In my view, globalization of the world economy is a given. Even North Korea, the hermit kingdom, is likely to join the world economy as did Vietnam, but the idea that complex global interdependence will emerge and help security regime building and dampen military preparations in potential flashpoints is simplistic. Two tracks have emerged in Asian continental relationships and regional sub-systems: one seeks to prepare against military uncertainty, the other seeks to engage in a dialogue with rivals. Both are important.

APPENDIX A: ATTRIBUTES OF MULTIPOLAR REGIONAL SECURITY STRUCTURES BILATERAL SECURITY INTERDEPENDENCIES

Power (military and economic capacity distribution	Asymmetrical/symmetrical
Indicators of chaos	Yes/no
History of war	High/low incidence of war
Number of security interdependencies	One/several
Nature of inter-state relations/pattern of alignments	Hostile/friendly/indifferent/difficult
Types of eelite/national interests in conflict/cooperation	Territorial and resource disputes/military security/prestige/arms control/economic security
Intensity of conflicting/cooperative interests	War-like/manageable pressures/ritual confrontations
Bargaining influence (leverage) of regional actors and decision-making strength	Asymmetrical/symmetrical/constant /variable
Relationship between great power policies/international regimes and regional inter-state arrangements	Yes/no
Relationship between domestic bargains and inter-state negotiations	Intense-continuous/variable
Boundaries of regional structure	Constant/well defined/variable
Strategic values or concepts	Isolationist/autarchic/interdependency-inducing within region and international system
Pattern of inter-state relations	Dyadic/multilateralist
Conflict resolution traditions or diplomatic, cultural or political thought	Yes/no

2 The meaning and importance of 'Asia' in international history and international politics

Why study Asia?

Asia has been important in the past, and it is of growing importance in the 21st century. In the 19th and the 20th centuries, Asia was a centre of gravity – point of commercial attraction as well as military and cultural conflict – between contending forces within it and from outside. Compared to Latin America and Africa, it is now a major economic and a geo-strategic region. No major power can afford to be indifferent towards Asia. It is now a core in the development of a major power's system of ideas (social and political thought), its economic, and its military strategies. 'Movement' or development of a country's interests in these spheres require an interplay with Asians. 'Eurasia' has emerged as a critical centre of international politics; Asia is a central place in world history as well as international politics.[1]

Asia has been the long-term object of Western as well as Russian attention. Since the 1500s, Western merchants, missionaries and military found Asia attractive. They facilitated empire-building. Russia's eastward and southern expansion produced the 'Great Game' among the imperial powers of the 19th century. The expansion of the powers into Asia at this time revealed the importance of land power and sea power in the development of East–West commerce as well as strategic relationships. Asia was a major centre of the military campaigns against Japanese power in the Pacific SE Asia and German power in North Africa and the Middle East during the Second World War. Asia remained a major point of engagement of competing powers during the Cold War period. It was a military battlefield (Korea, Indo-China, South Asia, Afghanistan), an ideological battlefield (US–USSR, Sino-USSR, Sino-US, Sino-Indian, among others) and the core of the Third World's strength during the Cold War.[2]

Asia is also important because East–West encounters have produced a *synthesis* between Western and Eastern values and state policies. Initially, Asia was an *object* of Western attention because opportunities to acquire profit, territory and power attracted European traders, missionaries and the military. As object, it became a fertile ground for *transplanting* Western institutions and methods of political and strategic behaviour, such as the development of modern democracy, and the use of modern industrial and military organizations and modern science. However, these transplants led to a synthesis between Asian and Western values and methods.[3] Asia has shown itself to be a better pupil of Western political institutions than say Africa or the Middle East.

Asia is an interesting laboratory for studying the negative and positive lessons of East–West strategic and cultural encounters. Western colonization disrupted the stability and autonomy of traditional Asian societies and Asia acquired a collection of 'conflicted' states – societies relationships following decolonization.[4] The colonial experience spawned two perspectives about its consequences. The first, the optimistic view, believes that, despite poverty, material weakness and the colonial experience, Asian states have managed the instabilities inherent in 'conflicted' or transitional domestic and external relationships; and furthermore, they have developed a position of autonomy in Asian political, economic and strategic affairs against the odds. The growth of autonomy shows the positive influence of nationalism and the stabilizing role of of an Asian civilizational base in managing conflicted relationships. In the optimistic view, Asian methodologies, religions, mysticism, lifestyle and spiritual or cultural influences challenge as well as attract the West to Asia; and they facilitate crisis management. The pessimistic view on the other hand sees Asia today as a region that is dependent on Western economic and diplomatic policies.[5] This book adopts the optimistic view.

Research questions

What is the international cultural and strategic *context* for the study of Asia today? Where are the geographical and systemic *boundaries* of Asia–Pacific in relation to Europe and North American (the Western World), the Middle East (the Muslim World) and the African world? Are these boundaries fixed or fluid? Have the boundaries of Asia expanded since Asia was integrated into the international system through the process of Western and Russian colonization, and subsequently through the extension of superpower rivalries into Asia during the Cold War? Following the end of the Cold War, have the boundaries of Asia continued to change as a result of the pattern of oil politics, drugs production and trade, arms trade, migration patterns, ethnic and religious conflicts as well as economic and military developments? Is Asia *nationalism* important? In the 20th century, Asia developed as the heartland of nationalism in the world. (Historically, Asia was developed by the Europeans for the Europeans: European military and political organization and racial superiority and European economic and military interests were the basis of empire-building. As a counterforce to European domination, Asian nationalism grew to undermine European rule.) Is Asian nationalism still a challenge to Western authority because nationalism in Asia now is accompanied by the growth of scientific, economic and military capacity in Asian hands? Are *Asian diplomatic and military strategies* significant? Historically, Asia was not taken seriously in the system of states.[6] It was treated either peripherally or with indifference and contempt in the West's idea of international society. While Western experts like A.B. Bozeman recognize the importance of Asian political and strategic ideas and ideals, still Greek, Roman and European experiences and thought were deemed to be significant in the development of Western political and strategic thought and the system of states. Is this still the case?

Themes

The book explores several propositions.

1. Historically, Asia has played an important role in East–West and North–South encounters and it is aware of its importance. The historic encounter between the West and the East, the older of the two and also the more significant, had two major axes or pathways.

The clash between Muslim expansion and the West – i.e. between 'Outer Islam' and the Christian world – established the Mediterranean as the frontier of the Muslim/Arab expansion westwards.[7] Out of the Muslim–Western clash and the threat perceived by the West, came the Western commercial and military expansion into the Indian Ocean. Here European sea power outflanked and defeated the Muslim challenge.[8] In combination with the Arabs of Saudi Arabia, the British promoted an intra-Muslim revolt against the Ottoman Empire. Here Britain supported the Wahabbis of Saudi Arabia against a common enemy, the Ottoman Empire. British sea power, military support for local allies and alliance politics paved the way for the entry of British (and European) influence into Middle Eastern, Indian Ocean and Asian affairs. This onslaught gave the Europeans a bridgehead in Asia and in most of what is now the Third World. It demonstrated that a highly motivated, organized and small military force could defeat a large population by the application of the principles of revolutionary violence.[9]

The second axis in the West–East encounter revolved around the emergence of the principality of Muscovy as the foundation of a secretive and expansionist empire; it grew westwards, southwards and eastwards in 500 years. The Russian empire acquired Pacific as well as Central Asian dimensions. It engaged a variety of powers on land: Britain in the Middle East and the Indian subcontinent, Germany, China, the Korean peninsula, Japan and America in the East. Whereas the European Muslim-European interactions produced a southerly axis for the European entry into Asia, as well as Indian Ocean and Middle Eastern affairs (here both sea power and land power were involved), Russia's imperial expansion revealed the existence of the northerly axis; here land power was the medium of expansion. It showed the central position of Eurasia as a centre of gravity in world politics. Consciousness of the Russian menace induced the European powers to contain Russia's eastward expansion towards the Pacific and towards the Middle East.

By the beginning of the 20th century, Muslim military power had been divided and curbed, and prosperous communities in the Indian Ocean world had been penetrated, plundered and conquered by the European colonial powers. But although the Europeans and Americans had established their ascendancy through sea power and land power in Asia, as well as the Middle East and the Indian Ocean world, the West/Eastern encounter was not the end of history; it was to be continued.

2. In the 20th century, nationalism, science and democracy were the core elements which formed a powerful combination in Asia.

After 1945, the North–South encounter emerged in the context of decolonization and the US–USSR Cold War. But to fully appreciate the meaning and scope of the North–South encounter, it is necessary to recognize that the Communist/anti-Communist ideology was not the fault line in the North–South encounter.

This encounter took shape in a dual context: the durability of nationalism in Asia, and the presence of incipient multipolarity in Asian conflicts since 1945. The belief that Asian regional and international relationships were primarily dependent or tied to bipolarity or to Cold War ideology missed the enormous influence of the three subtexts: nationalism, regionalism and multipolarity in Asia since 1945. Nationalism in Asia has challenged and undermined Western political and military authority and it continues to do so. It first inspired the dissatisfied peoples in the East to revolt against unjust colonial arrangements. Later Asian nationalism stimulated the desire to restructure political and strategic relationships between the satisfied Western powers and the dissatisfied but emergent aspirants to power and status in Asia. Japan's invasion of Manchuria showed the impotence of the Western powers, the weakness of the League of Nations and the problem of US isolationism.[10] Japan was the first industrial and military power in Asia to challenge both Russia and the USA (and its ally the Nationalists in China). Although Japan was defeated militarily in 1945, and it was occupied and brought under American authority after 1945, as Lattimore points out, Japan owes nothing to America. Its emergence as a major military power and autonomous economic and diplomatic force appears inevitable in the coming decade(s).[11]

Thus Oriental nationalism and despotism started the major revolt in world history against the authority of the Western powers. The guardians of world order at the turn of the century were under a major attack by militant Asian nationalism, despotism and expansionism for the first time in almost 500 years.

In the author's judgement, the Oriental challenge to Western authority is more profound than was the Bolshevik challenge to American authority. Bolshevism came from Marxism, and Soviet Communism was in its origins a Western idea that was planted in Russia and later in Asia. Stalinist Russia was an ideological rival to the West during the Cold War but it was also a military ally against Hitler's Germany during the Second World War, and it played a vital role in defeating Hitler's armies. Russia has a European dimension and it is open to persuasion and pressure by the West. Stalinist Russia was also a fellow practitioner of regional geo-politics with Churchill and Franklin Roosevelt in Eastern Europe. This was apparent from the nature and method of the political settlement in the Yalta Accord, and the manner in which the three great powers organized it according to the principles of European diplomacy and strategy. Later Stalin's successors became America's negotiating partners in international arms control and security arrangements (1950s to 2000). Soviet Russia never actually attacked the West physically, as did Japan in Pearl Harbour. During the Korean War, American and Chinese armies bloodied each other but American and Soviet armies were not physically engaged in a big way. (USSR pilots were engaged against US forces on a limited scale.) Moreover, the USSR never rejected America's right to be taken seriously as a great power; instead Soviet Russia sought for itself an international status as USA's co-equal. The Soviet problem during the Cold War, and the Russian problem today, is not the problem which nationalism in Japan, China and India poses for Western interests if the interests of the Asian powers are not satisfied.

Nationalistic powers in these areas do not simply seek an equal status with the US. Instead they pose a fundamental and insidious challenge to Western authority and prestige in the formulation of international and regional security arrangements which appear to sideline Asian interests. Japan, China and India elsewhere seek fundamental changes in Western behaviour as well as its social and political attitude towards them.[12] Here Japan's attack on Pearl Harbor, and Mahatma Gandhi's non-violent nationalism, were two different ways to rob the Western powers of their most precious assets: their power, their prestige and their self-confidence. This suggests that the end game for Asians was not simply to induce the retreat of Western dominance of Asia but to cause a rethinking within the West about their approach(es) to military strategy and to international relations. As Northrup points out:

> All this renders two things clear. First, each part of the Orient has left its traditional, passive, receptive attitude and is coming to impress its existence and values upon the Occident. Second, this coming can be evil and dastardly as well as it can be benign and beneficent. Which it will be in the future depends not merely upon the East but also upon the West, and in particular upon each knowing the other's values and interests as well as its own.[13]

This is an Asian challenge that impacts on war and peace issues. As Selig Harrison points out, America has continuously failed to understand the challenge of Asian nationalism to American interests.[14] The challenge of Oriental nationalism is profound because it has defeated the American strategic mind despite America's massive technological superiority and engineering feats, and its attraction as the centre of international finance and entertainment.

The meaning of Asia, or the genius of Asia, lies in the growth of a critical mass of three critical elements: nationalism, science and democracy. Nationalism is now a vital core of the Asian personality while science remains the essence of the Western genius. In Asia, democracy now reflects a blending of Asian and Western genius: 'Western', because of the reliance on Western political institutions and the principle of democratic consent; 'Asian', because of the faith in consensus politics; 'Western' as well because the doctrines of democracy and the Western/Russian doctrine of socialism have played an important role in economic planning in many Third World countries such as India. The critical mass of the three key elements was outlined by the Chinese leader Sun Yat Sen. He pointed out, in his *Principle of Livelihood*, that science applied to the soil and society – one basic value, and nationalism and democracy were the other two.[15] Nehru sought to marry Western science to the Asian cultural genius as represented by the institution of consensus politics. Nehru's India was blending Western science with Hindu-style discourse where superiority, conversion and holier-than-thou attitudes were considered irreligious by Hindu philosophers. Consider the following assessment of Hindu philosophy (by K. Shridharani).

> The very notion [of missionary evangelism] implies a superiority complex as well as an impulse of self-righteousness. Now that might be tolerable in other fields, but when it is brought into the realm of religion and the spirit, it looks very strange to the Hindu. To the Hindu philosophers, nothing is more irreligious than a holier-than-thou attitude – an attitude which of necessity provides the driving force of evangelism. One cannot describe it as a human desire to share with fellowmen things that are found personally precious. Such a desire would turn into fellowship, into discourse, never into a drive for conversion. In this respect I feel that all the great religions of the world have one thing to learn from Hinduism [and, it may be added, from Buddhism, Taoism and Confucianism]: a humility born of a profound philosophic insight into the relativity of knowledge of ideals . . . I think that in this Hinduism is more in harmony with the spirit of modern science than almost any other great religion. It is forgivable to insist on one God, but to insist upon *The Prophet* and *The Law* is intellectually wrong. The assertion of Louis XIV that 'I am the State' is quite innocent compared to anyone's assertion that 'I am The Law' . . . This exclusiveness is anti-spiritual inasmuch as it is overweening in the light of the limitations of human perception.[16]

This attitude in Hinduism makes it easy to combine discourse and political pluralism (democracy) with science that requires continuous curiosity and a quest for knowledge.

Why is the combination of the three elements necessary and why is it deemed to be the defining element in modern Asian international relations?

1 Without science, without industrial, conventional and nuclear explosive power which science provides, and without continuous reliance on the scientific method to assess and address problems, nationalism is merely rhetoric.
2 Without industrial and explosive power, a democracy cannot be independent. Explosive capability creates an ability to settle disputes by armed struggle, if necessary. Without possessing the legal right and the military means to escalate regional and international conflict by choice, a democracy cannot acquire and maintain its own space in a competitive and a dangerous international arena.
3 Nationalism without democracy is potentially Fascism.

The critical mass of nationalism, science and democracy is still developing in Japan, China and India. Japan possesses all these elements but it has lacked the political will until recently to give its scientific capability a military character. It is still under the US military umbrella, but it is developing a domestic consensus that favours an autonomous military position in the Asia–Pacific sphere. China has nationalism and science but its democratic base is weak, and its military technology, while formidable, is not entirely modern in comparison to Japan's and India's military modernization. India possesses all three elements of the critical mass but successive governments have shown a lack of political will to give its scientific potential a clear military character in comparison to China and Japan. However, in each case, the critical mass is developing and it has become the basis of engagement by the Asian powers with the West, and with their Asian rivals (i.e. PRC–Japan, PRC–India). This appears irreversible. In this perspective, the Cold War and its end was basically a sideshow in Asia compared to these developments in Asian states since the 1940s. The development of this critical mass among Asia's major and minor powers is a novelty in Asian political and social thought and its external behaviour. It is expected to undermine the ability of Western powers to set the international and regional strategic agendas and to implement them.

Asia's international position in world history and the international system has improved significantly since the colonial period. Today Asia–Pacific refers to half the world. This part of the international system is fast building the critical mass of *science* (the capacity to fight and escalate militarily as well as the capacity to increase economic strength), *democracy* (the ability to accommodate diversity and to adjust competing internal demands) and *nationalism* (the ability to mobilize public opinion against hostile foreign forces and to create a clear public identification with public policies and the common good).

3. Compared to other Third World Regions, Asia is vibrant but it must deal with its conflicted relationships

In comparative terms, Asia has arrived and it is dynamic, whereas the Middle East is stagnant. (Israel is the exception to this observation. It too has relied on a combination of democracy, science and nationalism to achieve its position in regional and global affairs.) In the past the Muslim world was a centre of world civilization, international commerce, scientific learning and achievement, and military expansion. Now it has lost its historical impulses. Instead, it is mired in politics of regime insecurity, sectarian fighting among the Muslims, the politics of the Jihad, and the management of dependency relations with the West (and during the Cold War with USSR and China as well). Since the retreat of European empires, the Muslim world has not been able to acquire the means and the vision to develop science, democracy and nationalism. Nationalism is at best a dream expressed in the form of slogans about pan-Arabism, Nasserism, pan-Islam, Jihad and Arab unity. The reality, however, points to deep divisions in the Muslim world between Arabs and Persians, moderate and radical Arabs (or moderate and fundamentalist Arab regimes), Israelis and Arabs, and 'Islam and the West'. Africa, too, is marginal as a centre of gravity of international, military and economic power. With weak state machinery, pervasive internal conflict, disorganized state–society arrangements and with endemic economic stagnation and corruption, Africa including South Africa, is a basket case – at best a peripheral region of the world system. Latin America, however, is now vibrant (with growing pains as in Mexico and Argentina) in the economic sphere and in its democratic development. But it does not possess the critical mass of the combination of democracy, civil and military science and nationalism that is driving the major powers within Asia and its sub-regions.

The improvement of Asia's position in the international system can be measured in the following way. The idea of Asia was created by Europeans for the Europeans and it led to Western domination of vast tracts of land and of large numbers of people who possessed wealth and a sense of history and culture, but who lacked effective military and political organization as well as a strategic vision to escape foreign domination. So Asia became an object of European attention and exploitation. It existed for the convenience and enjoyment of the West for over 300 years. Now Asia has emerged out of the humiliation of colonial (Western and Japanese) economic domination and exploitation, the degradation of European racialism, the civil war in China, US bombing of Hiroshima and Nagasaki, and US military action against Vietnam. From an object of Western exploitation, it has become an engine of economic development, democratic growth, nationalism and scientific-technological enterprise. Three of the seven nuclear powers are Asian (China, India, Pakistan). Asia's share of world trade/economic activity is increasing. Japan is a missile and space power and a potential nuclear power; despite major difficulties in its economic performance during the 1990s, it retains its position as the economic engine of Asia. China's economy is the fastest growing in the world and India has a respectable economic growth rate of about 6 per cent per year. By 2025, both are expected to overtake Germany. Regional multilateral economic arrangements and processes have emerged in the form of ASEAN, there are trade links among East Asian economies, and the possibilities are emerging for sub-regional economic cooperation among several SAARC members (India, Bangladesh, Nepal) and neighbours (Myanmar and Thailand). North Americans and Europeans are engaged in multifaceted debates about development of economic arrangements with the Asians. On the negative side, Asians are tied to each other by past grievances (such as Japan's war record), by regional strategic rivalries, poverty and internal conflicts. The balance sheet points to the emergence of a new and a proactive Asia that is both confident and vulnerable in its outlook and relationships with others.

Contemporary Asian international relationships reflect friction between a number of historical, geographical, political and cultural influences. The interactions between politics and cultures have intensified over time.[17] As a result, there are a large number of conflicted relationships in Asia–Pacific, with varying degrees of intensity and with varied prospects of conflict resolution or at least conflict management. Three theoretical constructs are presently relevant in the Asian strategic scene: that instabilities remain manageable; that instabilities become unmanageable and lead to inter-state war and/or internal conflicts; that an Asian balance of power emerges or that rivalries are managed and conflicting interests are dealt with by the classical methods of statecraft and by modern methods of conflict resolution or peace-making. This book examines the policies of players that shape sub-regional relationships in Asia–Pacific. My point is that now many parties are locked into regional (sub-regional) controversies. The players are great powers as well as minor powers. Because the costs of confrontation are high even for a great power like the USA, the parties need to develop wriggle space to negotiate political settlements. This requires clarity about the strategic agendas of the contenders and skill in determining the negotiation opportunities.

4. Asian international relations are a story of interactions between forces within and outside Asia in the last 500 years. This interaction has produced several significant tendencies which define Asian thoughts and actions.

These tendencies may be summarized as follows:

Japan, the first modern Asian power, is still a pole of power in Asia in the aftermath of its military defeat.

Within Asia the indigenous orbit of Japan's feudalism, imperialism and modernization shaped its emergence as a major power, and Asia's first industrial and military one, at the turn of the century. Japan's internal structures and policies before 1945 point to the vitality of Fascist, feudalistic and expansionist tendencies within Asia. Japan is now democratic and thus far, since 1945, it has pursued a non-aggressive military stance. However, it remains a major force with an ugly past in Asia. Consequently Japanese history and the pattern of its historical thought and actions justify its position as an independent orbit in Asia. As Lattimore points out:

> Japan then began to show an ambivalent ability to be both a part of the old system of keeping Asia under control and a part of the new process that eventually resulted in Asia's becoming out of control. As the most permanently anti-Russian of the maritime powers, Japan was essential to the working of the Open Door system. As a power within Asia, and so close to the mainland of Asia as to have almost the same kind of contiguity enjoyed by Russia, Japan sabotaged the Open Door. To the extent that support against Russia was useful, Japan worked with the Open Door powers; but step by step, as Japanese control was expanded over Manchuria and into North China, commercial opportunities and the exploitation of all resources were monopolized in favour of Japan and to the exclusion of other Open Door powers.
>
> This ambivalence of Japanese policy, which goes with Japan's geographical position, should not be overlooked now when it is so fashionable to think of Japan as a trustworthy ally. No necessity ties Japan down to be permanently an ally in Asia of powers outside of Asia. Nothing guarantees America against the possibility that while some Japanese demand American help against 'Communist imperialism', other Japanese, who could easily become a majority, may negotiate for an understanding with China, and through China with Russia, as an offset against 'American imperialism'. The propaganda of 'Asia for the Asiatics' was not silenced by Japan's defeat in the war. It is still a good line of propaganda, though it falls now on different ears, or ears differently attuned.[18]

In other words, the Japanese orbit has a history and Japanese politics and international affairs are dynamic today.

Taking the Asian countries into the Westernized system of States shows the power of statism and Western rules.

The second tendency had its origin outside Asia but it had a huge impact on Asia. In the last 500 years, Western dominance of Asia brought Western statist strategic and political thought as well as political-military organizations along with economic influences into Asian political, economic and social life. The colonial experience produced changing state forms in Asia and established the dominance of Western political values and political institutions among formerly traditional and tribal political entities. Now such entities were exposed to Western political thoughts and strategic actions that reflected the importance of statism as the modern form and basis of good government. Thus monarchical societies and city-states became larger political entities during the colonial era and, following decolonization, they voluntarily joined the ranks of the European/Western system of states. It was determined to be in their self-interest to do so.

So decolonization produced a growth in the size and number of independent states in Asia; this enlarged the size of the international system of states as well. This enlargement suggested that the Western system of states (with its conventions concerning war, diplomacy, commerce and peace) had emerged as a universal institution. Different cultures and political entities in Asia embraced the norms of state sovereignty as a basis of their international relations. Here, Asia was defined by its ties to the West: first, as an object of Western imperialism and, secondly, as a collection of decolonized state entities who had accepted Western international relational norms. However, the sub-text is that, having accepted Western statism, major and minor Asian powers have challenged Western diplomatic and strategic authority using Asian statism.

Asians have learnt to engage the West from a position of weakness.

The third tendency came out of the colonial experience. Western dominance humiliated the Asians who could not understand racialism as a basis of imperialism, who could not comprehend why self-contained traditional societies had become helpless against the Western penetration, and who could not understand how a massive transfer of wealth and loss of self-confidence could have occurred as a result of exposure to Western religious, commercial and strategic influences. Out of this sense of humiliation and helplessness against stronger or better organized Western forces came an awareness that Asian élites had to develop strategies which engaged Western forces from a position of weakness. Nationalism in China and India and elsewhere developed two forms. The Gandhian approach valued peaceful engagement of the British Empire while Japanese and Chinese nationalism emphasized armed struggle. Both reflected different shades of anti-Westernism. However, this was more pronounced in the Chinese case. Indians adopted British political institutions and parliamentary values, while Japan adopted Western technology and commercial/strategic links to make Japan into a major Asian force. In other words, nationalism became a defining element in Asia as a result of the colonial experience. This nationalism was primarily anti-Western rather than anti-Russian (despite Russia's big push into Asia in the last 500 years). So a link emerged between the Western colonial experience and the radical stimulation of nationalism among the Asians.

Asian societies are internally and externally conflicted and this inhibits Asian solidarity.

Following decolonization, the new Asian states and societies were politically independent and enjoyed the legal attributes of state sovereignty.

However, internal divisions afflicted their actions and their external relationships. Moreover, a gap existed between the élites and the masses. The leaders of independence movements occupied positions of power and influence after the countries became independent. New leaders in Asia like Mao Tse-tung, Chou en-Lai, J.L. Nehru among others represented the modernizers and the state builders. On the other hand, however, many influential groups in Asian societies remained tied to traditional modes of thought and actions. Even when the modernizing élites held the power to shape their country's political and economic life, their policies lacked consensus because traditional groups were influential and tied to old ways. The traditional versus modernizing divide still cuts into the fabric of most Asian countries today. As in the African experience, this produced political and social controversies that are divisive and durable, which can often lead to violent internal conflict, insurgency and civil war and, at the least, destabilize domestic politics. In other words, ethnic and religious conflicts are spawned by the encounters between the traditionalists versus the modernizing forces in many Asian countries; they are a manifestation of conflicted relationships that have dominated the internal politics and foreign policies of most Asian states and societies. They inhibit the development of Asian solidarity and they facilitate the growth of competitive sub-nationalism that is driven by ethnic, religious and regional considerations.

Despite the end of the Cold War, the 'Leninist' mode of thought and action still exists in Asia; it is still a powerful force among Communist and select non-Communist countries.

This tendency refers to the structure of thought and action in Bolshevik Soviet Russia, Communist China, Communist Vietnam, North Korea, Cuba and a number of leftist political parties and social movements in Europe, Asia (India and Japan), Africa and the Americas. Even though the USSR collapsed in 1989–90, a number of countries continue to follow the Leninist/socialist approach in organizing the country's political, social and economic life. My definition of the Leninist orbit refers to a system of thought and action which may be called 'revolutionary violence'. It refers to the development of politics on the principle of fanaticism and a belief that the state as a political institution is an agent of the rich and corrupt exploiters, that class rather than state ought to be the basis of international action, that the primary function of the revolutionary élite is to take advantage of contradictions within a country (which reflect the antagonistic interests of the rich and the poor). The approach rests on the *proposition that power alone is not enough; beliefs are also important and, indeed, they are essential to the exercise of power*. Beliefs provide the motive and the direction for the exercise of power. Power is ineffective unless its development and use are inspired by beliefs. On the other hand, beliefs alone are not sufficient unless their existence is accompanied by the availability of power. Beliefs create high motivation, and power alone creates a capacity to coerce and enforce, but this must be married to beliefs so that the level of motivation and the level of power are compatible and effective.[19]

There are major differences in thought and action between the Leninist and the Western approach to international and to state–society relations. In the West, the state is the primary institution. Here the Powers regulate external relationships, they establish the basis of international discourse and they define the methods of organizing international relations. Here the primary loyalty of the individual is to the state. As the primary institution, the government is presumed to represent the people. This presumption is validated by electoral means and by the development of transparent processes of decision-making and by the rule of law. In the Leninist scheme, the international system is deemed to be stratified along class lines; class not the state is the primary institution and the unit of behaviour. The government is presumed to be the agent of the ruling class and an enemy of the exploited people. So the Leninist scheme presumes the existence of antagonistic relationships or contradictions between the rulers and the ruled as well as the rich and the poor in politics and society. Even though the Bolshevik experiment failed, the idea of exploiting internal tensions is still relevant in modern political and military affairs. In the Western scheme, working through a system of politics and law, governments are supposed and expected to adjust conflicted interests within a country by compromise and compensation and to rely on diplomacy, negotiation and the principles of compromise and compensation to adjust conflicting interests at the international level or in a country's external relationships. In other words, diplomatic norms and methods of conflict resolution have a central place in the Western world-view. In the Leninist approach, there is no distinction between diplomacy and propaganda because both are tools of the class struggle. Propaganda and psychological warfare are highly valued norms and methods because they are utilized to increase the polarization or the contradictions within state–society relationships and to exploit international stratification. Propaganda is a tool that drives a wedge between the government and its people, and dislodges the loyalty of the individual from the state to an international cause. Here propaganda seeks to manipulate the psychology and the sociology of the enemy countries' population. Here loyalties of the élite and the public to the state are meant to be divided and used to disrupt the political and social unity of the enemy. Such divisiveness is helpful in building international support for the class struggle, socialism and peace. In the Leninist scheme, the emphasis is on terror and propaganda rather than law and diplomacy. The emphasis is on subversiveness and intrigue rather than public discourse. Finally the reliance is on war as an institution or on revolutionary violence because a revolutionary country is perpetually in a state of war in relation to domestic and international enemies. This brings out another important difference between the Western and Leninist approach. In the former, the emphasis is on the management of the external enemies. In the latter, because revolutionary regimes are born in terror and usually end through violent means (unless they collapse because of poor internal economic and social conditions), the problem of regime insecurity requires a continuous preoccupation with internal enemies, with external enemies and the links between the two.

Islamic revolutionary violence is good business and good politics in the Islamic belt in Asia. Isamic terrorism has adopted the Leninist pattern of secrecy and organization in its approach to liberation.

The Leninist approach is in play – for instance in North Korean activities vis-à-vis South Korea and Japan, as well as in Pakistani and Al Qaeda/Taliban military and intelligence operations in India, Kashmir, Afghanistan, the USA and Central Asia. So the Leninist formula is not limited to the thinking and practices of Communist states. The Islamic world uses elements of the Leninist methods. Its motivation comes from the Holy Book as interpreted by the mullahs and other practitioners. The Islamic orbit affects stability in the belt from the Mediterranean region to the Indian Ocean area. The Islamic orbit shows a pattern of global expansion as well as the growth of intensified and conflicted relationships. The conflicts are varied. They involve Arab states against Iran, Arab states against Israel, inter-Arab state rivalries and conflict, and internal cleavages within Muslim societies which pit the Shias against the Sunnis and, on the other hand, Islamic traditionalists against Islamic modernizers. Furthermore, they involve the USA and India, as terrorist attacks in September and December 2001 demonstrated.

Up to the late 1400s Muslim influence expanded into the Mediterranean and it continued to expand into the Indian subcontinent. In 1492, Muslim power was defeated by Spain and the expansion of the Muslim influence in the Mediterranean zone was arrested. Then followed the phase of European colonization of Muslim societies in the Middle East, North Africa and other parts of Africa. Following the end of the Second World War, decolonization gained ground and the Muslim countries emerged as independent political units. They joined the Western system of states and adopted the form of statehood and sovereignty. Hence decolonization produced a proliferation of Islamic states. This represented the extension of Islamic influence geographically – into all of Middle East (except Israel), North Africa, the Persian Gulf, parts of the Indian subcontinent and parts of South East Asia up to the Philippines. Muslim forces were also present in Soviet Central Asia, in China's border provinces in the proximity of Pakistan and Afghanistan and in parts of Western Africa.

Even though Muslim societies adopted the Western form of statehood, they did not accept Western political attitudes and political institutions and conventions. These emphasized the rule of law in state–society relationships, and the principles of state sovereignty and non-interference in the domestic jurisdiction of the state were important. In Islamic thought and action, Jihad is the central organizing concept especially among the traditionalists. Jihad has two meanings. On the one hand, it refers to internal purification and struggle; this meaning is a matter for the heart and the mind. However, the external meaning of Jihad requires the use of the sword and fanaticism to purify the world. The Islamic world-view distinguishes between 'Dar-al-Islam' (the communities of the believers and the zone of Islamic peace) and, on the other hand, 'Dar-al-Harb' where Islam is at war with non-believers. In the second sense of Jihad (external Jihad) Islamic forces are not bound by Western legal norms and conventions that emphasize respect of territorial or state boundaries. In other words, Islamic Jihad is not bound by Western norms attached to the value of statehood, rule of law, democracy and political pluralism. In Western political and international relations theory, secularism and the rule of law are emphasized; in Islam, religion and politics are meant to be two sides of the same coin rather than two separate compartments. In this perspective, what appears to be 'Islamic terror', appears to be a Jihad for a good cause, i.e. to propagate Islam and the norms and principles of the Holy Book, the Koran. In Islamic thought and action, there is no contradiction between seeking a temporary alliance between, say, Saudi Arabia (where Islamic principles prevail in the organization of state and societal arrangements) and, on the other hand, the United States where the rule of law is the norm. The politics of oil and strategic considerations justify the alignment and the uneasy existence between the two.

Despite the fundamental differences in the approach and concepts of the Western system of states and the Islamic orbit, it is noteworthy that the practitioners in the Westernized system of states are now tied to the problem of Islamic Jihad. Events such as the Iranian revolution (1979), the bombing of the World Trade Center in New York, the downing of the Pan Am plane in Lockerbie, the hijacking of the Indian Airline plane in Afghanistan, the bombing of US embassies in Africa, and the emergence of Islamic terror under Osama bin Laden point to an emergent pattern of engagement between Islamic and Westernized political and societal forces. This engagement appears to be inevitable and durable in the foreseeable future.[20]

To sum up, Asia has emerged as a centre of gravity in international relations and the combination of nationalism, science and democracy in Asia has created pockets of regional autonomy in Asia. The themes and perspectives outlined in this chapter show the meaning and importance of the Asian challenge to Western dominance of the international system.

3 Evolving international structures in Asia–Pacific and the Indian Ocean areas

Introduction and overview

As a region, Asia–Pacific has a dual reputation. This region has been outside the permanent control of major international powers but it has been a fulcrum of international conflict. Great powers have contended against each other in Asia, and Asian states have contended against the great powers. This has been the situation since the 1800s. The region displayed multipolar tendencies even during the Cold War and bipolar era (1947–90), and this has become a trend after 1990. During the Cold War and bipolar eras, durable and stable regional and strategic structures did not emerge in Asia. The rivalries among the major Asian powers (USA, USSR and PRC) provided the overlay in the organization of regional security structures in Asia (in North, South East and South Asia). However, a close inspection of the international relations of Asia–Pacific since 1945 shows three trends. (1) The superpowers failed to dominate the continent even though they possessed the power, the interest and the ambition to intervene in Asian affairs. (2) The major powers were not able to 'club together' and to create a joint condominium – through policies of great powers' balancing, compromise and compensation – in Asia. (3) The emergence of minor powers who could act independently in select regional and international issues and problems could not be prevented. Consequently, there is now a durable, public and predictable pattern of alignments in Asia that points to the growing importance of regional security structures in Asia. These indicate the importance of multipolarity. In Asia, multipolarity has taken shape at two levels: continental Asian relationships involve the major powers; sub-regional relationships involve major and minor powers in the key nodal points of conflict, in North East Asia, South and South East Asia. However, multipolarity in Asia at both levels is still evolving, particularly in the development of the parameters of the relationships among the great powers. In my judgement, regional (sub-regional) multipolarity, despite its evolutionary character, is entrenched in the sense that regional (sub-regional) powers are locked into neighbourly quarrels – be they deadly quarrels or ritual confrontations – in the nodal points noted earlier. The book argues that multipolarity at both levels has increased the costs of great power intervention in Asian affairs and, at the same time, a pattern of engagement between minor Asian powers and outside great powers has been created. Today, as never before, the great powers are not able to intervene in sub-regional affairs – alone or as a collectivity i.e. 'top–down' intervention has diminishing value for the great powers; at the same time the regional or the minor powers have a greater capacity to intervene at regional and international levels on select issues, i.e. 'bottom–up' intervention is growing.

Take the case of the USA, the 'sole superpower' after 1990. The ending of the Cold War has marked a change in the position of the United States, still the strongest military power in the Asia–Pacific region, from a proactive to a reactive force, unable to pursue its interests unaided. It has become dependent on regional partners such as Japan, South Korea, Australia and select South East Asian countries, and has sought to promote multilateral arrangements on trade, non-proliferation and security. The confrontation with Korea over nuclear missile sites in 1993–4 proved that the USA can no longer even contemplate war against 'pariah states' even when they are in breach of international treaties. The ability of the USA to act alone is circumscribed by China and by minor powers in the region who have become negotiation partners to whom the great powers have to pay the required price for cooperation.

This book points to the growth of regional great powers in the Asia–Pacific region today, and the enhanced freedom of action and bargaining opportunities which are available to regional powers like China, India and Indonesia, as well as smaller even so-called 'pariah' or 'rogue' states like North Korea. The USA is still the strongest military power in the region; however, the fundamentals of international relations of the Asia–Pacific region have changed. First, the USA alone cannot dominate or influence the distribution of power and the pattern of interstate relationships in the region. The USA is now reactive, not a proactive force, and it is one of many players. Its freedom of action is circumscribed by its domestic circumstances and by the growth of multipolarity in global and in Asia–Pacific affairs. Second, the great powers (the Big Five of the UN Security Council) are not able to club together and to fashion a dominant and a stable concert of powers in Asia–Pacific. America's regional partners, Japan and Australia, lack sufficient diplomatic and cultural authority, military weight and economic clout to manage a volatile continental and a maritime region. Their ambition exceeds their capability to organize Asia–Pacific regimes and relationships on an all-region or a system-wide basis. Third, the pattern of strategic alignments in the region is undergoing incremental and fundamental change. During the Cold War, military bipolarity and the 'communism versus anti-communism' divide gave the different parts of the region a definition and a structure. The nature of the enmities or threat perceptions, the distribution of power, the pattern of interstate alignments, the core strategic concepts and the national or élite interests reflected responses to the Cold War. During the Cold War, Asia–Pacific international affairs had a bipolar slant and the superpowers competed constantly in East Asia, South and South East Asia and in the Pacific and the Indian

Oceans. There was also a triangular slant in the form of attempted coordination of US–Soviet, Sino-Soviet and Sino-American rivalries under Nixon and Kissinger, so that a three-polar balance of power could be formed and managed by the USA. Finally, there was a loose part of Asia that was driven by Third World nationalism, non-alignment and zone-of-peace calculations.

A number of developments have changed the fundamentals of Asia–Pacific international relations. (1) The USSR's collapse and retreat as a diplomatic and a military force from Asia–Pacific has altered the region's bipolar overlay. (2) With the end of the Cold War, and of the necessity to mobilize America to engage the bad and big Russian rogue,[1] in the absence of other compelling rogues to replace the communist ones, the American preoccupation with domestic politics and economics has created a sense of drift in American strategic behaviour in Asia–Pacific.[2] (3) In these circumstances, and with the emergence of new centres of regional great power,[3] America's freedom to act is circumscribed whereas the freedom of regional powers to act has increased in local and regional situations. The testiness in US–China, US–Japan, US–India, US–Iran, US–North Korean, US–Malaysian, US–Philippine relationships is a sign of the growing capacity of the lesser powers to engage America and to reject unipolarity as the basis of international relations in Asia–Pacific. (4) The balance of power politics of the Nixon–Kissinger era revolved around the primacy of the three-powered triangle This is now irrelevant with the USSR's demise. During the Cold War era, there were five major rivalries in the Asia–Pacific region: USSR–USA, USA–China, USSR–China, China–India and USA–India. The first and the third ones ended with the USSR's collapse. The second one intensified after the end of the Cold War with controversies over trade, human rights and nuclear and missile issues. The fifth one showed an intensification of the dispute over Indian nuclear and missile policy even though both countries are democracies, but lately both countries have positioned themselves to establish a strategic partnership. The fourth one has been modified into a pattern of diplomatic engagement as well as military containment. China and Russia are the only powers in Asia–Pacific today that blow the whistle on American hegemony; and China and India are normalizing their relations because both require a peaceful environment to consolidate and restructure their domestic strength and external relationships. To a discussion of these aspects we now turn.

Great powers (declining), and rising regional great powers

The end of the American–Russian Cold War produced slogans about the 'end of history' and the emergency of unipolarity, but these perceptions are superficial. They mislead rather than clarify the realities of ongoing and profound power struggles in the Asia–Pacific sphere, especially in the South Asian and East Asian areas. The collapse of the USSR was a major event in East–West affairs but it did not eliminate power politics in Europe and Asia;

it did not eliminate the value of diplomacy and military strategy, and considerations of power, influence and prestige in international relations. War, military build-up, coercive diplomacy, intervention, economic and technological sanctions, psychological warfare, alliance activity and compensation remain the institutions or methods of work in the management of inter-state relationship.[4] Neither the Cold War nor its end changed the central position of these institutions of statecraft. The end of the Cold War loosened the rigidity of bipolar (between the two superpowers) and triangular (among the US, USSR and China) relationships which were strategically competitive and doctrinally driven during the Cold War. Now the power politics have intensified and shifted to the regional and local levels: for example, in former Yugoslavia, the Middle East, including the Gulf, Central Asia, South Asia, the Korean peninsula, the South China Seas and the Taiwan straits. Nor does the end of the Cold War mean the end of power politics in the relationship between the great powers. Containment and engagement are both at work in the relationships among the US, China, Russia, Japan and India.

In assessing major tendencies in the Asia–Pacific diplomatic and military sphere, it is prudent to revisit Martin Wight's definitions of three kinds of powers: great powers, regional great powers and middle powers in the system of states. Although Wight mostly illustrates his argument by examples of European diplomatic and military thinking and behaviour, his definitions are more likely than American scholarship to clarify the structure and process of Asia–Pacific international relations following the end of the Cold War.

Wight's work dealt with the relationships between independent powers. He distinguished between 'power' and 'influence', arguing that 'influence' is not power. It is concrete power in the end that settles great international issues.[5] There are different kinds of powers. A 'dominant power' (or a universal empire) possesses power and purpose 'to measure its strength against all its rivals combined.[6] Wight points out that a dominant power is not an accepted category in international thinking, and the 'only distinction in normal diplomatic intercourse is that between great powers and other powers'.[7] 'Great Powers' have 'general [system wide] interests' and can 'confidently contemplate war against other existing single power'. 'Minor powers' on the other hand have limited interests and limited power 'to protect or advance them by force'.[8] (Wight also discusses 'world powers', but this is not relevant for our purpose here.)

Wight is among the few who takes the category of minor powers seriously. There are two kinds of minor powers: regional great powers and middle powers. The former is a state 'with general interests relative to the limited region and a capacity to act alone'. Such a regional great power is a candidate, in the states system at large, for the rank of 'middle power'. A middle power was accepted as a category of power in 1815 among the German states. It has distinctive characteristics and appeal in the states system. It possesses 'such military strength, resources and strategic position that in peacetime the great powers bid for its support, and in wartime, while it has no hope of winning a war against a great power, it can inflict cost on a great power out of proportion to what the great power can hope to gain by attacking it'. According to Wight, middle powers appear when 'the qualifications of great power status are being revised', and the 'number of middle powers varies inversely with the number of great'. Still, there is a great gulf between the middle and the great powers. The former cannot unify continents, or rule the seas or control the international market. They have disputes with their neighbours and they possess limited interests and limited power. Wight recognizes the durability of middle powers because their ambitions are limited compared to great powers, and they appear to possess adequate power and influence to protect and manage their interests without risking the danger of over-reach as in the case of dominant and great powers.[9] Using Wight's definitions, it appears that the qualifications of great powers in the Asia–Pacific region are in dispute and there is an expectation about their declining influence and shrinking number. Compared to the Cold War period, even though Russia today possesses military strength to engage America, it has, in Wight's terms, ceased to be a great power temporarily.[10] Wight predicted that great power status is won and lost by violence. This is half true in the Russian case because it lost it non-violently as a result of internal economic and political defects. A 'great power does not die in its bed', Wight argued.[11] Russia is bedridden and needs Western injections to stay alive. Its experience points to the impact of domestic economic and political structures on a country's international position and its relationships with the states' system.

The USA is also a declining great power in Wight's terms, 'whose continued great power status depends upon an alliance, sometimes with a stronger partner'.[12] The American tendency to rely on its bilateral relationships (with Japan, South Korea, Australia and select South East Asian countries), and to promote multilateral arrangements pertaining to economic and security issues like trade, non-proliferation and regional security, is a sign of the American dependency on regional partners in Asia–Pacific.

There is a growing consensus in the literature about America's declining ability to pursue its interests unaided. Even though it is the sole superpower, it cannot settle international disputes by the use of its power and influence. The annual survey of the International Institute for Strategic Studies for 1994/5 expressed concern about 'drift' in American policy, an unwillingness to shoulder the burden of a 'lone superpower role', and wondered who is in charge?[13] Another work makes the point that:

> The era just after the Second World War has been an anomaly. Other nations had been bound to recover from the war and narrow the gap with the United States. By the 1990s, they clearly had. American who had grown up during the age of American predominance might not find their country's comparative decline easy to accept, but there was not much they could do about it.[14]

The semi-authoritative China Institute for International Strategic Studies offers the following assessment:

> The growth and decline of the strength of the major powers in the world have been obvious since the end of the Cold War. One of the superpowers passed away and the other is wounded, the former Soviet Union has disintegrated and the United States has also been relatively weakened. During the Gulf War, the United States had joyfully declared that it would establish a new world order under its own leadership and the so-called 'one-pole world'. However, the response was cold and detached, even some of its allies expressed disapproval. Owing to its ability not equal to its ambition, the United States could not but adjust its policy in many international events over the past year.[15]

Can America protect its interests by force in Asia–Pacific today? During 1993–4, it became clear that the USA could not confidently contemplate war against even a 'pariah' state like North Korea which had apparently violated its Non-Proliferation Treaty obligations. When the controversy erupted, the USA thought about using force as it had done in the Iraqi case. It found that its military could not guarantee the destruction of nuclear and missile facilities which were buried in granite tunnels and, politically, it could not form an international alliance with China as it had done in the Iraqi case. Despite the broad international consensus against nuclear proliferation, the USA could not act by war against a smaller power. Can it do so with China which is at least a regional great power and a middle power if not a great power? Can the USA permanently contain China's push by forceful measures into the South China Seas and Taiwan? Can the USA defend Vietnam if it runs afoul of the Chinese leadership again? Can the USA stop China's nuclear and missile supply to Pakistan and Iran? Can the USA get India and Pakistan to settle their differences? Can the USA persuade India, Pakistan, Iran and Israel to disarm? Can the USA get Japan to accept its economic demarches? In each instance, American leverage is limited, forcing the USA to redefine and narrow the list of its core strategic interests; and it is increasingly finding itself locked into bilateral and multilateral negotiating processes. The lone superpower is not able to function alone. By testing and hypothesizing America's ability to pursue its interests by war and diplomacy in important situational contexts, the point could be made that America is a front rank power in military and economic terms but it lacks the ability 'to monopolize the right to create international conflict' in the name of international security, which is a sign of a great power according to Wight.[16] Its freedom to act is being circumscribed by China and other minor powers in Asia–Pacific.

The distribution of military and economic power as well as the patterns of relationships (polarities and alliances) has been in the process of continuous evolution since the period of European colonization in Asia and the Indian Ocean area. This evolution continued after the retreat of Western empires.

This chapter outlines the pattern of structural change in the context of global and Asian history. The aim is to establish the interface between history and the analytical constructs. This chapter is not theory, nor is it history. It is a step towards the development of an explanation of the nature and character of Asia–Pacific international relations today, and how they came to be the way they are. The emphasis is on the direction and the movement in the last fifty years. The chapter locates the history in the context of widely used but not clearly expressed Western international relations approaches such as balance of power, multipolarity, unipolarity, regional great powers and regionalism. The analytical constructs will be used to organize Asian international relations history, and the historical data will be used to tease and develop meanings and nuances out of the widely used but not well understood or well developed Western constructs. Hence it is expected that a basis for theory or at least hypothesis building will emerge.

Table 3.1 outlines the spatial, temporal and cultural framework of the emergence and evolution of the nodal centres of power in Asia. 'Power' means military and economic strength, autonomy and influence of Asian political and strategic thought, independence of strategic action in Asia, and ability of major and minor powers in Asia to develop and change strategic alignments. It means the ability to engage the powers and to shape the pattern of alignments. Asia is now an integral part of world history and world politics. First, Asian states and societies were affected deeply by the encounter with the West and by the penetration of Western economic, strategic and cultural influences into Asian experiences since the late 1400s. Secondly, a pattern of engagement occurred when Asian statist and social forces developed strategies to reshape and to challenge Western thought and behaviour in their dealings with Asian countries. This encounter has been extended in both space and time; it continues to occur at the level of competing values as well as conflicting interests among Asian states as well as between Asian powers and the international great powers. These encounters have inevitably involved debates, dilemmas and decisions within Asian states and societies,between select Asian countries and select foreign powers (i.e. USA and Japan, Britain and India) and in international institutions such as the Commonwealth of Nations and the United Nations. The encounters have a durable quality.

There appears to be a commitment among rivals in Asia to develop multiple points of discourse with each other so that conflicting trends or tendencies can be managed and resolved and conflict is accommodated. This book locates the study of Asian inter-state behaviour in a paradigm of three extremities: unmanageable instability, manageable instability and stable multipolarity at the sub-regional and continental levels. The book explores the prospect of manageable instability transforming itself into a process of stable multipolarity as a result of mature conflict management and conflict resolution policies of the major and minor powers in Asia. That is, Asia was out of control in 1945. Nearly sixty years later, it is seeking a pattern of stable diplomatic and military relationships. For example, the situation in the Korean peninsula is stabilizing, as is the situation in the Indian subcontinent. The pattern of relationships which have evolved in these sub-regions indicate that a stable pattern of 'conflict formation' and 'power formation' has emerged, and now state-level processes are in play to dampen the military and social conflicts and convert deadly quarrels into ritual confrontations as a starting point for conflict resolution. However, there are major 'ifs' in the road map to stability in these areas as well as in other parts of Asia. In South East Asia, ASEAN has emerged as an institution where particular Asian values are the basis of conflict management and resolution, in a secondary zone of international conflict, but ASEAN is not our prime example of 'conflict formation' and 'conflict resolution' strategies. The Indian subcontinent and North Asia are better examples.

The experience of Asian/Western engagement is unique in the sense that it is both broad and deep. Table 3.1 shows the dynamics of the historic engagement between the West and Asia. A similar pattern of engagement is not to be found in the history of relations between the Western world and other parts of the Third World other than the US in relation to Latin America.

Periods and themes

The history of Asia–Pacific international relations may be divided into different periods. Each had a distinctive theme and consequences in terms of structural characteristics, i.e. distribution of military and economic power, pattern of relationships or alignment patterns, internal characteristics of the major and minor players and their external orientation, core strategic values of the major and minor players, or the organizing principles of their strategic behaviour.

Pre-1945 and the inter-war era: the great powers are contenders[17]

At this time, Asia–Pacific was the centre of fierce contention among the great powers' (European – particularly British, Dutch and French – Russian, American and Japanese) expansion. Their ambition was driven by economic and strategic motives and interests. Secondly, since the late 1400s, there was domination of Asian states and societies by forces outside Asia. Here the main fights among the great powers involved a number of pairs: Britain/USA, USA/Japan, Japan/Russia and Russia/China. This period had two dominant themes. The first involved a search for position and advantage by the great powers. The analytical paradigm was that of the classic balance of power. The second involved Western domination of Asia through colonialism.

In this period, Asia was the great vortex after Europe. It was the primary international centre of gravity where many great powers clashed. There was significant movement in terms of political and strategic ideas, economic and

Table 3.1 Asia's staying power in world history and world politics

Period	*Academic paradigm*	*Centre of activity*
Pre-1945 (1500s–1940s)	Balance of power activity within Europe involved European powers during and between the two world wars.	Europe
	The European quarrels were extended to the Asia-Pacific and Indian Ocean spheres. European colonialization and domination of Asia–Pacific and Indian Ocean areas occurred on a massive scale.	Asia, Africa, & Middle East
(1920s–1940s)	Balance of power within Asia–Pacific involved European powers, especially Britain, the USA and Japan.	Asia–Pacific
1945–90	Bipolarity in Europe shifted from 'tight' bipolarity and confrontation (1947 to early 1950s) to 'loose' and competitive bipolarity (mid-1950s to 1960s) and later it became a relationship of limited conflict and limited cooperation between two military and social systems (1960s–1990).	Europe
1945–90	'Loose' multipolarity started to emerge in Asia–Pacific. Despite the ideological Cold War overlay in Korea and Vietnam Wars, and in the US–USSR naval rivalry in Pacific and Indian Ocean areas, there were autonomous centres of power and independent decision-making which challenged the dominance of the two Bloc leaders. China's independence of thought and action was revealed in the Korean War. Asian states reacted to US–USSR rivalry, many took sides as allies but nonetheless maintained an independence in their strategic and political thought vis-à-vis the great powers (superpowers) and in their external actions, albeit in a circumspect and circumscribed way. So precisely when the US and USSR were active and intrusive in Asia–Pacific affairs, other Asian states (especially China, Japan, Vietnam, ASEAN states, India, North Korea) were seeking autonomy in their international relations. That is, multipolar tendencies emerged in Asia–Pacific during the US–USSR Cold War period. Even as bipolarity and the Cold War was the most obvious framework of action, multipolarity was emerging as a significant tendency in Asian international relations. *A three-layered system of Asian international system was discernible during the Cold War era. The first layer* expressed the important role of the US and USSR and their alliance activities in Asia–Pacific. This layer	Asia–Pacific

Table 3.1 – cont.

Period	*Academic paradigm*	*Centre of activity*
1945–90 – *cont.*	revealed *horizontal* competitive, and later, cooperative relations between the US and USSR in relation to Asian questions; and a quest to develop inter-bloc politics in Asia. *The second layer* – at the continental level – involved the pattern of triangular multipolar relations between the US, PRC, USSR; this emerged during the Korean War and was expanded into US–USSR–PRC activities in Eastern Europe, South Asia, South East Asia, and Africa in the 1960s. *The third layer* concerned the growth of regional multipolar linkages within East Asia, South East Asia and the Indian subcontinent.	Asia–Pacific
1990–present	The end of the US-USSR Cold War led to the mature formation of regional security structures (i.e. 'conflict formation' and 'regional power formation' were clearly evident. Bilateral and/or multilateral relationships were *consolidated* along two tracks: competitive and cooperative. The parameters of relationships became stable and predictable but they were not in an equilibrium or harmony state. The ground work for a 'tight and safe' multipolarity has been established in a way that elements of social and military conflict are manageable (negative peace) and cooperative relationships are taking shape among regional rivals (positive peace). The decoupling of US–USSR conflict from Asia–Pacific and the Indian Ocean areas facilitated regional conflict formation/stabilization and conflict resolution because the former superpowers were less able to manage Asian problems by great powers intervention or by clubbing together, i.e. acting in concert.	Asia–Pacific

military activity. There were recurring wars, arms races and interventions because of competing interests between the great powers, and between great powers and local Asian élites and societies. Only one major issue was settled in this period. Britain, the foremost imperial power in the world, between 1500s and 1900s, lost its pre-eminent position in Asia. Even though the sun never set on the British Empire in the 1900s, Britain was unable to function as a balancer or the pre-eminent international force in relation to Japan and the USA. Britain's international authority started to decline in the 1860s, and in its contention with American power, Britain found it necessary to seek Japanese aid through the Anglo-Japan Treaty (1905). So the high point of the

British Empire, globally and in Asia in the late 1800s, was also in hindsight the beginning of the end of Britain's international position and authority.[18]

This period settled the question of Britain's leadership position in Asia–Pacific by confirming its pattern of decline but it did not settle the position of other great powers. Their ambition and power remained in contention. This included the contention between Japan, USA, the Chinese Nationalists and Chinese Communists, and Soviet Russia (through a civil war) within China. The relationship between China and Stalinist Russia from the late 1920s onwards was also difficult. The future of Japanese territorial and strategic ambitions in Manchuria, Korean peninsula, China and the Pacific also remained unsettled in this period.

Effects of the Second World War

The Second World War produced a settlement of sorts in Asia but it is uncertain if after fifty years, this can be viewed as a permanent settlement concerning Japan's power and ambition in Asia–Pacific.[19] The Second World War was a bloody fight between American and Japanese power which established American hegemony over Japan's affairs. The US changed Japan's internal political structure as well as its external orientation in 1945 following Japan's military defeat at American hands. This was done by the establishment of a new Japanese constitution in 1945. The Second World War also settled in a way the future role of Stalinist Russia in Japanese affairs. President Truman decided to use the atom bomb in Hiroshima and Nagasaki to force Japan's military surrender. This effectively put an end to Stalin's ability to participate in the war against Japan and to have a voice in the Japanese peace settlement. This way, the US government established a pattern of American unipolarity in Japanese affairs. However, the Korean division (after 1945 into North and South Korea as zones of Soviet and American influence respectively) established a pattern of bipolarity in the Korean peninsula, while China remained an arena where American, Russian, Chinese (Communist versus Chiang-Kai-Shek/KMT) and Japanese influences contended up to 1949. The dominant themes of this period therefore reflected the emergence of American unipolarity in Japan and the area surrounding it, bipolarity in the Korean vortex, a power vacuum within China that was filled by the ascendancy of the Chinese Communists in 1949, and the rise of politics of US–Soviet containment, bipolarity and Cold War in other secondary zones of conflict in Asia–Pacific after 1947.

Cold War era, 1947–90: obvious bipolarity but significant multipolarity

Several themes were prominent during this era.

- *Soviet–American rivalry is the most obvious public theme in international relations of Asia–Pacific and the Indian Ocean areas in this period* but it was not the most significant theme, as the following discussion indicates.

- *Asia was out of control during the Cold War.* The superpowers never acquired a position of supreme dominance or physical control in Asia as the European powers had done. They did not acquire the legal and political authority over a territorial jurisdiction in Asia, unlike the European empires since the 1500s. So even though the Americans and the Russians possessed considerable nuclear and conventional armament and economic strength, their political, legal, diplomatic and military authority in different parts of Asia was less permanent compared to the Europeans. Moreover, with the growth of Asian nationalism that led to the end of empires, the asymmetry in the distribution of power between Western and Asian states did not seem to matter in shaping the pattern of alignments among major and minor powers.
- This era demonstrated *that Asian nationalism was the most powerful and durable force in Asia–Pacific and Indian Ocean areas.* Of course, Communism existed in China, Vietnam and North Korea, and the communist parties had influence in Japan, India and Indonesia. Nonetheless, Asian Communism had a nationalistic foundation. So even though the Cold War was played out on Communists versus anti-Communist lines, nationalism remained the more powerful impulse.
- *Asian capitalism has strong historical and institutional roots in different parts of Asia.* Asian countries recognized the importance of the free market and economic reforms and the value of joining the global economy. In this sense, Asian economics are wired with the Western world. However, there is an indigenous Asian basis for the attraction of the world market for Asian political and business élites. The capitalist tradition in Western India can be traced back to the 1500s if not earlier. The Indian Ocean area (that touched Africa, Middle East, Persian Gulf and South East Asia) was a lively trading and a cultural arena before the arrival of the European colonialists. The coastal regions in China have also enjoyed a long history of capitalistic development and international trade; this included the development of smuggling syndicates and coastal traders. Japan acquired a trading personality after its penetration by the United States from the mid-1800s. Earlier Japanese society and imperial authority was based on a healthy link between feudalism and capitalism. These examples indicate that the growth of Communism in Asia did not diminish the vitality of capitalism in the Asia–Pacific and Indian Ocean areas. The Western belief that Communist states were anti-capitalist (because Marxists said so) was misplaced because many Asian states either adopted the path of state capitalism or of a mixed economy, or adopted the private enterprise path with strong state direction (as in the case of Japan) during the Cold War. In other words, Asian politics and economics developed in a framework of statism,

nationalism and capitalism (profit motive) in Communist and non-Communist states.

- *During the Cold War era, the global context was overtly bipolar but multipolarity was the basis of inter-state behaviour in Asia.* Multipolarity – mostly 'loose' – existed on a continental scale in Asia and in each sub-region (South Asia, South East Asia and North Asia). At the regional level multipolarity challenged the bipolar overlay in Asia–Pacific international relations. The Korean War revealed the emergence of three major powers (the US, Soviet Russia and China) and two smaller powers (North and South Korea). Each had its own set of strategic interests, threat perceptions and a pattern of behaviour and relationships with each other. These did not fit neatly into the bipolar scheme. In South Asia also there were three major players (as above) and two regional rivals (India and Pakistan) and a number of smaller South Asian states. Finally, in South East Asia, a number of autonomous regional influences were in play along with the international powers and the Europeans. In each instance, the multipolarity was loose, just as Soviet/American bipolarity was also loose and not tight in Asia. It was tight in the superpowers' confrontation in Europe in the late 1940s and early 1950s but not so in Asian affairs.

Regionalism grew in the Cold War era. It revealed the presence of three major centres of regional (or sub-regional) gravity. By 'gravity' I mean the emergence of centres of strategic/diplomatic/economic actions that altered the distributions of power and the pattern of relationships among major and minor powers. Here a centre of gravity refers to the pattern of developments and the sequence of events that have high impact and the likelihood of great danger and instability unless constructive strategies are formed to achieve stability and growth in conflict-prone areas. A centre of gravity has a number of well-defined characteristics. The interactions within clearly defined areas are intense, continuous, durable and significant. The interactions are driven by the attitudes, interests and policies of the major and minor players who are mindful about the actions of their geographic neighbours and their consequences for the neighbourhood. Even though each region (sub-region) has defined geographic boundaries, the boundaries of the system are dynamic in the sense that they respond to changing problems and issues and changing behaviour patterns and alignments among the major and minor powers. Although *ideologies* are important, they are *secondary in comparison to the impact of interests* (i.e. Vietnam, a former enemy of the USA is now an American strategic partner in the post-Cold War era).

The point being made is that such regional (sub-regional) systems started to emerge in Asia–Pacific during the Cold War era. The three principal centres of gravity were North East Asia, South East Asia and South Asia. In each case, countries were locked in their respective regions as a result of geography, strategic and economic issues, the impact of neighbourly quarrels on their internal well-being, the impact of outside intervention on regional politics and the opportunities to develop international alliances in the context of regional quarrels.

In other words, precisely when the super powers appeared to be the dominant players in Asia–Pacific, the Cold War era, regionalism and regional multipolarity emerged as a significant parallel trend to East–West bipolarity in Asia–Pacific.

- Finally, this period also saw *the growth of the number and influence of minor powers in Asia–Pacific*. North American scholarship does not take seriously the idea of minor powers. North American scholarship relies heavily on the 'dominant–subordinate states' system paradigm or on the 'great powers' – small state' paradigm. These paradigms distort scholarly and policy analysis. My work relies on British scholarship, especially the work of the late Professor Martin Wight that offers insights about the grading of different kinds of 'powers' and the relational context in which major and minor powders function. Wight's definitions and categories require elaboration, and this is done in Table 3.2. This table helps us locate Asian 'powers' in the grading scheme, and the important role they play in the Asia–Pacific and Indian Ocean areas.

Table 3.1 shows the staying power of Asia–Pacific in world politics. Table 3.2 shows the grading of 'powers' (great ones and minor ones, regional, middle and small). The criteria in this table will be used to assess the proposition that the number of and influence of minor powers increases precisely when the qualifications of the great powers are in dispute; and this is the trend in Asia–Pacific since 1945. Furthermore, Tables 3.1 and 3.2 help us examine the nature of regionalism and the multipolar regional linkages in Asia–Pacific. Here we visualize the minor powers getting out of their country boxes, and into the region or into their strategic neighbourhood; here a geo-political pattern of thought and behaviour is indicated. Secondly, we visualize the minor powers, especially the regional great powers, emerging as candidates for middle power status and influence. These suggestions imply that the great power(s) (i.e. the US or Russia) no longer enjoy a commanding presence in Asia–Pacific. They have the strongest power in comparative and notional terms but they cannot pursue their interests unaided and they cannot alone shape the pattern of relationships or alignments in Asia–Pacific. The US is no longer able to fulfil the criteria of a great power laid out in Table 3.2.

The foundation of 'soft regionalism' in ASEAN was established during the Cold War/bipolar era in Asia–Pacific. 'Loose regional multipolarity' in the Korean War and in Far East international relations also emerged during the Cold War/bipolar era. US practitioners also became preoccupied with the issue of 'regional hegemons' in Asia–Pacific at this time. This indicated an awareness of the threat to US authority and prestige from potential regional hegemons. Historically, great powers have relied on a set of classical strategies

Table 3.2 Grading of powers

Criteria	*Type of Power*				
	Great power	*Regional power*	*Middle power*	*Small power*	*Failing state*
1. Ambition to be world Leader	Yes	Maybe	No	No	No
2. Scope of general interests extensive (globally and/or in a region)	Yes	Variable	Variable	No	No
3. Capacity to act alone	Yes	Yes, regionally	No	No	No
4. Possess strength over neighbours	Yes	Yes	No	No	No
5. International role(s) differ	Yes	Leader within region	Follows diversion of labour with global leader	No	No
6. Possesses technological edge in military and	Yes	Yes, in region	Yes, in some areas	No	No
7. Has ability to create and maintain international and/or regional institutions	Yes	Yes, within region	No, but participates actively in such institutions	No	No
8. There is external recognition of its superior important position	Yes	Yes, in a regional context	Yes, as a middle power	Yes, as a local power	No

Note: Excluded from this list are 'failed states', and 'nobodies' (i.e. who lack motivation and capacity to shape/alter the pattern of global/regional relationships (e.g. Somalia) to manage the international environment: namely, creating a great powers' concert by 'clubbing together' to set the rules or the norms of good international behaviour vis-à-vis dissatisfied states or the new challenges to world order. Alternatively, a great power could act alone and intervene coercively to create order. These options are now costly for the great powers.

Asia–Pacific is outside control of great powers

In the context of the developments discussed in Tables 3.1 and 2, the situation in Asia points to an overarching theme: that is, no combination of international powers has been able to dominate the major and minor Asian powers in Asia since the 1950s. Neither the US nor Russia nor the Europeans have been able to tame Asian powers and to integrate Asian states into their orbit. Since 1945, Asians have gradually acquired the characteristics of minor powers in Table 3.2. Chapter 2 outlined the importance of nationalism, science and democracy in Asia since the turn of the 20th century. In the last fifty years, this combination has taken shape. It has emerged as the basis of the growth of regionalism as well as regional great powers in Asia–Pacific. Nationalism means the growth of political consciousness and political organization among the Asian powers. It creates a public identification with a country's political and social thought and its economic, social and military interests and strategies. The development of science in Asia–Pacific has led to the growth of technological prowess, an ability to reduce dependence on Western scientific and technological imports. The growth of independent scientific and technological capabilities implies an ability to work around a variety of Western technological controls and barriers to Asian scientific development. The development of science in Asia reflects a recognition that science is the ticket to modernization as well as the way to gain political and strategic independence. The question 'Can you be independent in thought and action without possessing a stable and growing industrial and technological infrastructure along with chemicals and nuclear explosives capacity?' has been answered by the Asians. The answer is that armed struggle, or the acquisition of the means to wage war and act alone, and to achieve technological independence, are the bases of national independence; cultural and political discourse has to be built on such capacity. Democracy is the third element in the equation. Democracy is not simply about having fair and regular elections. Rather it is a practical method to accommodate diversity, to adjust conflicting interests and diverse perceptions or world-views within the state and society or in international society. So faith in democracy is both a method and an attitude. It now has appeal even in Communist and authoritarian regimes. Communist powers emphasize the importance of inner-party democracy. In China, even when there is only one candidate up for election, democracy exists in terms of the debate that proceeds the selection of the single official candidate. In Communist states, even if Western type electoral democracy does not exist at the national level, it exists at the local level. In this sense, the seed of democracy has been planted in the Asia political landscape. The expectation is that the seed will grow.

Earlier I indicated that Asia has been out of control since 1945. What do I mean by this? After the USSR's collapse in 1989–90, the US declared that it had won the Cold War and that it was now the sole superpower. This was a rash and premature prediction because there is no evidence that the US can pursue its interests unaided in Asia. Indeed, there is contrary evidence that the US government has increasingly found itself locked into negotiating relationships with the North Koreans, Chinese, Indians, Vietnamese, Russians and the Japanese. The US government needs their cooperation to pursue its strategic and economic agenda. So the American declaration that the end of the Cold War had created the unipolar moment has fallen by the wayside. Furthermore, even American partners in Asia are engaging the US with a view to checking its influence. China talks with the USA but it wants to check its influence in Taiwan, the Korean peninsula, the South China Seas, South Asia and South East Asia. Russia is down but not out in Asia. Boris Yeltsin's successor, Putin, has savaged Chechniya, he is negotiating with China, talking with the Japanese, pushing for a new strategic relationship with India and Vietnam and talks with the US in a cool detached business-like way; he seeks a new basis for a relationship that locks America into the Russian strategic and political agenda. China and Russia have taken steps to form a new strategic relationship. Its goal is to contain the possibility of American unipolarity, and to contain Western influence in the Russian and Chinese strategic neighbourhoods. In attempting to develop a new relationship, Russia and China are both pressuring America. Russia wants China's support against USA and China is telling USA that a new Sino-Russian bloc is an option. In other words, the two giants in the Eurasian landmass are using each other to pressurize America. The Great Game continues to be played on the Eurasian continental scale.

Japan also has a complicated attitude towards the West. It is an American ally but its attitude to America is ambivalent. The realities are that the USA needs Japan to promote its interests vis-à-vis China, Russia, North Korea, Taiwan and the protection of the sea lanes in Northern Pacific. At the same time, Japan needs American military protection against China and Korea. These circumstances point to a relationship of constant bargaining and at times disharmony when perceptions and interests vary. Japan owes America nothing. Japan is currently going through a big domestic defence debate. At issue is the future nature of Japanese defence organizational and technological infrastructure and the future pattern of Japan's strategic relationship with its senior partner, USA. For almost fifty years, Japan had a defence allergy. As a result of Japan's war time experience, Japan's political class and public opinion hesitated to create a clear public stance on defence issues. Japan's political class was content to leave defence questions in the hands of the Americans. Following North Korean nuclear development and missile tests across Japan in 1997–8, there is unease in Japan about North Korea's intentions but also about possible differences in the strategic priorities of

USA and Japan. For instance, the North Korean missile program had an immediate impact on Japanese élite and public opinion because of geographical proximity, whereas the impact on American thinking is long-term. Japan relies heavily on American military intelligence inputs in assessing major developments in its neighbourhood. Now doubts exists among Japanese practitioners whether American intelligence inputs are timely and complete, and whether Japan should be developing independent intelligence means through satellite development and other sources. The North Korean missile program and the reaction in Japan has gone a long way in shedding Japan's defence allergy. Now defence issues are openly debated in the Japanese parliament (Diet) and in the media. Defence decision-making is being reorganized and coordinated better among the bureaucracies. The centre of decision-making has now moved closer to the prime ministerial and cabinet levels and plans are under way to break down the compartmentalization in intelligence acquisition among the different branches of the Japanese armed forces. In other words, the Japanese domestic structure is undergoing fundamental and subtle shifts that reflect heightened defence consciousness and planning. The nuclear allergy is still there but one should keep in mind that Japan, unlike Germany, is not a convinced non- proliferator. It has all the means to go nuclear at will, although at present, it does not have the incentive to do so. Consequently, Japanese non-proliferation is a product of the strategic situation in Northern Asia, and the level of confidence in the military relationship with America. One should be aware that the issue of nuclear proliferation has not been put to rest in Asia. There are five declared nuclear powers in Asia: the US, China, Russia, India and Pakistan. Japan is a potential nuclear power or a latent nuclear state; and North Korea has an active albeit primitive missile program and a nuclear weapons capability. Given the growing list of nuclear proliferators in Asia and the absence of a stable strategic structure in Asia, the future of the nuclear question in Japan is hence unsettled.

This discussion indicates that Asia is full of high impact and high probability strategic situations that are potentially destabilizing. Russia and China are important for a variety of reasons. (1) If they come together, they form a powerful critical mass, which can undermine the Western security as well as many Asian states. (2) If they fight each other or remain rivals, they obviously neutralize each other's strength, but this scenario also creates a danger of instability in the region. (3) If one or both were to collapse internally, a powerful vacuum would emerge. This would likely unleash conflicts and instabilities or civil war-like conditions. All these possibilities are dangerous in different ways. Furthermore, in assessing external strategic relationships, one must be mindful of the impact of internal politics of external affairs. China, Indonesia, India, Pakistan, North Korea are examples where political instability and internal dissent leads to social and economic tensions that undermine the fabric of civil society and external stability. If the Far East is one major centre of high impact, high probability strategic danger(s), other

Paradigm | Global | Flow of Power

1. Global bipolarity/Cold War 1940s–90 (dominant-subordinate system)

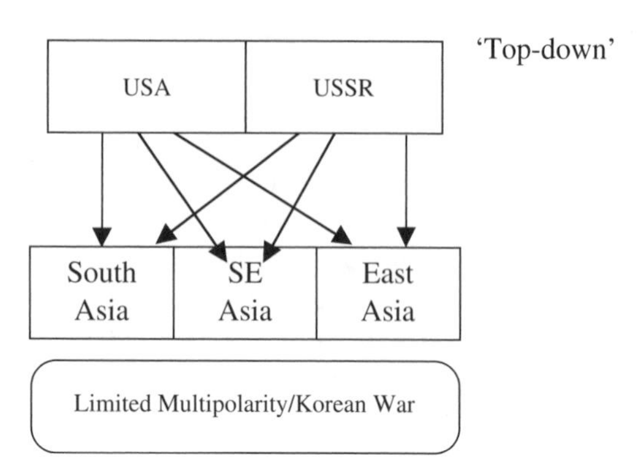

'Top-down'

2. Loose multipolarity, 1950–1990 (Dominant–subordinate system)

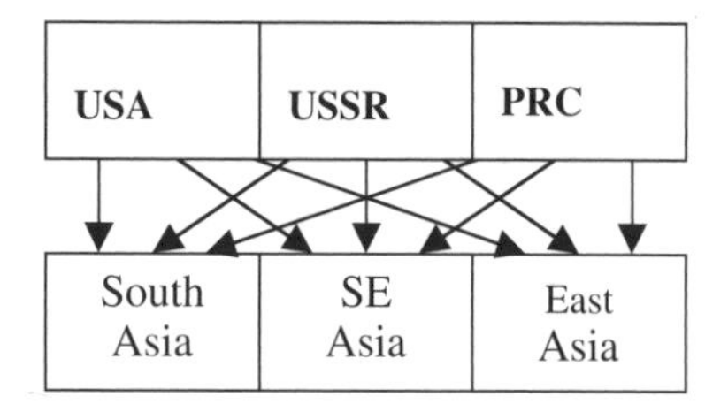

'Top-down'

Growth of limited power and limited autonomy by minor Asian powers

3. Loose multipolarity during Cold War & following its end, 1947–present

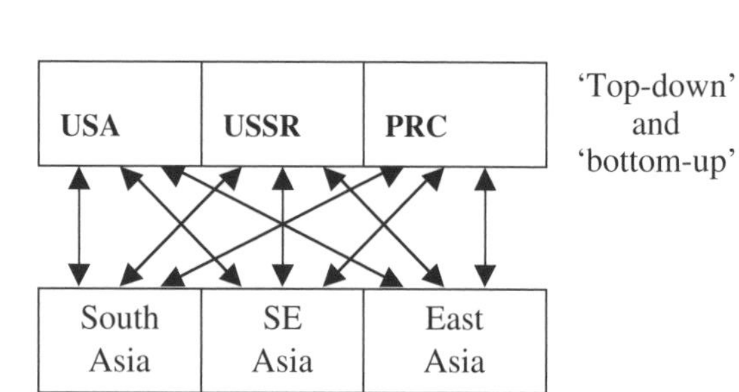

'Top-down' and 'bottom-up'

Figure 3.1 Overview of international structures in Asia–Pacific 1915–present

areas contain similar dangers. A Talibanized or a failing Pakistan obviously opens up a scenario of intervention by Pakistan's neighbours and the great powers whose vital strategic interests are engaged in the region. The future of maritime security in the Taiwan straits, the South China Seas, and the Indian Ocean – the arc from Japan to Israel – is vital to the interests of several Asian powers including the US, Japan and India. This points to the growing importance of naval security in the policies of Japan, India and China in Asia–Pacific today.

The first paradigm in Figure 3.1 represents the dominant view in Western scholarship. However, in the author's judgement multipolar tendencies became apparent, for example in the Korean War. See *The Cold War in Asia*, (Cold War International History Project, Woodrow Wilson International Center for Scholars, Washington, DC, Winter 1995/6).

The second paradigm reflects the emergence of PRC as the third voice in international security issues, e.g. in arms control and disarmament negotiations, in East European international relations and Communist states' and Communist parties' relationships during the Cold War (1960s–1990), in SE Asia from 1940s to present, in South Asia from 1949 to present. This paradigm emphasizes the rise of multipolarity at the global level, and in the Asian continent. It was evident in international conference diplomacy e.g. in Indo-China accords and Bandung conference (1954), in the flow of military and diplomatic activity during conflicts and wars, e.g. during the Vietnam War, in interventionist activities by the great powers, e.g. in Indonesian affairs. That is in each instance, the great powers acted with an awareness of rivalry among the three powers. The rivalries affected their behaviour at the global, regional (Asian) and sub-regional (South, South East and East Asian) levels. This paradigm notes the development of multipolarity at the sub-regional level as a result of the rise of minor powers in Asia who were acquiring the characteristics of a regional great power, a middle power and a small power. However, there was limited engagement and challenge by the minor powers vis-à-vis the great powers.

In hindsight, 'loose multipolarity' in Asia–Pacific was safe. The great powers' rivalries created manageable instability and mutual accommodation. They did not go to war. They compromised and compensated each other. Also in hindsight, 'loose multipolarity' at the sub-regional level during the Cold War era led to wars; it was not safe until the emergence of a regional great power in East Asia (Japan), South Asia (India) and in SE Asia (Australia/Indonesia), and a number of small powers (North Korea, Taiwan, Singapore, Malaysia).

The third paradigm rests on the proposition that multipolarity exists now at all levels: global politics; regional (Asian continental) politics and sub-regional politics in Asia. This paradigm expects the flow of power to go two ways: 'top–down' and 'bottom–up'. Despite the asymmetry in the distribution of military and economic power between the great powers and the minor powers, the paradigm predicts that the ability of great powers to act alone, or through great powers' concert or club, to wage war, to create and to maintain international institutions or regimes, to enforce discipline among minor powers has declined: i.e. their qualifications as great powers are in question. At the same time, the autonomy and the influence of the minor powers – their ability to shape regional security structures and to occupy space in the international system has increased significantly.

Figure 3.1 shows the development of complex relationships and functions of international structures in Asia–Pacific, from 1947 to the present. They indicate the emergence of processes and institutions that result in manageable instability or a stable form of 'regional power formation' and 'conflict formation'. That is, the parameters of military and social conflict are well defined in different sub-regions of Asia–Pacific and there is no expectation of general war or a nuclear holocaust in Asia. These structures do not predict the emergence of total harmony, or positive peace, or equilibrium in Asia. Rather 'moderate stability' among warring states, and attempts at peace settlements are the expected norms. This is a situation of temporary military truces between states engaged in deadly quarrels rather than one of a substantial political settlement. In this context, the tactical aims are to extend the truces, to find ways to convert deadly quarrels into ritual confrontations, to discover the negotiating space among the warring factions within and between states and to develop strategies to settle disputes. This is not an easy task because limited stability is being sought in a complex context. There is asymmetry in the distribution of power and influence among the major and minor powers in Asia. Among Asian rivals, hostility, mistrust and a search for revenge for past grievances shapes the worldviews of the élites and the public. The élites preside over fragile, fragmented and competitive domestic coalitions. Consequently, a combination of cultural differences and political controversies, mutual mistrust and dilemmas of 'limited peace' require two paradoxical strategies: military modernization to guard against dangerous contingencies and, on the other hand, methods to secure confidence building and peaceful political settlement(s). The first strategy rests on the proposition in classical military and realpolitik thought that one must prepare for war if one wants peace. The second strategy rests on the proposition of peace researchers that one must prepare for peace if one wants peace. Both approaches are relevant in Asian affairs, and this book treats them as two integrated tracks, and not as an either–or proposition.

Towards development of bargaining relations between great (declining and ascendant) powers and minor ones

Asia–Pacific international relations today face a choice between two approaches. The first seeks a new balance of power or a multipolar system. Western and Chinese think-tank publications favour this approach.[20] This approach requires rule by condominium or by a competitive balance among great powers and a curb on the ambitions of new entrants to the great power club. Here international competition is eventually accommodated by compromise among the powers so that the vital interests of each are satisfied;

and then ways are found to intervene against the lesser powers or the small states or to co-opt them into the great power definitions of stability and security. Clubbing together of the few powers is the preferred method of action in the Security Council, in G-8 affairs and in international conference diplomacy concerning security issues. Divided power and great power concerted action is preferred to the alternative of a single power hegemony or imperialism.

In Asia–Pacific today, a balance of power approach is attractive in the context of two choices. Dibb defines these as:

> [on the one hand] a peaceful Asia characterized by a growing sense of economic interdependence with a rough balance between competing great-power interests; and a less stable and more unpredictable Asia in which strategic competition and tests of national interests are the dominant forces.[21]

Dibb foresees the possibility of a five-sided balance of power across Asia, with the USA, Russia, China, Japan and India as the key players. Some of these are continental powers and the others are maritime ones. There are, of course, difficulties: 'There is no wider pattern of Asian security that embraces balance of power, conflict resolution, alliances and arms control'. Dibb offers realistic assessments of the capacities and interests of these powers. China is an ascendant power and it is suspicious of others, so cooperation is not easy. There are doubts about American leadership in Asia–Pacific. It seeks a zone of peace in the region based on democracy and economic interdependence (which requires US military strength in the background) but its ability to function as a balancer is problematic, as is the future of its bilateral security ties in the region. Japan is not a great power in the traditional military sense. India has internal and regional problems, as does Russia. At the same time, there are a number of Asian middle powers: a unified Korea, Taiwan, Vietnam, Thailand and Indonesia. (Dibb, an Australian, is silent about Australia's position.[22])

The second choice is the basis of the argument of this book. It rests on several premises. Great powers are in decline in Asia–Pacific; this refers to Russia and America. China is an emergent power. However, its ambition is greater than its present capacity to exert its influence on a global or an all-Asian basis. It undoubtedly is able to bargain with the Russians and the Americans but any sign of expansionism attracts adverse attention from its neighbours. The declining and ascendant great powers have a tendency to club together but, to the extent it exists, the collective strength of this club is not sufficient to marginalize the interests of the minor powers. The latter manage real estate in Asia–Pacific, they are also ambitious and powerful in limited ways and they can escape punishment and isolation in select circumstances; that is, they cannot be ignored. Their existence reveals limits to great power intervention. Finally, Dibb is partly wrong to say that:

> The relations of the principal Asian nations to each other bear most of the attributes of the European balance-of-power system of the 19th century. Any significant increase in strength by one of them is almost certain to evoke an offsetting manoeuvre by the others.[23]

Of Dibb's five key Asian players, the Chinese respond to fears of American and Japanese power, and since 1998 to the growth of Indian nuclear and missile power. Indians react to growth of Chinese power but not to growth of Japanese, American and Russian power. The European analogy must be used with great care, and the classical meanings of balance of power do not appear relevant in the Asian case. Wight distinguishes between different meanings: an even distribution of power exists, or is desired, or there is a tendency in international politics towards evenness; it means the status quo; the responsible power ought to have a margin of strength to keep the peace, and a margin of strength in the enemy camp is undesirable; it means the existence of a balancer.[24] None of these meanings is relevant for Asia–Pacific today, given our premises noted above.

Instead of an all-Asian or a multipolar continental balance, Dibb's conclusion that the national interests of the great powers 'will underscore an uncertainty and basically competitive strategic outlook'[25] is the basis of my argument. The emphasis of both scholarship and policy development should be to develop new bargaining relationships between great and minor powers in Asia–Pacific today in the context of emerging regional systems or sub-systems. Dibb predicts a northward shift in the centre of gravity of Asia–Pacific strategic affairs.[26] Presently, there are five regional sub-systems or 'worlds' with distinctive characteristics, i.e. threat perceptions, pattern or alignments, élite and/or national interests, core strategic values and distribution of power. Each aspect, and none is unimportant, is dynamic and it shapes the rivalries and the negotiating opportunities within each sub-system. Each sub-system is a centre of gravity of conflict and action. In North East Asia, the critical mass comprises the two Koreas, Japan, China, Russia and America. In Taiwan–South China Seas, the critical mass comprises China, Taiwan, the USA and Japan. In South East Asia, the critical mass comprises ASEAN nations, especially Indonesia, Australia, Vietnam, the USA, China. In the Myanmar–Bay of Bengal area, the critical mass comprises China, Myanmar, India, Thailand, the USA and eventually may include Indonesia. In northwest Indian/subcontinent-Gulf area, the critical mass comprises India, Pakistan (including the northern areas which border the Karokaran range and the China–Pakistan highway), China, the USA, Russia and Iran. Significant change in the distribution of power and the pattern of alignment has the potential to change the boundaries, the nature and the stability/instability of each sub-system. Their existence indicates that the 'northward shift' in Dibb's analysis is one of several ongoing and potential shifts. To take an example, if China seeks and achieves a wedge between South and South East Asia by inserting its primary influence into Myanmar and the Bay of Bengal, and if it achieves the same in the South China Seas (these are big ifs but they are not entirely fanciful),[27] China could become the primary balancer of the Asia–Pacific region with the USA as the co-director. In such a scenario, the North East Asian sphere would remain accessible to American power, it would function as a point of pressure against China but it would be isolated from the rest of the Pacific maritime world.

The second and the preferred choice then is to take a part of the balance of power idea and to fashion a proactive strategy which produces stability and security for great and minor powers who participate in the regional sub-systems. This approach has two aims. The first is to encourage the development of economic and military strength of major and minor powers as per their threat perceptions. The USA should contribute intelligence to internal debates about threat perceptions but it should not try to foist globalist security regimes that are not relevant to local and regional politics and security planning.

However, the development of economic and military strength in the context of uncertain contingencies within our five regional sub-systems requires a second leg as well: the development of stabilizing patterns of relationships between competitive states. Specifically, this requires a security architecture with two channels to develop bargains. The approach rejects the value of great power concerts *à la* Henry Kissinger and Alastair Buchan as the way to organize regional international relations. Instead, the approach relies more on bargains between great powers and regional great powers; and second, to develop bargains between regional great powers and the local powers and small states. The basis of these bargains should not only be the distribution of power and the self-importance of the great powers or the lesser ones. Rather, to endure, the bargains require the voluntary, negotiated consent of the regional great powers/middle powers and the local powers/small states respectively.[28] Regional hegemons should also be recognized by the US as legitimate players because they provide countervailing influence against expansionist tendencies of other hegemons in neighbouring regional sub-systems; e.g. Japan should be inducted into the China–Taiwan–South China Seas area, and India into South East Asia. Attempts to equalize military and economic power within regional sub-systems will fail because the regional hegemons will regard such action as an invitation to self-immolation, a denial of power, security, influence and prestige, and a form of great power intervention and containment in the name of international security. Regional military balances are meaningless because often the members of regional systems or sub-systems are from outside the geographical boundaries of the region. (That is, to achieve a regional military balance, a regional state will borrow power through external military aid and alliance activity.) Note that the distribution of military and economic power in all our five regional sub-systems is asymmetrical. By itself, the power distribution neither explains nor predicts the patter of relationships in each system or subsystem and as such, it is not useful to rely on old balance of power thinking that highlights military balances between regional rivals. My preferred strategy rests on the pattern of balance of power activity as outlined in Tables 3.3 and 3.4.

Table 3.3 'Balance of power' activity by major powers in Asia

Players	*Key events*		*Key issues*	*Power shifts*		
				Military	*Economic*	*Strategy*
Japan	1945	Defeated in 2nd World War	Rebuild Japan, its power & prestige	↓↑	↓↑	↓↑
China	1949	Victorious in Revolution	Rebuild its power & prestige	↑	↑	↑
		Promotes revolutionary violence in Asia & Africa				
		Emerges as a third force in Asia				
Russia	1945	Shut out of Japan	Build USSR's Asian power	↑	↑	↑
	1949	Builds Indian & other Asian links		↑	↑	↑
	1990	End of Cold War		↓	↓	↓
	1999	Putin presidency revitalizes Russia's internal & international position		↔	↔	↔

USA	1945	Pre-eminent power in East Asia & in Pacific	↑	↑	↑
	1960s	Lost Vietnam War & authority in Asia	↓	↓	↓
	1972	Engages in triangular diplomacy with PRC & USSR: USA can't pursue its interests unaided	↔	↔	↔
	1990	End of Cold War reverts USA's pre-eminence but USA is engaged with PRC, Japan & India who all challenge USA's authority; USA can't pursue its interests unaided	↔	↔	↔
India	1947	Gains independence	↑	↑	↑
		Gains international diplomatic status			
	1971	Breaks up Pakistan			
	1974–98	Tests nuclear weapons			

Table 3.4. Characteristics of Asia–Pacific system of states

Characteristics	*Examples*
1. There are multiple powers at international, continental and sub-regional levels.	US, China, Japan, India, Russia and others
2. The distribution of military and economic power at all three levels is changing.	China, India, Japan
3. Alliances shift and are stable; conflicts/ instability is manageable/are limited.	Yes, in all regions
4. Regional interdependencies have emerged.	Yes, in all regions
5. Non-ideological, interests'-driven policies and attitudes are dominant form of inter-state behaviour.	Yes, in all regions
6. Coordinated, interactive diplomacy is the norm.	Yes, in all regions
7. There are an increasing number of regional great powers.	India, Iran, Japan, Indonesia (?)
8. There are an increasing number of Asian small/local powers.	Yes, in all regions
9. The qualification of great powers are changing and some are downwardly mobile.	USSR is example
10. The autonomy of minor powers is increasing vis-à-vis great powers.	North Korea–US bargaining relationship
11. The Asian balance of power is taking shape and it has particular meaning(s) or characteristics.	Still evolving

4 Tied together by power politics and notional realities

The great powers in Asia in the 19th and 20th centuries

Introduction

The chapter deals with a number of important geo-strategic and geo-political questions. The theme is that the powers often couch their policies in abstract and ideological generalizations or notional realities (like making the world safe for democracy and fighting communism) but these are only tenuously connected to the real conflicts. My concern is the focus on the latter. A geo-strategic region is an area 'large enough to possess certain globe-influencing characteristics and functions'. It symbolizes an inter-relationship of 'location, movement, trade orientation, and cultural or ideological bonds'. Its raison d'etre is to embrace a single-feature region over which power can be projected but, in reality, it is composed of a multi-feature region connected by strategic land and sea passageways. In contrast, a geo-political region has unified geographic features notably proximity of location and complementarity of resources, which serves as the platform for common political and economic actions. Geo-political regions exist within geo-strategic regions. In this regard, it is important to understand that geo-strategic regions connote a strategic role, while the geo-political region is tactical.[1]

1. What were the sources and patterns of strategic thought and strategic 'movement' of great powers into Asia–Pacific and the Indian Ocean area before the 20th century. (According to Cohen, 'colonialism, as a process involves settlement from a mother country, generally into empty lands and bringing to these lands the previous culture and organization of the parent society'. 'Imperialism as distinct from colonialism refers to domination over indigenous people, transforming their ideas, institutions and goods'.[2])

2. *Where did the great powers compete in* Asia–Pacific during the 19th and 20th century? What were the areas in contention and why (issues and interests)?

3. What were/are the *principles of great powers' behaviour* in the development of pattern of relationships in the 19th and 20th century?

4. Have 'globalization', 'economic interdependence', nuclear weapons and arms control replaced 'geo-politics' and 'cultural conflict' in Asia–Pacific in the 20th century?

5. What are the sources and patterns of strategic thought and strategic

movement that shape international relations of Asia–Pacific and the Indian Ocean areas since the 20th century?

The chapter deals with the general patterns of strategic movement and organization of power and principles in geographically defined spheres. The chapter is not centred on a single country or single power. References to the pattern of European, American and Russian expansion are meant to illustrate the enormous impact of internationalist forces on Asia–Pacific/Indian Ocean affairs in the 19th century. They provide the necessary historical context to the contemporary pattern of nation-building, power-development and diplomatic-military strategies. My focus is on activities which engage the international forces (i.e. powers outside Asia–Pacific and the Indian Ocean area) by coercive and diplomatic means and which have altered the pattern of relationships and the distribution of power between Asian and non-Asian powers. The temporal divide is between the 19th and the 20th century. The spatial boundaries of Asia–Pacific and the Indian Ocean areas cover almost half the globe now. They have a dynamic history. Before 1945, the boundaries were determined by the points of engagement and the limits of colonial/imperial power. After 1947, the boundaries were shaped by the points of engagement and the limits of American and Russian power and interests and the emerging pockets of autonomy and multipolarity in the Asiatic buffer belt of the 19th century. Now, following the end of the Cold War, the boundaries in Asia are being shaped by the policies of major and minor powers in Asia. They show the influence of full-blown multipolarity in the Asia–Pacific and Indian Ocean spheres. In the 19th century, the boundaries were drawn in a world of open land and sea frontiers. In the 20th century, they reflect the reality of closed frontiers. In other words, the boundaries are changing but the major and minor powers must now seek to discover the wriggle space along fault lines of regional and international strategic systems which rest on an almost universal acceptance of the territorial demarcations of the colonial and imperial eras. In other words, in accepting political independence, the new states in Asia accepted the territorial borders along with the territorial disputes of their former imperial/colonial masters.[3] Bangladesh is the only example of a new state being formed by force in Asia–Pacific and the Indian Ocean area after 1945. 'Changing boundaries' refers to changes in frontiers or zones of competing influence involving rival major and minor powers within the existing states' system in Asia–Pacific and the Indian Ocean area.

Sources and patterns of movement of great powers into Asia–Pacific and the Indian Ocean areas before the 20th century

Three major international forces intruded into Asia–Pacific and the Indian Ocean areas before the 20th century. Map 4.1 outlines the pattern of movement of the European powers that resulted in colonialism and imperialism as

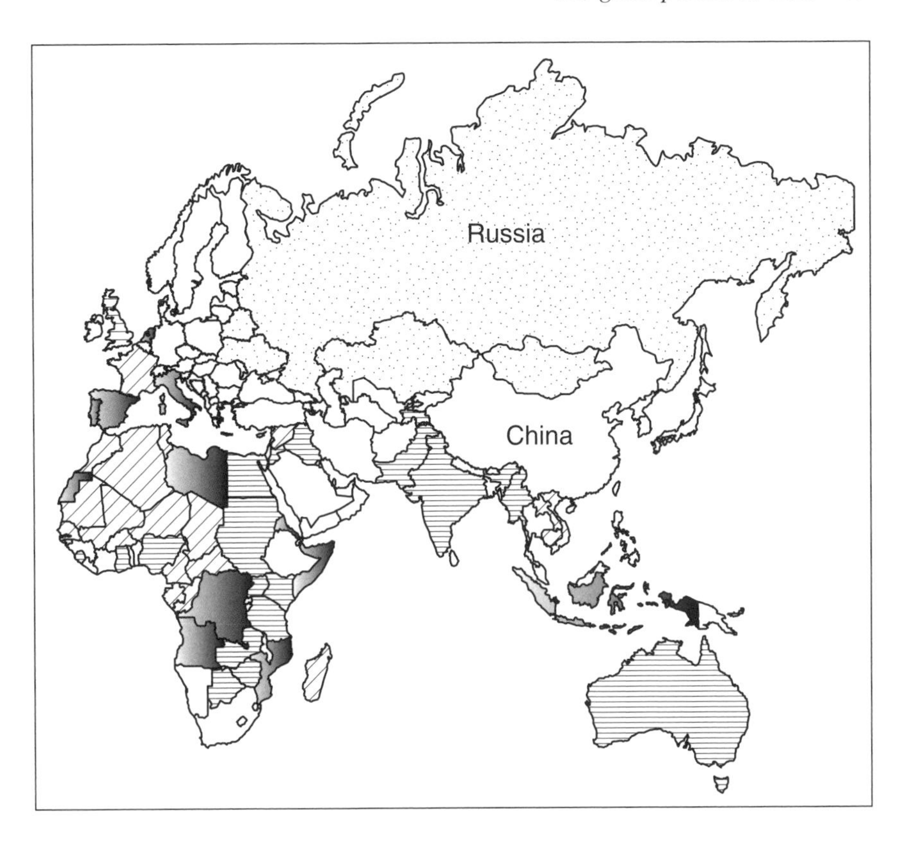

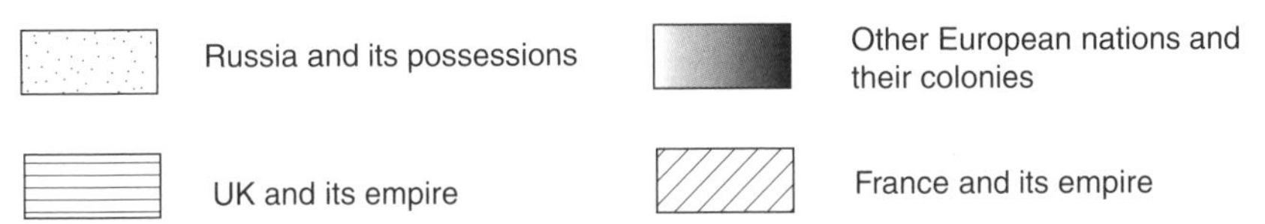

Map 4.1 The world's geo-strategic regions and their geo-political subdivisions. Adapted from S.D. Cohen, *Geography and Politics in a Divided World*, 1973, p. 67.

the dominant form of authority and order in these areas. This movement involved sea power. Map 4.2 outlines the pattern of movement of the Russian Empire into Asia. This movement involved land power. Map 4.3 outlines the pattern of movement of American power into the Far East. This movement involved sea power.

Where did the great powers compete in the 19th to the 20th centuries?

In the 19th century, the great powers competed in the Asiatic buffer belt that extended from the Middle East through the Indian subcontinent, South East

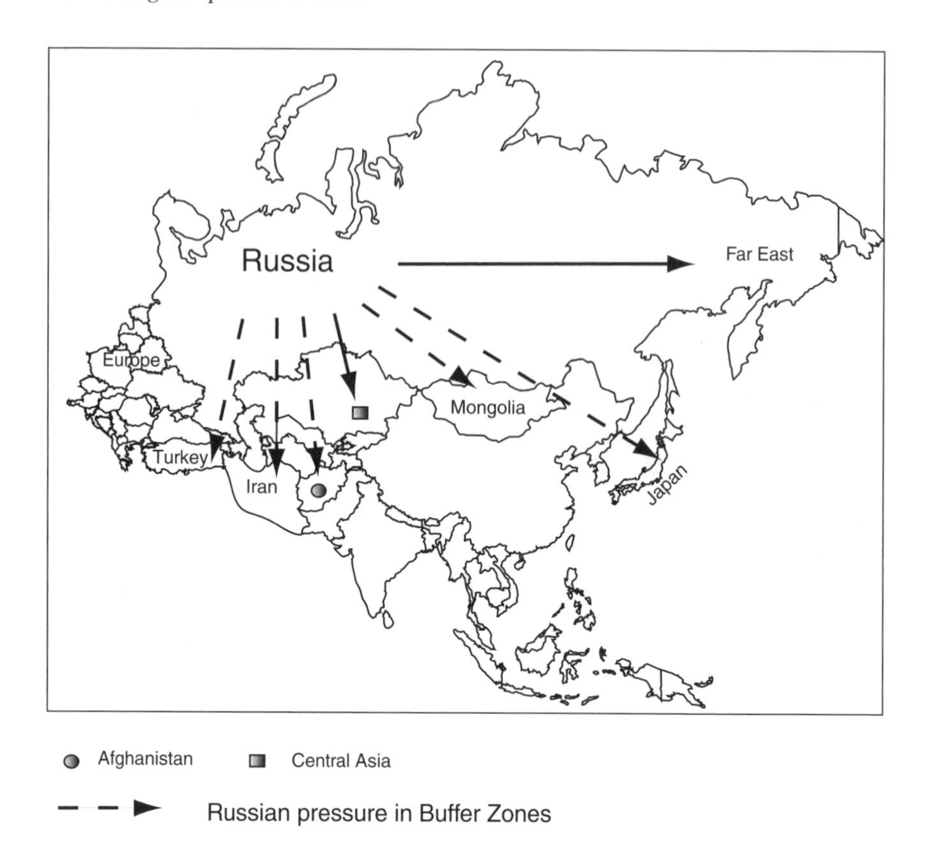

Map 4.2 Russia's movement into the Far East. Adapted from G. Chaliland and J.-P. Rageau, *Strategic Atlas: A Comparative Geopolitics of the World's Powers,* 1983, p. 95.

Asia to the Far East. According to Martin Wight, buffers played an important role in the competition among Great Powers. Maps 4.4 and Map 4.5 show the points of contention between the British and Russian Empires during the 19th century according to Alastair Lamb and Martin Wight respectively.

In the 19th century buffers were used to manage international conflict among the great powers.

Table 4.1 shows the points of contention and the role of buffers in the 19th century involving British, Russian, Japanese and French Empires. Table 4.2 shows the role of buffers both the 19th and 20th centuries. Buffers played a vital role in great powers' imperial strategies in the 19th century according to Martin Wight.

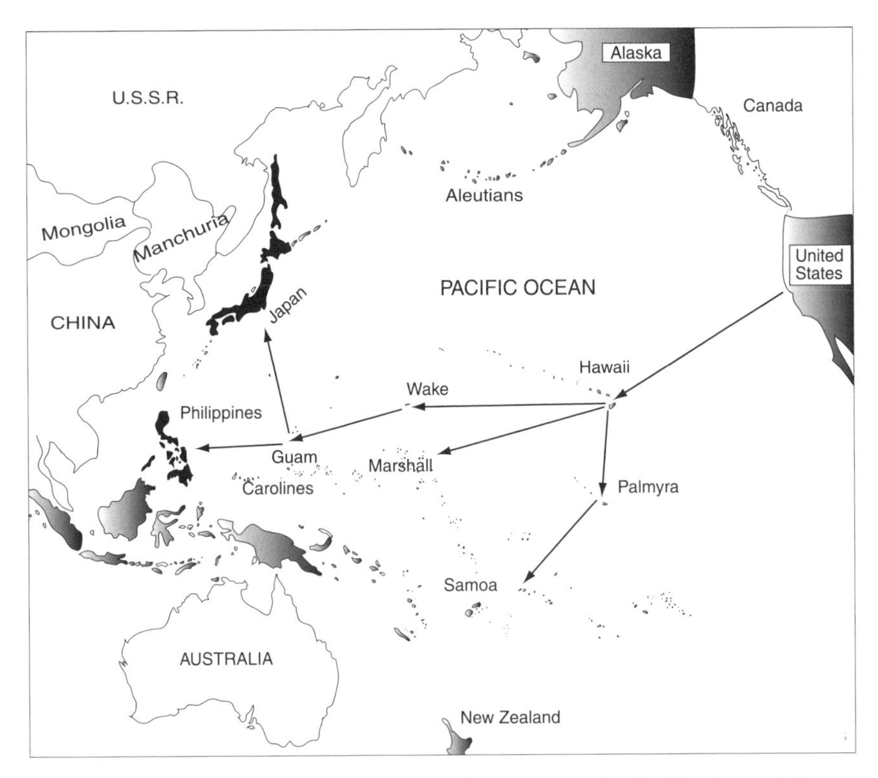

Map 4.3 Movement of the US into the Far East. Source: G. Chaliland and J.-P. Rageau, Strategic Atlas: A Comparative Geopolitics of the World's Powers, 1983, p. 79.

> A buffer state is a weak power between two or more stronger ones, maintained or even created with the purpose of reducing conflict between them. A buffer zone is a region occupied by one or more weaker powers between two or more stronger powers; it is sometimes described as a 'power vacuum'. Each stronger power will generally have a vital interest in preventing the other from controlling the buffer one, and will pursue this buffer zone as neutral and independent, or to establish its own control, which may lead in the long run to its annexing the buffer zone and converting it into a frontier province. Buffer states may therefore be divided into trimmers, neutrals and satellites. Trimmers are states whose policy is prudently to play off their mighty neighbours against one another; . . . Satellites are states whose foreign policy is controlled by another power. If the weaker state has formally conceded this control by treaty, so that in law as well as in fact it has surrendered a measure of its sovereignty, it is known as a protectorate.[4]

A related idea is that of a frontier. According to Alastair Lamb:

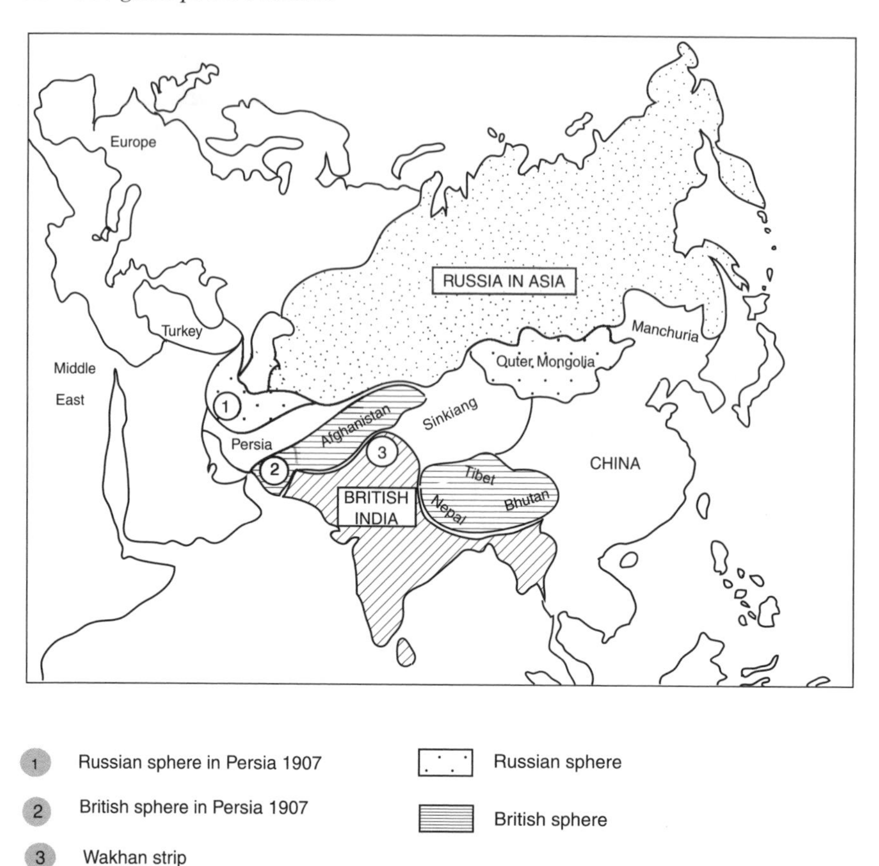

Map 4.4 Buffer zones between the British and Russian empires in the 19th century. A Persia, B Afghanistan, C Tibet, D Outer Mongolia, E singkiang (Chinese Turkestan). Source: Alistair Lamb, *Asian Frontiers*, pp. 62–7.

Frontier is *a zone rather than a line*. It is a tract of territory separating the centers of two sovereignties. A frontier zone may well be a very extensive area, and a dispute over the exact whereabouts of a boundary line through a frontier can involve large tracts of territory. A frontier must be distinguished from a boundary, which is a clear divide between sovereignties that can be marked as a line on the map. It has length, but not area. If the boundary is capable of being set out on the map, and if it is explicitly accepted by the states which it divides, even though they have not got down to the task of setting up boundary posts or otherwise laying down the boundary on the ground – a situation which frequently arises where the boundary passes through difficult country – then that boundary is said to have been *delimited*. A properly demarcated

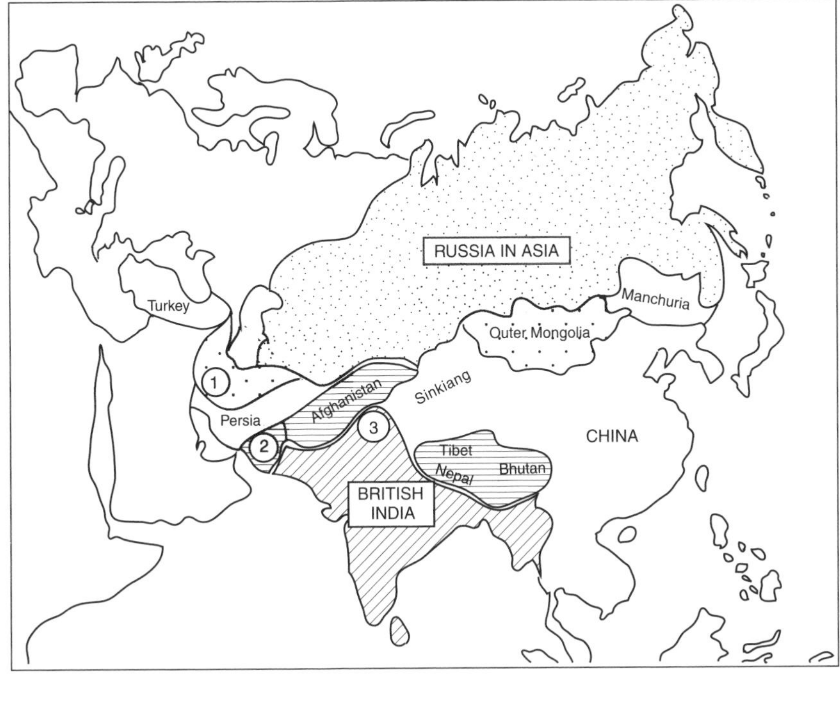

1 Russian sphere in Persia 1907

2 British sphere in Persia 1907

3 Wakhan strip

Russian sphere

British sphere

Map 4.5 Buffer zones between Britain and Russia in the 19th century. A Turkey, B Persia, C Afghanistan, D Tibet, E Manchuria. Source: Martin Wright, *Power Politics*, 1978, pp. 160–5, adapted from Alistair Lamb, *Asian Frontiers*, p. 63.

> boundary should be free from disputes if the parties concerned accept the validity of the act of demarcation. A delimited boundary may well produce disputes arising from differing interpretations of its verbal or cartographic definition.[5]

Finally, Map 4.6 shows the size of the Asiatic buffer belt, extending from Iran to SE Asia and the Korean peninsula.

What were/are the principles of great powers' behaviour?

My assessment of regional and international relationships in Asia–Pacific and the Indian Ocean area relies primarily on the *pattern of power* and less so

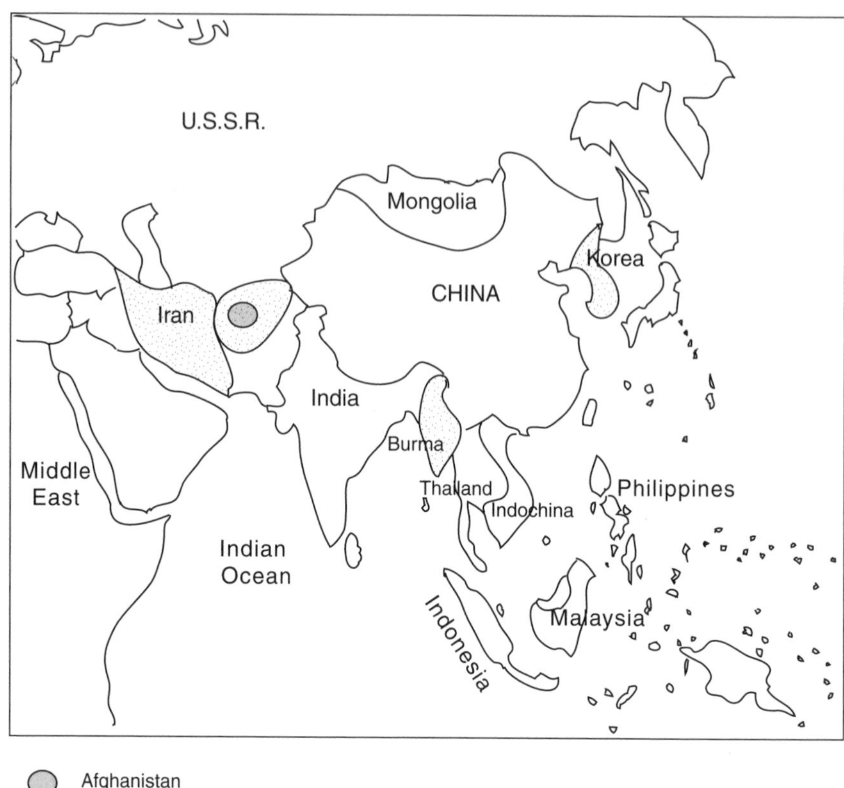

Map 4.6 Buffer zones in the mid-20th century. A Iran, B Afghanistan, C Pakistan, D India, E Burma, F Indo-China, G Thailand, H Indonesia, I Malaysia, J Philippines, K Korea

on the distribution of power. My work assumes that there is asymmetry in the distribution of power even among the major powers and between major and minor ones. The *first premise* is that no power can make policy or pursue its interests without reliance on other powers and without a reference to local and regional conditions in countries which are designated as buffers, neutrals and satellites. The conditions are dynamic because buffer states can become neutral or satellite states, and neutrals or satellites may be able to develop a policy of a buffer state (discussed below). So major and minor powers need to be continuously attentive about developments in regions and countries, and they need to be constantly engaged. Hence no power is able to act in complete detachment because no power is completely self-sufficient even if it enjoys a massive advantage in the distribution of power. Self-interest requires cooperation. Expediency and rationality is the basis of international and

Table 4.1 Buffer zones in the 19th century

Country	*Buffer zone between*
Turkey (1978); Persia Afghanistan, Tibet (1907); Sinakiang (Chinese Turkestan), Outer Mongolia	British and Russian Empires
Nepal (after 1816); Tibet (1886–1914)	British and Chinese Empires
Manchuria (at the end of the 19th Century)	Russian and Japanese Empires
Siam (Thailand) 1867–1896)	British and French Empires
China (because of the weakness of the Chinese Empire during the late 19th and early 20th centuries)	British, Russian, French and Japanese Empires

Sources: Alastair Lamb, *Asian Frontiers: Studies in a Continuing Problem*, New York: Frederick A. Praeger: 1968, pp. 62–7; and Martin Wright, *Power Politics*, Leicester: Leicester University Press, 1978, pp. 160–6.

Note: The British and French definitions of the boundaries of Thailand were a combination of three separate arrangements, namely the 1896 Burma–Laos border along the Mekong; the 1867 Thai–Cambodian border; and the 1896 Thai–Malaysian border. See Lamb, pp. 161–5.

regional cooperation.[6] Even a superpower is tied to the behaviour and interests of other major and minor powers. The *second premise* is that powers are natural rivals because of ambition, jealousy, competing interests and a preoccupation with their vital interests, prestige and domestic as well as public opinion.[7] Territorial neighbours also tend to be rivals, e.g. Russia–China, China–India, India–Pakistan, Israeli–Arab neighbours, Iran–Iraq, Iran–Saudi Arabia. If countries are not geographically contiguous, they may be connected by sea frontiers, e.g. China–Japan through the Sea of Japan, China–Taiwan through the Taiwan straits, USA–China through the Taiwan straits, the South China Seas and the Pacific as well as the Indian Oceans generally.

There are two *exceptions* to the premises, according to Wight: (1) if competing powers reach a permanent political settlement (which is rare but not unknown in history, e.g. USA–Canada) the countries become interdependent or/and indifferent in select areas; (2) the competing powers develop a joint interest in relation to a third country or a lesser power or on a major issue. This results in the development of a cooperative or a changing alignment, depending on the durability of the issue and the sentiment. For example, in the 18th century Prussia and Russia had a joint interest in suppressing Polish nationalism. The result was Prussian–Russian friendship for 100 years.[8] Today, despite their mutual rivalry and differences in foreign and military affairs, Turkey, Iran and Iraq have a joint interest in suppressing Kurdish nationalism and keeping it partitioned. In the 1950s, USA joined

Table 4.2. Buffer zones in the 19th and mid-20th centuries

Buffer between	*Early 19th century*	*Late 19th century*	*Mid-20th century*
British and Russian Empires	Turkey (1978); Persia Afghanistan, Tibet (1970); Sinakiang (Chinese Turkestan), Outer Mongolia		
British, French, Japanese and Russian Empires		China	
British and French Empires	Siam (Thailand)		
Japanese and Russian Empires	Manchuria		
America and Russia			Iran, Afghanistan
America, Russia and China			South East Asia Indonesia, Thailand, Philippines); Indo-China (Vietnam, Laos, Cambodia); Burma, India
Russia, Pakistan and America			Afghanistan
China and Britain		Malaysia	
China, Japan and Russia	Korea and Manchuria		

Notes: By 1907, the four major powers in territorial contact with China were all so tied to each other by a complex of treaties that no one power could move without giving the other compensation elsewhere. The Russo-Japanese War (1905) compelled Russia to retreat to the 1858–60 frontier line along the Amur and Ussuri Rivers.

France to suppress Vietnamese nationalism but the effort failed. The British Empire wisely retreated when it confronted Indian nationalism but, on the other hand, the history of the development of the British Empire in India was a story of constantly changing alignments in relation to Indian princely states where the British Crown aligned with one side at the expense of a third party.[9] After Indian independence Pakistan, USA and China tried repeatedly to divide Indian nationalism by promoting Indian regionalism and balkanization. This strategy could succeed if Indians remain internally divided and confused about the future of the Indian Union.

The development of *joint interests as the basis of a temporary friendship* between or among the powers is not rare. For e.g. the US–USSR were against China in the 1950s and the 1960s. The US–PRC opposition to USSR in the 1970s and the 1980s was a basis of US–PRC normalization in the 1970s. The Security Council permanent members were against India in the non-proliferation and comprehensive test ban negotiations. There is speculation that the US and the USSR were against German and Korean national unification movements because they preferred partition and the preservation of their respective spheres of influence to the growth of German and Korean unity and autonomy.

The search for temporary friendship at the expense of third-party interests accommodates or adjusts rivalries between powers but it never ends them. For example, the end of the Cold War does not mean the end of American–Russian or Russian–Chinese or Sino-Indian rivalries. So the second exception noted above is a strategy of conflict management among the powers. It does not reflect a false sentiment or expectation about harmony and peace; rather it rests on an expectation of changing alignments among the Powers as a result of changing interests and changing circumstances. In other words, developing a policy that benefits the powers and injures the lesser power or the third party is an acceptable way for the great powers to compensate themselves and to achieve a 'compromise peace' or temporary friendship. (This is also called 'negative peace' i.e. there is an expectation that war will not occur.) In the 19th century colonization and imperialism helped the great powers to compensate each other and themselves by expansion, exploitation and domination of Africa, Asia, Middle East and the Caribbean. Here the existence of open frontiers – open spaces as well as weak societies – helped satisfy great powers' ambitions.

Thus far it has been argued that the powers have employed two strategies to adjust their rivalries. First in the development of interdependent relationships through a permanent political settlement. This is rare. The second strategy is by changing alignments and securing temporary friendships to suppress third-party interest and ambitions. The second strategy may be studied from the perspective of the 'sandwich system'. This system implies the existence of a buffer zone between two equal or semi-equal powers (in the distribution of military strength and in the level of each sides ambition). Martin Wight provides the definitions.

> The pattern of forces in international relations, then, resembles a checker board of alternating colours. But in practice, it is indefinitely modified and complicated, becoming a Looking-glass chessboard, where the squares usually have less or more than four frontiers, and vary in size. The *simple sandwich system is found only between powers of similar strength*: that is to say, powers of which no one could conquer any other

> single-handed. If a sandwich system of small states comes under the direct pressure of a great power, it is apt to be gradually transformed. The *great power itself will take part in the rivalries of the small powers, simultaneously encouraging and controlling them, on the principle of 'divide and rule'*. This *method of hegemony* was employed by France in the seventeenth and 18th centuries among the German states, and by Germany between the World Wars among the states of Eastern Europe. There is evidence that Russia has had to pursue the same policy to control her East European satellites since the Second World War, in spite of their façade of Communist uniformity, and this in particular was why in 1948, it forbade the Yugoslav-Bulgarian federation desired by Tito and Dimitrov. When a sandwich system of small powers is *brought under pressure by two rival great powers at once, it tends to become obliterated.* At this point, *local rivalries are largely ironed out by the pressure of greater rivalries; the small powers are reduced to a buffer zone* between great powers; and the sandwich system is reproduced on a wider scale in the alignments of the great powers themselves.[10]

Buffers are a vital component of the 'sandwich system'. *A buffer has two qualities*. It is a *point of friction or contention between or among* rival powers; and it is a *geographical area* which is *available for the powers* to play out, and to accommodate, their rivalries. Buffers are like shock absorbers that manage the friction between the powers. A buffer is either a power vacuum or a weaker/weak power which is available for the use of great powers on a non-exclusive basis. It is an arena, a plaything of great powers who can intervene at will and they possess the means to escalate the level of conflict in the buffer zone.

Traditionally, a buffer state could behave in three different ways in relation to the great powers. It could be a neutral, in which case the scale and intensity of external intervention is circumscribed by great powers' agreement (e.g. Switzerland and Austria); and the neutral state, by policy as well as capacity, is able to manage external intervention. Another option is that a state is so weak that it seeks protection as a satellite of a external power. This protection prevents the conversion of the weak state, a helpless pygmy, into an arena of contention between two or more powers. A satellite is, however, playing a buffer role in the sense that it insulates two contending powers from direct confrontation; the satellite state becomes the trip wire between the two rival powers. This was the role played by Eastern Europe in superpower relations during the Cold War. In the third instance, the buffer area was occupied by a weaker or a minor power which was nonetheless ambitious to increase its power and its influence in regional and international affairs; and it had the means to enlarge its power base and its interventionist potential. This was a trimmer. It occupied a buffer zone. It did not have the military and the economic strength to prevent great powers' intervention (singly or collectively) but it possessed the ambition and the limited capacity to raise, for the great powers, the anticipated costs of their planned intervention and it was able to convert this fear of high costs into a deterrent relationship. Additionally, if it could develop its internal strength and to build productive alliance relationships, it could make great power intervention counter-productive. Trimmers could thus become regional great powers or middle powers under these conditions. Trimmers were activists with a knowledge of the fault lines or the cracks in great powers relationships. They knew the pressure points and they had the skill to manipulate great powers' relationships (their policies, attitudes and their interests) through the development of temporary friendships with one or the other great power. However, trimmers' actions were circumscribed by their limited strength and by circumstances.

Did 'globalization' and 'economic interdependence' replace geo-strategy (geo-politics) and cultural conflicts in the 20th century?

Adda Bozeman's powerful review of international history reminds us about the historical and contemporary importance of cultural conflicts and orbits in international relations. Martin Wight's insightful analysis of power politics reminds us that international economics has not replaced international politics. Subsequent chapters show that geo-politics is a powerful basis of modern Asian international relations and economics has not replaced geo-politics.

Following the collapse of the European empires in Asia, the Middle East, and Africa, the superpowers acquired a global military reach in the 1940s and the 1950s by their possession of missiles and strategic bombers. They held a terrible power over humanity by their possession of nuclear power. They sought to control the nuclear menace through international arms control. In hindsight, nuclear weapons and arms control are a distraction from the geo-politically and national interest driven pattern of changing alignments and temporary friendships that preoccupy governmental practitioners. The arms race did not replace foreign policy. Turkey, Iran and the Persian Gulf, Afghanistan, the Sino-Soviet frontier, Indo-China, the Korean peninsula and the Far East, the Sino-Indian frontier, among others, remained the points of friction and contention in Asia–Pacific.

Despite the hype about the Cold War, the central balance and a bipolar world, and the pre-eminent position of the superpowers in world affairs since 1945, the latter never attained a dominant position as full or unquestioned successors to the power and authority of the empires in Asia–Pacific. Unredistributed power remained in play, and power rivalries continued among major and minor powers. The superpowers were able to develop economic, military, diplomatic and cultural presences in many former colonial states but paradoxically and simultaneously a number of states in the Asiatic buffer belt of the 19th century were able to develop the qualities of a trimmer. Between the 19th and the 20th centuries the number of great powers shrank from six (USA, UK, France, Russia, Germany and Japan) to two (USA and

USSR); UK and France became secondary powers; Germany and Japan were defeated. The number of minor powers – regional great powers as well as small or local powers – increased in the Asia–Pacific region. Several ex-colonial states emerged as trimmers in regional and international relations. They were able to play the superpowers against the middle, e.g. India vis-à-vis USA and USSR in the 1950s, and Vietnam vis-à-vis USA, USSR and PRC. They participated in regional military conflicts and in diplomatic deliberations concerning international security issues. They raised the costs of great power interventions in regional affairs (e.g. note the results of policies of PRC and North Korea in the Korean War, India in the 1971 Bangladesh War, and Vietnam in the Vietnam War).

The 19th-century Asiatic and the Middle Eastern buffer belt remained an active arena for the superpowers in the 20th century: their rivalry was played out there. However, the 20th century also saw the emergence of this belt as a breeding ground for minor powers. They were adept at playing trimmer roles. They had the ambition and the skill to develop policies and alignments which reduced the scope of great power intervention in regional wars and crises; they reduced the margin of diplomatic manoeuvrability of the ex-European powers and the new superpowers. In 1502 Vasco de Gama bombed Calicut because he was displeased by the behaviour of the Hindu prince in the murder of Portuguese merchants. America likewise punished Japanese bad behaviour by inflicting nuclear holocaust on the Japanese population. The standard was to inflict harm on the enemy when Western norms of acceptable behaviour were deemed to have been violated.[11] The ability of great powers to inflict such punishment for 'bad behaviour' has declined progressively. Now 'bad behaviour' requires negotiated solutions. Unilateral demarches or concerted actions by great powers either reveal divisions in the great powers' front or the actions taken by consensus are ineffective. The history of nuclear non-proliferation and missile control regimes makes this clear.

How did weaker Asian states located in the Asiatic buffer belt become adept in engaging stronger military powers? First, the former natives and objects of imperialism were quick learners of the Western practice of coercive diplomacy. The Chinese forces attacked General MacArthur's troops in the Korean War and pushed them away from the Chinese border; their human wave tactics had a tremendous shock value on the American mind, and after this bloody engagement, the USA was never again to seek a physical engagement with Chinese military manpower. Vietnam also defeated massive American military power in the 1960s and left an imprint on the American psyche. Thereafter, the line was drawn against US military fights on Asian soil. In 1971, India broke up Pakistan by force and broke an international convention against the creation of a new state by force. Again in 1998 India undermined the international norm against further nuclear and missile proliferation. The former natives and subjects of foreign powers were learning how to radically alter the pattern of relationships in the Asian buffer belt, and create situations by coercive measures whereby minor powers could be expected to engage and to challenge the authority of the major ones, and to foster a 'bottoms–up' restructuring of regional powers relationships and a pattern of engagement between minor and major powers.

Secondly, the superpowers not only failed to emerge as the full successors to the European powers in Asia but they also were unable to prevent the growth of regional great powers. This was facilitated by the importance of nationalism and its relationship with modern science in Asian countries. Wight characterizes nationalism in a number of ways.

> The moral cohesion of powers is often spoken of in terms of nationality or nationalism. But this can cause confusion, since these words have several meanings. First, in its oldest sense, a nation means a people supposed to have a *common descent* and organized under a *common government*. Here the word nation is almost interchangeable with the words, state or power; . . . Secondly, after the French Revolution, the word nation came to mean in Europe a *nationality*, a people with *a consciousness of historic identity* expressed in a *distinct language* . . . The principle of *national self-determination* asserts the right of every nationality to form a state and become a power, and the peace settlement of 1919 attempted to reorganize Europe in accordance with it. Thirdly, in Asia and Africa, since the First World War, the word nation has come to mean a political unit asserting its right of independent statehood *against European domination.*[12]

Fairbairns calls it an anti-Western revolt, thus highlighting the role of race, and colonial history. In Asia nationalism has an attachment to land, it expresses a particular sense of identity and destiny, and it carries a baggage of historical grievances.[13] As noted earlier, in the history of Asian international relations since 1945, nationalism has revealed itself as the more fundamental social and political force than communism or a particular religion. My point is not that every Asian country is nationalistic or equally nationalistic. Those countries who aspire to the role of trimmers in the 20th century (following decolonization and following the rise of the superpowers, the Cold War and bipolarity) tend to be nationalistic. That is, Asian practitioners in public and private sectors are both traditional (nationalistic) and modern. They are learning the importance of marrying nationalism with science: nationalism provides the beliefs because power without beliefs is meaningless or lacking in purpose and direction. Cutting-edge science provides the basis of a modern industrial organization and technological as well as military capacity to engage stronger external forces. This is why great powers constantly urge a halt to the arms race after they have secured their strategic interests and their international position, but this position is doomed to fail for reasons discussed by Martin Wight.[14]

Great powers constantly strive to handcuff the development of cutting-edge science in foreign lands as it would undermine their military and scientific superiority and their agenda about 'international security'. In other words, the combination of nationalism and Asian military science has enabled the trimmers and the minor powers in Asia to engage the major international powers. This combination has had two results. First, it has immunized the former against coercive intervention by the latter; or at least it has reduced the scope of, and raised the opportunity-costs of great power intervention in regional affairs. Secondly, the minor powers have developed the means to intervene in areas that are vital to the interests and prestige of the major powers.

What are the sources and patterns of strategic thought and actions that shape international relations in Asia–Pacific and the Indian Ocean areas in the 20th century?

To answer this question, we revisit the works of Owen Lattimore and other specialists who have analysed the historical context and who have identified the mistaken elements in the American approach to Asian strategic affairs. America is highlighted because of its leading role in Asian international relations since 1945. America is important because other powers relate to it or react to its policies. These analyses provide the crucial 'prehistory' and the context in which Asian states have functioned since 1945.

Lattimore makes a number of points.[15] The part played by Asia in changing international relations since 1945 is greater than the role played by Europe. Asia's growing importance pertains to the rate, type, impact and the probability of future change, which has a high likelihood and high impact in issues of war and peace in relation to USA, Russia and Europe. The rate of change is measured by a number of indicators: the growth of Asian economies, political organizations and political attitudes, military development and scientific expertise, and finally by the ability to act independently in initiating, managing and terminating regional conflicts, and in shaping the regional and the international security agendas. Here growth is measured in relation to power, negotiation skills and cohesive ideas. The rate of change is also measured by the trend towards diffusion of power centres in the world since 1940. Then the major power centres were USA, UK, USSR, Japan, Germany and France. In 1945, the major power centres changed as follows. USA became the number one international power and its international position appeared to be upwardly mobile. UK was a wartime victor, but its international economic and military position declined because of the devastating effect of the Second World War on UK's economy and the impending loss of its imperial possessions. It was downwardly mobile after 1945 but it possessed a seat at the table of the UN Security Council. Japan and Germany were defeated and eliminated from the power game at the time. France was downwardly mobile even though it had a seat at the UN Security Council table and a voice in European and colonial affairs. USSR was clearly the number two international power and it appeared to be upwardly mobile. By the early 1950s, Soviet Russia reached the limits of its expansion in Europe and America reached the limits of its policy of containment in Europe and in Korea. But, as Halle points out, the USA and the USSR were locked into an ideological debate that was global but secondary in importance, and the real conflict was about the balance of power in Europe (not Asia).[16]

By 2000, a number of major and minor Asian powers had emerged following the rebuilding of Japan, the consolidation of Chinese Communist rule, and the emergence of India. These later became the major regional power centres in Asia. The two Koreas, Taiwan, Hong Kong and most South East Asian states were at the time emerging as the minor power centres, of which Singapore was to emerge as a major economic and military powerhouse. The trend towards diffusion of international power and the growth in number and strength of Asian powers was accomplished in a short span of fifty years. This rapid rate of change had an impact in the sense that it contributed to the decline in a number of great powers outside Asia who had influence within Asia. The number of minor powers (regional great powers, middle powers and local powers as per the definition of Martin Wight) increased in Asia; and Asia emerged as a centre of growing strength and volatility since 1945 compared to Europe, America and Russia. Finally, by the end of the 20th century Asia had the potential to create high impact, high probability changes in the future. Several key issues loomed large on the Asian strategic landscape. Internal developments within the Peoples Republic of China had the potential for social and economic instability within China and the danger of its export into the Asia–Pacific region. Japanese military policy in Asia was changing rapidly through the growth of its power projection capabilities in the direction of South China Seas and the Indian Ocean. America's leadership in Asia had an uncertain future and this uncertainty was causing the USA to reposition itself in relation to traditional and non-traditional strategic partners. In addition to the likely impact of statist forces (USA, China, Japan, India and Russia as well as the minor powers in Asia), several significant non-governmental influences were in play, religious militancy (e.g. Islamic), competitive ethnic and sub-national forces (e.g. a variety of insurgency movements), criminal syndicates (drug and arms trade cartels) that operate in the South China Seas and the Indian Ocean areas) and state-sponsored terrorist organizations (e.g. Pakistan's intelligence organization and Afghanistan's Taliban). A measure of the rapid rate of change is that the diplomatic, strategic and economic space of these powers in Asia, and the international system, had grown rapidly; that of Europe had shrunk comparatively; and that of the US is constant (i.e. the US is still the premier power in Asia since 1945) but it is under attack from Russia and Europe as well as Asian powers.

The type of change reflects the growing integration of scientific, nationalistic and democratic forces in the internal development of the major and minor Asian powers. This combination has created a fusion of internal power that has an impact on external relationships. It has established the basis of independent policies among regional, middle and local powers in Asia. This process of integration started in the 1940s and it is still ongoing. This combination was the basis of European and American international expansion but, comparatively speaking, it has peaked in Europe. Now European states are preoccupied primarily with domestic social and economic issues, with European integration and, to a limited extent, with geo-political concerns (i.e. French/Russian strategic dialogue at present focuses on a concern with Germany's increasing power and influence). Bozeman accurately analyses the problem of small states and small-minded states in Europe. They lack the capacity and the strategy to strike and/or negotiate major international issues; that is, European states no longer appear to possess a geographical-cultural-military strategy concerning major international security issues, as they did in the 19th century and in the age of colonialism and imperialism.

> The determined Anglo-American pursuit of these conjoint policies throughout the 20th century led automatically first, to the liquidation of the West's geo-strategic frontier that had held enemies at bay because its human guardians knew when to mediate East–West conflicts and when to strike; second, to the transformation of the small states into satellites of the Soviet Union; and third, to the paralysis that gripped the West's policymaking in 1989–90.
>
> In accounting for this epochal failure, one can single out many reasons, but all converge in the final analysis on one: the Anglo-American West did not and does not know either the continental West or the Soviet Union.[17]

To this judgement, we add that the Anglo-American West did not understand Asia or know how to deal with it.

Bozeman emphasizes that the problem of provincial and insular thinking is endemic in Anglo-American thinking. She maintains:

- U.S. policymakers were intellectually not prepared either for the victorious outcome of the German-led Eastern European revolt against the Soviet Union or for the collapse of the latter.
- The Anglo-American coalition lost the war it fought on behalf of the West.
- The European state system has lost credibility at home because it has been deeply divided throughout the century between continental European and Anglo-American states. The issues in contention relate to Germany's place and role in Europe and to the defence of the invisible frontier separating Europe from Asia.
- The Western civilisation has suffered serious loss and its orbit is contracted and uncertain at the threshold of the 21st century.[18]

It is appropriate here to recall Henry Kissinger's assessment of the sources of power and the pattern of relationships in the foreseeable future. He makes the following points.

1 In the post-Cold War world, the United States is the only remaining superpower with the capacity to intervene in every part of the globe. Yet power has become more diffuse and the issues to which military force is relevant have diminished. Victory in the Cold War has propelled America into a world which bears many similarities to the European state system of the 18th and 19th centuries, and to practices which American statesmen and thinkers have consistently questioned. The absence of both an overriding ideological or strategic threat frees nations to pursue foreign policies based increasingly on their immediate national interest. In an international system characterized by perhaps five or six major powers and a multiplicity of smaller states, order will have to emerge much as it did in past centuries from a reconciliation and balancing of competing national interests.
2 The end of the Cold War has created what some observers have called a 'unipolar' or 'one-superpower' world. But the United States is actually in no better position to dictate the global agenda unilaterally than it was at the beginning of the Cold War. America is more preponderant that it was ten years ago, yet, ironically, power has also become more diffuse. Thus, America's ability to employ it to shape the rest of the world has actually decreased.
3 The international system of the twenty-first century will be marked by a seeming contradiction: on the one hand, fragmentation: on the other, growing globalization. On the level of the relations among states, the new order will be more like the European state system of the 18th and 19th centuries than the rigid patterns of the Cold War. It will contain at least six major powers – the United States, Europe, China, Japan, Russia, and probably India – as well as a multiplicity of medium-sized and smaller countries.
4 In the Cold War, when the Soviet Union was the dominant security threat Japan was able to identify its foreign policy with America, thousands of miles away. The new world order, with its multiplicity of challenges, will almost certainly oblige a country with so proud a past to re-examine its reliance on a single ally. Japan is bound to become more sensitive to the Asian balance of power than is possible for America, in a different hemisphere and facing in three directions – across the Atlantic, across the Pacific, and toward South America. China, Korea, and Southeast Asia will acquire quite a different significance for Japan than for the United States, and will inaugurate a more autonomous and more self-reliant Japanese foreign policy.
5 As for India, which is now emerging as the major power in South Asia, its foreign policy is in many ways the last vestige of the heyday of European imperialism, leavened by the traditions of an ancient culture.

Before the arrival of the British, the subcontinent had not been ruled as a single political unit for millennia. British colonization was accomplished with small military forces because, at first, the local population saw these as the replacement of one set of conquerors by another. But after it established unified rule, the British Empire was undermined by the very values of popular government and cultural nationalism it had imported into India. Yet, as a nation-state, India is a newcomer. Absorbed by the struggle to feed its vast population, India dabbled in the Nonaligned movement during the Cold War. But it has yet to assume a role commensurate with its size on the international political stage.

6 At the same time, Wilsonian idealism has produced a plethora of problems. As embodied in the Fourteen Points, the uncritical espousal of ethnic self-determination failed to take account of power relationships and the de-stabilizing effects of ethnic groups single-mindedly pursuing their accumulated rivalries and ancient hatreds.

7 There has been a surge of American interest in Asia as symbolised by the proposal for a Pacific Community made by Clinton at a meeting with the Asian heads of government in 1993. But the term 'community' applies to Asia in only the most limited sense, for relationships in the Pacific are fundamentally different from those in the Atlantic Area. Whereas the nations of Europe are grouped in common institutions, the nations of Asia view themselves as distinct and competitive. The relations of the principal Asian nations to each other bear most of the attributes of the European balance-of-power system of the 19th century. Any significant increase in strength by one of them is almost certain to evoke an offsetting manoeuvre by the others.

8 Military expenditures are already rising in all the major Asian countries. China is on the road to superpower status. At a growth rate of 8 percent, which is less than it has maintained over the 1980s, China's Gross National Product will approach that of the United States by the end of the second decade of the twenty-first century. Long before that, China's political and military shadow will fall over Asia and will affect the calculations of the other powers, however restrained actual Chinese policy may prove to be. The other Asian nations are likely to seek counterweights to an increasingly powerful China as they already do to Japan. Though they will disavow it, the nations of Southeast Asia are including the heretofore feared Vietnam in their grouping (ASEAN) largely in order to balance China and Japan. And that too is by ASEAN asking the United States to remain engaged in their region.

9 America's capacity to shape events will therefore, in the end, depend primarily on its bilateral relations with the major countries of Asia. This is why America's policies toward both Japan and China – at this writing, much buffeted in controversy – assume such critical importance. For one thing, the American role is the key to helping Japan and China co-exist

> despite their suspicions of each other. In the immediate future, Japan, faced with an aging population and a stagnating economy, might decide to press its technological and strategic superiority before China emerges as a superpower and Russia recovers its strength. Afterward, it might have recourse to that great equalizer, nuclear technology.[19]

Bozeman's and Kissinger's comments indicate that the end of the Cold War shrunk America's diplomatic and strategic space in the international system, even though America remains the foremost military and economic power in the world, it participates in the major alliances and in international conferences, and it has the scientific edge in the civilian and military spheres. Still, its authority is constantly challenged by a variety of major and minor powers: Indian nuclear missile tests challenge American-led international non-proliferation regimes, North Korean missiles threaten American and Japanese security interests, China openly challenges American interests and presence in the South China Seas and in relation to American non-proliferation goals in Pakistan and Iraq. Russia is seeking a new strategic partnership with the USA. Its naval 'show the flag' activities in the Pacific and Indian Oceans, and its quest for new alliance ties with India and Vietnam indicate that, under President Putin, Russia is rebuilding its Asian presence. So the end of the Cold War did not mean the end of power politics in Asia or a decisive American victory in the international system.

To sum up this point, I note that, today, most European states neither know when to strike militarily and when to mediate in relation to major centres of international and regional power and conflict. They lack an independent policy or the capacity or the ambition to do so. They are small-minded because they lack a grand strategy, a geo-cultural strategic plan to deal with major conflict systems. On the other hand, Asia is currently the centre of three major international conflict systems: Islamic, Leninist-Russian, Maoist-Chinese. I call them conflict systems in the sense that each orbit, as Bozeman points out, is dedicated to the use of conflict as the primary method to achieve a change in the pattern of regional and international relationships which organize state and society. So conflict is the medium to effect change given the absence of a philosophy in these orbits that relies on diplomacy and negotiation. In comparison, Europe is home to the development of a new scholarly and policy orientation that stresses peace research and human security. Both are ill suited as methods to engage the world's largest conflict systems.[20] In other words, peace research and human security strategy are unable to engage the forces of regional and international conflict that are of deep and long-term character in Asia.

The rate and the importance of change that Asian powers are bringing into play reflect an ability to develop geo-cultural-military strategies that are based on the combination of science, nationalism and democracy. These methods are being employed in relation to international powers who are now looking from outside into Asia following the retreat from colonialism to imperialism; and secondly, they are used in relation to powers who are tied to Asia by permanent land frontiers. Russia is tied by a land frontier that extends from Northern Europe through the Middle East, Afghanistan, and the Indian subcontinent, China's border provinces, the Mongolian region, the Korean peninsula and Japan's northern islands. The rate and type of change also involves the development of new relationships between the major and minor power centres within Asia and their respective neighbourhoods. To a discussion of these relationships, we now come.

Lattimore points out that Russian influence in Asian affairs is unavoidable. The Eurasian continent has two major strategy loops or channels for the flow of power. They are the points of engagement among the major powers. The first strategic loop goes from Northern Europe through Europe, the Mediterranean, the Arab world, Iran, Afghanistan, Singkiang, Mongolia and Korea. This loop corresponds to the Russia land frontier. The second strategic loop goes from Europe, Mediterranean, Arab world, the Indian subcontinent, South East Asia and, through the Pacific, it goes into Okinawa and Japan. This loop predominated in the days of European colonialism and imperialism (1500s to 1960s). This loop has been the object of continuous American strategic attention. Historically and during the Cold War era, Russia was preoccupied primarily with the first loop and Russia entered the second loop during the Cold War period as a part of its Cold War strategy.[21]

Historically and during the Cold War and its aftermath, American policy has been preoccupied with the stabilization of its position in the second loop. However, the motives of Russia and America varied. Russia, as in the case of Turkey, was interested in the reduction of predominant Western (British) influence rather than in its replacement by predominant Russian influence. This remained the Soviet motivation during the Cold War. Although the two loops overlapped in Europe, the Middle East and the Indian subcontinent, they should be studied separately because the two loops have a different directions and implications in Asia–Pacific strategic affairs. The first loop is land orientated while the second one is sea orientated. These two loops have been central to the study of international relations of the area in the last 500 years. Following the end of the Cold War, Russia is still engaged in the first loop and under President Putin, it is seeking a strategic presence in the second loop. The US remains committed to its interests in the second loop and it seeks a presence in the first loop by its activities in the central Asian republics after the collapse of the USSR. In other words, Russia is an Asian insider that is looking out from the first loop to the second loop. The US, on the other hand, is an outsider in Asia which is looking into Asia from the second loop to the first one. The major and minor powers in Asia are located in the proximity of both the loops and are, accordingly, preoccupied with developments in both. As such, both loops are crucial today as in the past for understanding the strategic motives and the pattern of relationships in areas in the proximity of the two axis of power. The policies of the major and minor powers in Asia – the use of their capabilities, their diplomatic strategy and their strategic ideas – correspond to the international policies of the two loops.

The new element, however, is that the current major and minor Asian powers are weaker in military and economic strength compared to Russia, American and European power but, despite their weaknesses, the Asian powers have increased their room to manœuvre in relation to America, Russia and Europe. The increased manœuvrability is being effected in a number of ways. First, the Asian powers are ambitious and leadership policies are sensitive to domestic public opinion. In other words, there is strong public identification for the external policies of the Asian powers. Secondly, in the last fifty years, there has been significant growth in their economic, military and organizational capacities. They are able to act independently despite the asymmetrical distribution of power. Thirdly, competition between European, Russian and American powers creates opportunities for them to bargain and enlarge their presence and influence. Even the greatest powers have limits in their ability to control or influence events or other countries. Weaker Asian powers have the knowledge and skill to play one against the other. They know how to discover and use wriggle space to enhance their positions and to reduce the advantages of others, including the great powers.

Fourthly, in every strategic situation, major and minor powers participate in the politics of attraction and the politics of repulsion. Countries are attracted and repulsed as a result of who is accommodating, who is threatening, who is a potential ally and who is the enemy. Weaker Asian powers are attracted and repulsed by the great powers just as the great powers themselves are attracted and repulsed by the activities of their rivals and allies. The politics of attraction and repulsion play a big role in Asian affairs. It often involves triangular relationships between weaker Asian states and the major powers. In triangular US–USSR–Asian country relationships, the politics of attraction and repulsion revolve in relation to specific policies of the superpowers. For instance, American aid was often tied to support governments and leaders who were anti-Communist and who were authoritarian (with a preference for law and order at the expense of democracy). Such a policy created a repulsion within the domestic politics of a country with a nationalistic history. As a result, American policies created friction and maintained it between the pro-US law and order government leadership on the one hand, and nationalistic forces on the other: in other words, an internal fracture developed between nationalistic and pro-US forces, and on the other hand, pro-Soviet and Asian nationalistic forces. In this way, a fault line was created in domestic politics that affected the weak Asian countries' external relationships. After 1945, for while pro-US, pro-law and order forces were strong in places like South Korea, Philippines, China, Taiwan, Japan and Indonesia. Later, nationalistic forces gained ground and captured leadership positions that reflected local nationalism, and in many cases, they were tied to democratic countries. In these cases, the United States had failed to connect with Asian nationalistic forces whereas the Russians did. The American approach encouraged the politics of repulsion. As long as the Asian leaders can tap into the nationalistic sentiments, and the Russians identify themselves with Asian nationalism, there is politics of attraction between the Russians and the Asians, and the politics of repulsion between America and Asia nationalistic forces. This is ironic and counter-productive because the US is the number one international power and Russia has been the number two power since 1945.

The politics of attraction and repulsion reveal three principles.

1. Neighbours are natural rivals, i.e. Vietnam–China, China–Russia, China–Japan, China–India, India–Pakistan, etc. Here politics of repulsion is likely, assuming that an inter-dependent relationship based on a political settlement has not emerged as in the case of US/Canada.
2. Proximity creates a temptation to control the neighbour. The greater the control, the greater is the likelihood of repulsion, assuming that the controlled élite or population is nationalistic. Here politics of repulsion is likely, assuming that an inter-dependent relationship based on a political settlement has not emerged as in the case of US/Canada.
3. The further away an outside power is, the less likelihood that it will be able to dominate an area of interest. In this situation, politics of attraction are at work because the relationship is based on mutual interests.[22]

America's past mistakes still permeate its approach to Asia–Pacific today. So it is worthwhile reviewing them on the basis of Lattimore's analysis.

Mistake 1: the fight between America and Russia was bipolar and ideological

American policy suggested that the fight with Soviet Russia was more important than the issue of Asian development, Asian nationalism and unification of divided societies. In other words, big power quarrels are more important than the peaceful development of formerly colonial Asian societies. Most Asian powers however (China, Japan, India, etc.) functioned in the context of multipolarity and nation-building which required strong public identification with the link between domestic and international politics and a link between nation-building and power development.

Mistake 2: the recovery of Europe was more important than the recovery of Asia

This was a mistake because it revealed a pro-European bias in American policy, and hence an anti-Asian bias in the view of the practitioners in Asia and Asian public opinion. In the Asian mind, the continent should have been taken seriously because the rate of change in Asia was greater than that of Europe.

Mistake 3: the Truman Doctrine created an expectation that Soviet Russia could be defeated

This was a mistake because, despite internal difficulties, neither Russia nor any other major power in Asia could be defeated. America can no more defeat Russia than Russia can defeat America. Accordingly, it was a mistake to claim that America won the Cold War when Russia could not be defeated and is now in the process of rebuilding its international position in the Asian sphere. Russia was down but never out.

Mistake 4: the US is constantly preparing to fight the next war instead of developing peaceful relationships

Emphasizing a preoccupation with war planning rather than the development of the politics of attraction and reduction of the politics of revulsion in a post-war atmosphere is the mistake. Even after the end of the Cold War, the United States is still preoccupied with building its defences against new threats in Asia, i.e. against North Korean missiles, Indian nuclear weapons, Chinese military capabilities, Iranian missiles, etc. There are, of course, opportunities for America to recalibrate the imbalance that currently exists in favour of war preparation rather than peace preparations. But to make these opportunities real, the United States would need to revise its approach and to rely more on trust and negotiations and less on war preparations and pressure to secure compliance by Asian states. This however is not likely to happen.

These four mistakes are the context for the next chapter which examines the situation in Asia and the growth of multipolarity and regionalism in the Asia–Pacific and the Indian Ocean areas.

5 The situation in America and Asia and the growth of regionalism in Asia

An overview

Introduction

Since 1945, the situation in Asia has been one of great turbulence as well as constructive change. There are a number of indicators of turbulence and positive change.

Wars

Asia has been the scene of major international and regional conflicts: Korea, Vietnam, Afghanistan, the Indian subcontinent and the Persian Gulf. These were not simply proxy wars of the great powers. Regional and local powers were active participants, and competing interests of major and minor powers were engaged in these conflicts. The war behaviour and the strategic interests of the major and minor participants in each war created new centres of independent power and multipolarity in different parts of Asia. They stabilized regional situations which had a potential for chaos. In popular thinking, an outbreak of war is deemed to be a negative event. In Asia, wars have been contained; they have been limited; Asian wars led to the development of 'stable regional conflict formation' and to the rise of responsible regional great powers. Generally, the consequences of Asian wars have been positive in confirming the ascendency of regional great powers and in stabilizing regional conflicts. For example, Vietnam was recognized as a regional great power in the aftermath of its military encounters with USA and PRC. India gained the position after the defeat of Pakistani Army, in 1971 and in Kargil.

Revolutions

Massive revolutionary changes in China, Vietnam, North Korea, and Iran showed the importance of armed struggle and mass politics in Asia. Asian revolutions shrank the freedom of independent strategic action of the great powers. At the same time, it enlarged the freedom of such action by Asian regional great powers and local powers in Asia after 1945. Revolutions revealed the importance of nationalistic upheavals. The Asian revolutions were positive events to the extent they were followed by the development of internal reforms and non-expansionist external policies.

Autocratic military governments

Asia has produced a number of home-grown autocratic and repressive regimes: South Korea (1950s–1970s); Taiwan (under KMT rule); Philippines until the 1990s; Indonesia (under Sukarno and Suharto); Burma (under its military, especially since the 1990s); Bangladesh (with bouts of military rule and democracy since 1971); Pakistan (mostly under military rule since 1947, with bouts of democratic experiments); and Iran which, until the 1990s, was under autocratic rule of the Shah and then the Ayatollahs. In most cases during the Cold War era, these regimes had strong links with the US and other Western governments because of their anti-Communist, pro-Western and pro-law and order policies. Now such governments are under attack by democratic forces. Such governments had a negative impact on the prospects of democracy and internal reforms but their persistence also stimulated a quest for internal economic, political and social reforms. By the end of the 20th century, most non-Communist authoritarian regimes had embraced the reformist path. The Communist states have adopted economic reform policies (e.g. China and Vietnam) and they are under domestic as well as international pressure to accept political pluralism as the basic principle of governance. So the consequences were both negative and positive in this case.

Peaceful international change

India's non-violent route to independence, democratic ethos, and its political culture which emphasizes a commitment to peaceful accommodation of conflicting interests, showed the possibility of synthesizing Western and Asian political cultures. After 1945, Japan rejected policies of militarism and imperialism and embraced democracy and peaceful international change as its new path. Taiwan, South Korea, and many South East and South Asian states have also restructured their internal politics in favour of democratic values and peaceful change. Only Asian Communist states remain wedded to one-party rule and authoritarianism. So, despite the history of autocratic rule, imperialism and war in Asia, the seed of peaceful change has been firmly planted in Asian social and political thought processes and the governmental policies of a majority of Asian states. The push for reform comes from the political classes as well as progressive social forces in many Asian countries.

Ethnicity

The pervasiveness of ethnic conflicts in different parts of Asia showed the importance of sub-national primordial loyalties that challenged the idea of the nation-state. Such conflicts undermine the primary loyalty of the citizen to the state. They also show the enduring attachment to land as a primary motivator of political action in the modern states' system at two levels: those who would carve out homeland out of existing states; and those who would avoid a breakdown of existing states. In Asia, ethnic sub-nationalism is being dealt with within the framework of national democracy and territorial sovereignty. The creation of Bangladesh is the only case of a forced breakup of an existing state. The issue in Asia is being addressed less in terms of self-determination and more in terms of meeting the aspirations of the sub-national groups.

Border disputes

Asia has an inventory of territorial disputes that show the vitality of territorial nationalism and devotion to state sovereignty by the nation-states in conflict. Most border disputes in Asia now are ritual confrontations rather than deadly quarrels. They are not likely to trigger general war between the rivals.

Regional rivalries in Asia

Asian rivalries involve America, China, Russia, Japan, India, Pakistan and South East Asian countries and they show the importance of geo-politics. Rivalries are good to the extent that they stimulate competitive scientific, economic, political and military development among rival nation-states that contributes to the public good. On the other hand, rivalries are counter-productive if the rivals cancel out each other's power and influence. Both types of rivalries have existed in Asian international relations since 1945. Nevertheless, there is a struggle to reduce the importance of the second type of rivalry and to increase the appeal of the first type of rivalry. Currently, both types are in play in Asia. In other words, the 'clash of civilizations' in Asia has positive as well as negative connotations in Asian experiences.

Military build-ups and arms control

All major and minor powers in Asia are involved in military buildups, including nuclear and missile proliferation. These developments show the linkage between modern technology and international politics. Various attempts under Ronald Reagan and George W. Bush to develop missile defences indicate that international arms control arrangements such as ABM Treaty, Outer Space Treaty, the Non-Proliferation Treaty and the Missile Technology Control Regime are fragile. Regimes are vulnerable to changes in US defence policies, as well as changes in the intentions and capabilities of rising Asian powers. At the beginning of the 21st century, the US under the new Bush administration recognizes the necessity to forge strategic partnerships with non-traditional allies. This reflects uncertainties about the future direction of PRC's strategic capabilities and intentions, and the inability of the USA's traditional allies (e.g. Japan and Australia) to keep the peace in Asia. The interface between modern military technology, regional geo-politics and international politics is likely to grow in the coming decade(s). It is likely to challenge the major and minor powers in the Asia–Pacific and Indian Ocean spheres. Such build-ups, and the policies associated with them, are viewed positively if they stabilize international and regional relationships. They do so in Asia.

Religious fundamentalism and criminal transnationalism

Fundamentalist forces have grown in importance in Asia. They have emerged within the framework of the Asian states' system, and paradoxically they undermine the integrity of the states' system. For instance, state-sponsored terrorism undermines the fabric of international society. An Islamic system of conflict is now a major undercurrent in the vast region that extends from Chechniya and Dagestan, through Central Asia, and the Indian subcontinent; it touches China's Singkiang province, and it extends through South East Asia into Malaysian and Philippine politics. Talibanization of regional power politics is a reality. It challenges the authority of the state as an institution. It reveals the growing importance of subrosa links between terror groups and state authorities that sympathize with the goals of the terror movements. Osama bin Laden is a prime example of such links. The link-up between drug trade, arms trade and terror networks in the Indian subcontinental and Central Asian areas, along with the growth of piracy and smuggling in the islands (e.g. Indonesia) and the seas (e.g. South China Sea and the Bay of Bengal), points to a pattern of criminalized Asian international relations. This is a negative development in Asia which is drawing a response from regional as well as international powers.

Great powers' competition in Asia

Asia was an arena of great powers' competition during the colonial and imperial era and during the Cold War. After 1945, the great powers learnt to tame their competition and to apply the principle of compromise and compensation in regulating their relationships with each other. War is no longer an option for the management of great power relations in Asia; the advent of weapons of mass destruction have capped great power conflicts. The rise of regional great powers has also altered the matrix of opportunity costs of great powers' intervention in Asian affairs. The changes are a positive development.

Asian nation-building

In many parts of Asia, Asian states are committed to nation-building and reconstruction. Nationalism is being used for constructive purposes that reform state, society and economy. This is a positive development.

Volatility and Change in Asia

Asia is volatile, but compared to the situation in 1945, Asia today has the character of 'conflict formation' (or structured/organized conflict) and 'regional power formation' in key areas. Table 5.1 outlines the points of comparison and the macro indicators. It shows the rate and the types of changes in Asia–Pacific and the Indian Ocean areas in the past fifty years. Before the end of the Second World War the Asiatic buffer belt was occupied and dominated by the great powers; their capabilities, their interests, skills in war and peace and their ideas and organizations were in full play. Fifty years later, the rise of a number of major and minor Asian powers has transformed this belt into geo-political pivots where their capabilities, their interests, skills in war and peace, and their ideas and organizations are effective. From their erstwhile position as objects of great power attention and manipulation, the Asian states are now players in their own right.

Asia's new geo-political pivots

Brzezinski[1] distinguishes between geo-strategic players and geo-political pivots. The players are states that have the capacity and the national will to exercise power and influence beyond their borders in order to alter – to a degree that affects American interests – the existing geo-political affairs. The pivots are states whose importance comes not from their power but from their sensitive location and the consequences for the geo-strategic players. They may be able to deny access to important areas or resources to a major player. A pivot may function as a defensive shield for a major player or region.

My definition of a geo-strategic player differs from Brzezinski.

- They possess capabilities (military, economic and organizational) to exert themselves outside their borders and to engage friends and foes.
- They possess an array of skills to strike by forceful means and to negotiate at will. The skills relate to an ability to initiate, conduct and terminate war, to intervene by diplomatic, covert, economic and psychological means short of war, and to engage in peace-making.
- They possess ideas, philosophy and a vision which underlines their activist approach in the international arena.
- They are able to engage the attention of major and minor powers by affecting their definition of interests, their decision processes and their policies.

We also add two new points to Brzezinski's definition of a geo-political pivot. The first is that a pivot includes autonomous regional powers. They can initiate, manage and end conflict, (e.g. India in South Asian wars, especially 1971; and Vietnam in Indo-China conflict in the 1950s and 1960s). They can

Table 5.1 The enormous pace and the scope of change in Asia–Pacific and Indian Ocean areas

From	*To*
Western domination (colonialism and imperialism)	Decolonization and growth of pockets of regional autonomy and internal reforms.
Political independence	Growth of combination of nationalism, science and democracy, and growth of regional cultural–military strategies that develop the public good.
Bipolar and Cold War superpower-dominated international system	Growth of multipolarity at the continental and the regional (sub-regional) levels that can manage external and internal conflicts.
Top–down approach to management of instability in the international system	Diffusion and decentralization of power, increase in the number of regional, middle and local powers and emergence of a 'bottom–up' approaches to manage conflict and instability in regional and inter-regional affairs have emerged.
Great power-dominated international system	Great powers are in decline, regional power centres and regionalism are growing. Since 1945, there is a decrease in the number of great powers and an increase in the number of lesser powers. The system is more polyarchic.
Soft regionalism of the 1950 and the 1960s	The growth of coerced linkages in some cases (South and North Asia) and regional communities in others (ASEAN) indicates a pattern of 'stable conflict formation' and 'regional power formation' which facilitates regional cooperation.
Stable conflict and regional power formation in the 1990s	Growth of formal as well as informal conflict management and resolution processes and norms.

participate effectively in international economic relationships. They can establish norms of acceptable behaviour within their region. In other words, a geographical pivot has the quality of acting as a benign regional hegemon and as a legitimate regional police force. Secondly, the pivot is an object of great powers' attention and competition on a non-exclusive basis because several great powers' have vital interests in a region of conflict and disengagement is costly. For example, the US cannot detach itself from the Middle East, the Persian Gulf, Central Asia, the Indian subcontinent, East Asia, South China Seas and so on for a variety of reasons. But engagement is not easy. On the other hand, the enormous military strength of the great powers is not enough to safeguard their vital interests in these areas. Hence their interests and consideration of their prestige tie them to a policy of engagement in the zones of conflict in Asia. Moreover, the great powers are not able to dominate these areas as they did in colonial and imperialistic times; nor can they club together with other great powers and institute a great power concert of powers to dominate regional relationships. Hence their engagement in regional conflict zones is inevitable.

Brzezinski's definition is similar to Martin Wight's and Alastair Lamb's 'buffers and frontiers'. In 19th century international relations, the great powers could secure their competing interests through the development of the 'sandwich system'. With our amendments, the great powers still compete with each other, but the pivots are not simply arenas of great power competition; they are also centres of independent regional thinking and power in select issue areas. Two points follow. First, the great powers are locked into the future of the pivots because their interests would be adversely affected if they walked away from these areas. That is, disengagement would cost more than engagement. It is now costly for USA, PRC, Russia, Japan and India to disengage from the international politics and international economics of the major geo-political pivots in Asia. The major pivots are:

1 Korean peninsula and the neighbourhood
2 Taiwan straits and South China Sea and the neighbourhood
3 the north-west zone of the Indian subcontinent
4 the Eastern zone of the Indian subcontinent
5 the ASEAN area

Secondly, the pivots represent areas where diffusion of power has occurred, and major challenges to the international and regional interests of the international powers exist. Map 5.1 shows the main centres of gravity in Asia today.

The geo-political pivots are important from the point of view the policies of powers outside the areas as well as powers within the areas. Brzezinski defines the world today as a state of unrivalled US hegemony. To quote him, 'Most of that system emerged during the Cold War, as part of America's

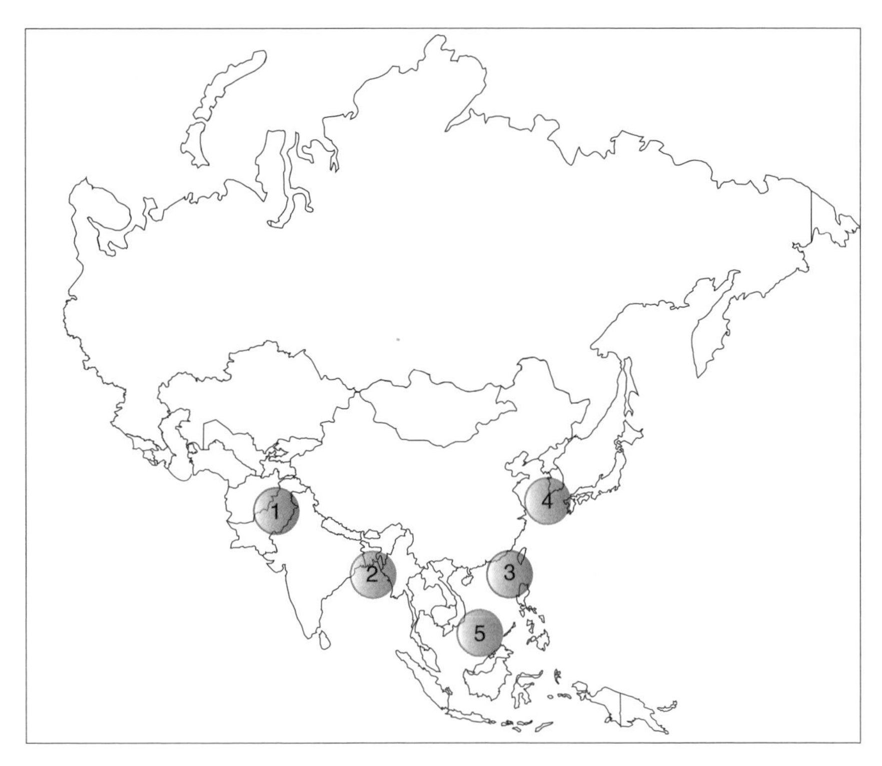

1. Northwest Indian Subcontinent. Players: U.S., Islamic militants, Afghanistan, Pakistan, India, Russia and others.
2. Myanmar and Bay of Bengal Region. Players: Myanmar, U.S., China, India, Thailand, Russia and others.
3. Taiwan Straits. Players: China, Taiwan, Japan, U.S. and others.
4. Korean Peninsula. Players: North Korea, South Korea, China, Japan, U.S., Taiwan, Russia and others.
5. South China Sea and sea lanes. Players: China, U.S., Japan, India, Vietnam, the Philippines, Indonesia and others.

Map 5.1 Main centres of gravity in Asia today

effort to contain its global rival, the Soviet Union. It was thus ready-made for global application, once that rival faltered and America emerged as the first and only global power.' Its essence has been well encapsulated by the political scientist G. John Ikenberry:

> It was hegemonic in the sense that it was centered around the United States and reflected American-styled political mechanisms and organizing principles. It was a liberal order in that it was legitimate and marked

> by reciprocal interactions. Europeans [one may also add, the Japanese] were able to reconstruct and integrate their societies and economies in ways that were congenial with American hegemony but also with room to experiment with their own autonomous and semi-independent political systems . . .[2]

However, Brzezinski is pessimistic about the future of American hegemony. He recognizes the limits of American power and feels that it will diminish over time.[3] I agree with Brzezinski's assessment but with one major amendment. Despite its victory over Soviet Russia in 1989/90, and its possession of enormous power, it cannot alone keep the peace in troublesome regions, it cannot prevent the rise of regional hegemons, it cannot alone manage the ethnic and Islamic battlefields, and it cannot prevent the growth of new interregional alignments (Russia–Iran, Russia–India, Russia–Vietnam, China–Pakistan, China–Iran etc.). To a discussion of the American strategic dilemma I now turn.

The American defence dilemma and growing importance of regional powers and regionalism in Asia

The American situation merits attention for several reasons.

- The US is not only the pre-eminent power in the world today, it is also the reference point for other powers. They reposition themselves in relation to and in response to changing American power and policies.
- Despite its many weaknesses, the US still has the capacity to initiate international changes.
- The US hegemony in the globe is temporary and its defence dilemma is primarily a dilemma of its Asian policies – as they concern developments in China, Japan, Taiwan, India, Myanmar, Iran, Central Asia, Russia and the sea lanes in the Pacific and the Indian Oceans.
- The US retains the technological edge in the military and the industrial spheres.
- Fundamental errors in American strategic thinking create opportunities or wriggle space for other powers and facilitate the loss of American pre-eminence in international relations.

According to Halle, great powers like the US are victims of their self-created and self-serving mythologies and notional or subjective realities. To quote:

> All nations cultivate myths that endow them with dignity and, when occasion arises, give nobility to the causes in which they fight. A simple view would have it that myths, being fictional, must therefore be false. In a more sophisticated view, myths belong to the conceptual world by which, alone, we are able to interpret the existential world that constitutes

> our raw environment. This conceptual world, even if fictional, provides interpretations of the existential world that we must assume to be true in some degree.[4]

In America's case, the notional realities include an over-confidence in the importance of military policy and military technology in securing national security; and Americans underestimate the role of political measures to achieve security or manageable instability. To quote Lattimore:

> Military security is a necessary part of a stable peace; but military security alone cannot assure the safety of a nation which is confused in its political thinking. On the other hand, a nation which is clear in its political thinking can overcome the handicap of military weakness to a surprising extent.[5]

A policy based on notional or subjective assessments creates two limitations in the American case. First, when national security machinery is meant to deal primarily with international wars or sub-critical situations like most post-1945 situations (except the Cuban Missile Crisis), policy thinking is geared to preparations to fight the next war or to handle the next crisis, rather than to establish peaceful relationships. In these circumstances, military forces or budgets may be determined in a strategic vacuum or with a predisposition about the inevitability of international conflict in general, and about particular enemy or rogue states. A number of important questions and international trends may not be dealt with explicitly and publicly. Who is the real enemy? What is the nature of the problem? Who are the secret enemies? What are the vital interests that must be defended? Is the aim of the great power to address all sub-critical crises in its sphere of interests? Is it to maintain a situation in which no great power or hostile coalition can threaten its physical security? If the preoccupation is with sub-critical issues such as North Korean and Iraqi possession of weapons and mass destruction, then the policy aim is to prevent the escalation of a sub-critical situation into a major crisis that leads to confrontation among the major powers. This requires active and continuous intervention in a variety of situations that may or may not come to pass. Such interventions take place during peace-time and in secondary zones of conflict. On the other hand, if the aim is to ensure that no hostile coalition emerges to threaten America's physical security, then the solution is to ensure that the US always maintains a clear and a convincing military edge over its great power rivals. This could be done by staying ahead in the technological sphere and by reducing overseas commitments. The absence of clarity about the nature of the strategic problem may create a mismatch between force structures, threat assessments, domestic and international imperatives (challenges and opportunities) and its technological capabilities. Confused strategic thinking, a confused understanding of international and regional situations as well as the motives and decision processes of regional and local powers, is likely to produce such a mismatch. A disconnection between national policy that is based on 'notional realities' on the one hand and 'objective' realities on the other hand produces policy responses which cannot manage the real international and regional problems.

Second, a manifestation of the dominant effect of notional realities and preferences is America's faith in its military and technological superiority, its faith in the benign nature of its global hegemony, and its refusal to accept the idea of a benign regional hegemon or regional great powers. American scholarly and government practitioners have failed to recognize the regional imperative in Asian politics. Their preferences substitute for analysis. The idea of a regional great power is alien in American political and foreign policy culture. Island nations like America and the UK suffer from three defects. The first one stems from the belief that they are important and central to the orderly functioning of the international system and they represent the winning side. Note the fixation in the British mind about the importance of the British Empire (1500–1945) in world affairs, and a similar fixation in the American mind that it won the Cold War and that faith in its role as a global hegemon is warranted. I call this the 'ethnocentric', 'moralism' and 'victory' defect. ('We are the greatest, we are right, and we will prevail' is the notional reality or the mythology.) The second defect refers to the preoccupation with finding military solutions even for political problems; and a preoccupation with the development of superior military technology (for yourself) and legally verifiable rules for the road of arms control and disarmament measures for enemies or potential enemies. This is the problem of militarism, and legalism. Finally, following the end of the Cold War, many American official and academic practitioners were smitten by the economic disease, i.e. a belief that economic liberalization and globalization was the way of the future. This was expected to lead to interdependence as well as to tame armed conflicts. In this assessment, geo-politics and nationalism were deemed to become irrelevant in the modern world. As the US enters the 21st century, objective realities have begun to impinge on American policy consciousness. The new Bush administration recognizes the importance of geo-politics in the Asia–Pacific and the Indian Ocean areas today. The Clinton administration did not.

The return to geo-politics followed the end of the Cold War and it dwelt on the pattern of change in Eurasia. Two schools of thought have emerged which form the background to the current American strategic debate. The first school is that economics still drives the world and economic liberalisation creates a vested interest in peace, democracy, human rights; it is likely to marginalize or defeat nationalism. This school is presently under attack. With Russia, Western economic and political engagement got mired in corruption and the growth of xenophobic nationalism. Then came the ascendancy of Vladmir Putin as the new Russian President. This signalled the revival of Russian nationalism and a geo-political approach to international affairs. With China, economic reforms and engagement with the West gave the PLA and the Party the ambition and the means to push China towards a leadership position in Asia, to assert China's military presence in the South China Seas and the Indian Ocean area, and to contain India through a combination of Chinese and Pakistani missile and nuclear power, as well as support of insurgency in Indian border provinces and supplying missiles to Iran. Despite 'constructive engagement' with the West, Chinese Communists remain ruthless at home, more so than before, as evidenced by their treatment of the religious sect Falun Gong; and the human rights situation remains disturbing in China. The second school argues that economic globalization has not made geo-politics obsolete, nor has it replaced the imperative towards the development of regional (e.g. NAFTA, European Union) as well global (World Trade Organizations) economic arrangements; and such arrangements have a social, economic and geo-political context as well as strategic, economic and social consequences.

In the second school, the priority is to maintain the American military and technological edge in relation to other great powers as well as in relation to the sub-critical problem areas like 'rogue' states, terrorism and proliferation. This school emphasizes the looming challenges to the American interest by Russia, China and regional as well as minor powers. Regional allies must be found as the USA cannot act alone to defend its global and regional interests. In this school, geo-politics is still the main game in town and arms control, regime-building as well as non-proliferation are sideshows.

Despite the ascendancy of the second school in American thinking under the Bush administration, confusion still prevails in American views about the situation in Asia. The Bush administration is unclear about its strategic priorities. Who are the enemies (Osama Bin Laden and Islamic terrorists, the rogue states or the big Asian powers)? What is the strategic problem (Islamic terrorism, human rights violations, nuclear and missile proliferation, great power geo-politics, America's pre-eminence in outer space and in the oceans, management of regional situations as in the Balkans, the future of China's internal and external policies and orientations, future of Russia's internal and external policies and orientations)? Is the primary threat to American interests from secondary powers or from other great powers? Is it in the American interest to nip the rise of secondary powers or to put out fires in secondary zones of conflict, such as Kashmir; or is it to buy time in relation to rival great powers and to co-opt regional powers and possibly even the rogue states (Iran? North Korea? Iraq?) as formal and informal allies in the looming great power competition? Will reduction of US overseas troop deployments, and increased reliance on advanced military technology (such as stealth, long range precision munitions, space based satellite imaging and battlefield robots, and national/theatre missile defence) help contain American adversaries abroad and maintain America's military edge in the international system? Will this approach require new regional coalition partners such as India, and new policies in relation to existing allies such as Japan who are seeking the means to an independent military policy (such as acquisition of air refuelling planes)? Will the US retreat from a forward presence in

Germany (from the existing level of 100,000 US troops), from Korea (from the existing level of 100,000 US troops) and from the Gulf area (from the existing level of 25,000 US troops) and cut back its force levels (ten aircraft carriers instead of twelve at present, eight army divisions instead of ten at present) and cut back its marine corps amphibious forces? Will a scaled back US forward military presence stimulate regional military build-ups, regionalized power politics and increase alliance activity? What are the negative and positive implications for American interest and prestige?[6]

The Bush administration's position on the missile defence plan shows the dilemma of developing and altering a force structure without achieving a consensus about priorities in strategic threat assessments and the nature of enmities as they affect vital US interests. So I will review the list of complex American motives in announcing the intention to mount an anti-missile defence system as well as outline America's defence dilemmas. The missile defence idea is a part of new American defence thinking. It reflects an awareness that the US faces challenges to its position in outer space, and challenges to its space-based satellite communications capability could cripple its defences. It also reflects an awareness that the rate of change of threats to American interests in Asia including Central Asia and the Gulf region is far greater than threats to American interests from Europe or other parts of the world. Eurasia is now the major centre of gravity that is seen to challenge American interests, and, as Brzezinski points out, Eurasia is the new major international chessboard. In this prospective, the anti-missile defence proposal has a variety of uses as follows.

1. It is a safety net against rogue states such as North Korea and Iraq. As well, other unnamed 'rogue' states would get the message that America can do to them what it is able to do to North Korea and Iraq. It is good domestic and external politics to demonize the rogue states even though the actual threat may be minimal. For instance, North Korean missiles are few in number and the technology is primitive. China and Russia are constraining North Korean missile development by holding back on technological assistance to them. North Korea has a powerful incentive to secure American economic assistance and diplomatic support so that North Korea can escape international isolation and join the world community without sacrificing the current nature of the regime. It makes no sense for North Korea to confront the USA but it does make sense for North Korea to use missiles as a bargaining chip in its international negotiations. The US also wants to deal with North Korea so that the American presence reaches the Yalu River, extends America's reach to the China border, and completes the unfinished business of the Korean War. North Korea may be fashioning its approach to the USA along the lines of Vietnam although there are similarities and differences and the comparison is not exact. Vietnam won the war against America; North Korean military action during the Korean War led to a stalemate and an armistice. On the other hand, both countries are Communist states seeking constructive engagement with fellow Communist states as well as the

leader of the capitalist world. Such facts and considerations must occupy the attention of American strategic planners and leaders. But it is not good politics to bring out the nuances because it would undermine the public US case in favour of anti-missile defence. Here notional and subjective realities are in play in the development of the new preferred US defence posture.

2. It builds a theatre missile shield for allies such as Japan and Taiwan so that these countries do not feel compelled to adopt an independent strategic policy and force structure. Here the context is the belief expressed by Owen Lattimore (discussed earlier) that Japan is nobody's ally. Another context is that Japan has been adopting defence positions such as acquiring air refuelling planes that indicate an awareness of the need to be able to mount military operations in the 'area surrounding Japan' in the future. The political cover for such actions is provided in the US/Japan military guidelines that are periodically revised.[7] This gives Japan, the junior military partner, an expanded role in an enlarged military sphere where Japanese strategic and commercial interests are engaged, i.e. the Taiwan straits, the South China Seas and the maritime lifeline of energy leading to the Persian Gulf. For Taiwan, a theatre missile shield is timely given the PRC's efforts to strengthen its air power in relation to Taiwan. It increases Taiwan's sense of security and its negotiation space in its relations with the mainland. It buys time for Taiwan to build its international profile and to expand its international links.

3. It promotes the American goal of emerging as the pre-eminent space power at a time when few countries have already developed space launch and anti-satellite capabilities, i.e. Russia, China, Japan, India and the Europeans.

4. It will promote the well being of the American industrial military complex because the anti-missile defence technology is untested and it requires extensive research and development.

5. It puts a distance between the strategic orientation of the Democratic Clinton administration and the Republican Bush administration regarding American's attitude to the great powers. The anti-missile defence program lends weight to the second school of thought that emphasizes the central importance of great power geo-politics. It shifts USA's posture towards China from the Clinton view of China as a 'strategic partner' to the Bush view of China as a 'strategic competitor'; and it shifts the US posture towards Russia: from Clinton's neglect of Russian strategic interests and international prestige to an acknowledgement of Russia as a negotiation partner in arms control and bilateral relations.

6. It degrades China's missile capability. It signals an intention to mess with PRC's strategic mind and its decision process concerning its military modernization and related costs. It undermines Beijing's smugness that it is the natural leader of Asia, and that America and China are strategic partners in the Asia–Pacific sphere. By mounting an anti-missile defence strategy, the Bush administration is rewriting the international agenda on the ABM Treaty (1972), the Outer Space Treaty (1967) and its non-proliferation and missile

technology control policies (1960s–). Furthermore, Bush administration actions cast doubt on the viability of multilateral arm control agreements and negotiations. Ability to rewrite the international agenda is a sign of international power. The context for America is that PRC has a problem. Its self-image or its mythology that it is a natural leader in Asia and a potential world power does not correspond with the reality of internal problems and its economic and military weaknesses. Beijing is not prepared at the moment to manage the American challenge without investing heavily in its defence sphere. This, however, has internal social, economic and political costs. In other words, the US can escalate and act independently in terms of rhetoric as well as policy in relation to China. China cannot do so easily. China is circumscribed in many ways. It depends heavily on overseas investments. It has not secured vital resources like oil that are free of hostile intervention. At the same time, regional powers like Japan and India are acting as rivals to China because they are preparing to meet the possible danger of China's military expansion and its international pressures. Regional military and alliance build-ups affect China's range of choices and decision processes. The reality that Russian–Chinese, Sino-American, Sino-Indian and Japan–China interests are in contention means that China, like America, must develop means to manage its continental as well as sub-regional relationships in addition to its internal politics and economics.

These points indicate that the Asian strategic context is volatile and multilayered. It points to the vitality of geo-politics in Eurasia. There is an awareness in the American strategic mind that American hegemony of the international system in the 21st century is temporary. It will diminish as new power centres emerge in Asia, and something must be done to maintain the American position. An emphasis on an anti-missile defence is also a statement about the nature of American political culture. It relies on technological and military solutions and power build-ups rather than building political security, as Lattimore has pointed out. The anti-missile defence reflects a new orientation (but it is not a done deal). This orientation carries several assumptions: rivalries among great powers are rapidly growing; regional great powers have emerged in southern Asia and the Persian Gulf (Iran); Japan is improving its defensive capability and the subtext of US/Japan alliance ties is that a significant section of the Japanese élite no longer feels that it can rely on US for protection. This orientation points to the growing importance of regionalism in Asia.

Regionalism in Asia

Regionalism differs from local nationalism on the one hand, and internationalism or globalism on the other hand. It is a valuable and an intermediate link between the two levels of activity, and it is a centre of critical discourse among states. Figure 5.1 illustrates the place of regionalism in relation to

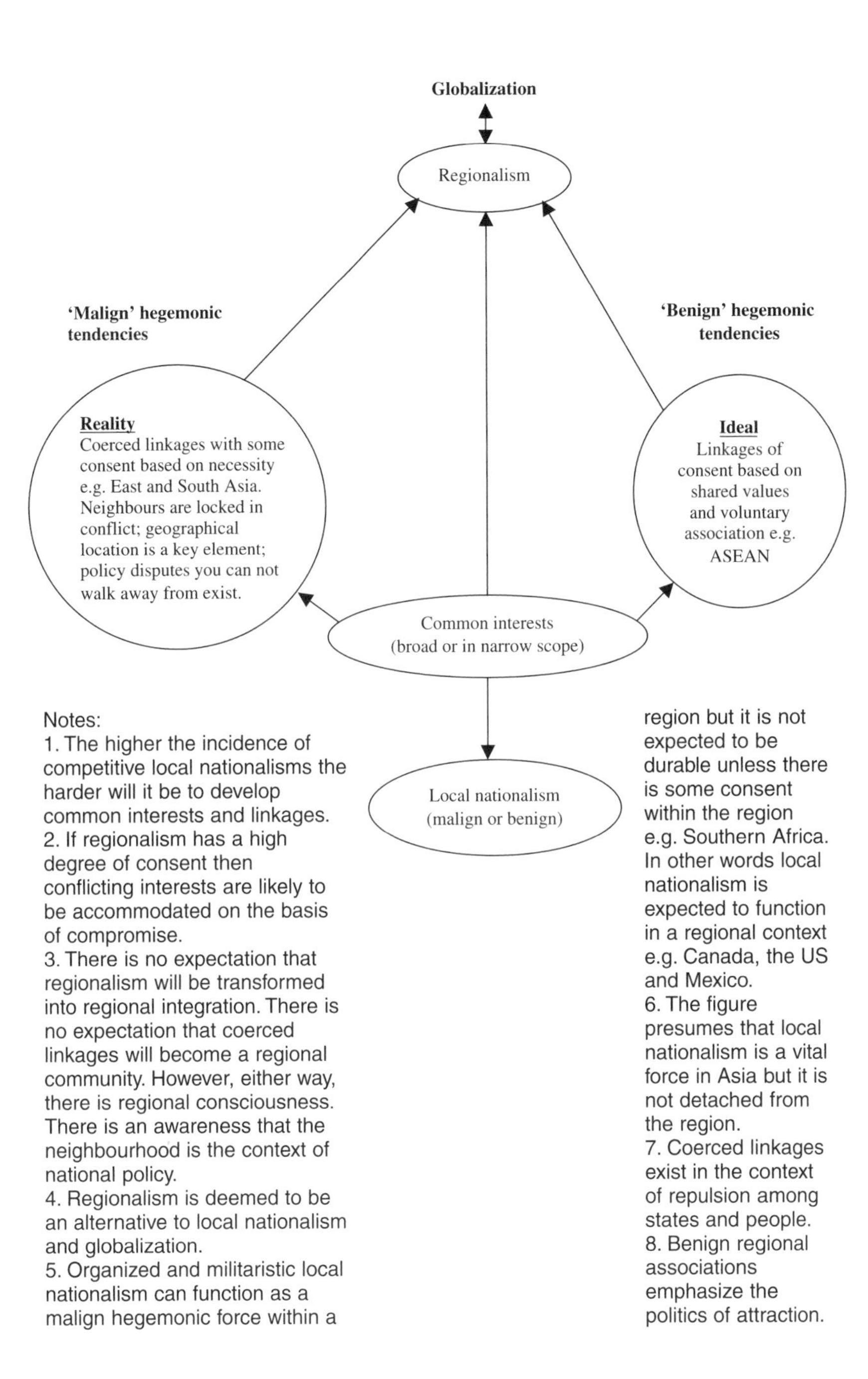

Figure 5.1 Regionalism

local nationalism and globalization. Secondly, it shows the two faces of regionalism: 'malign/coercive'; and 'benign/consensual'. Thirdly, it emphasizes the importance of relationships rather than the distribution of power.

Regionalism is a fundamental impulse in the modern world for at least three reasons. First, culturally, peoples are tied together regionally more than internationally even though regional states may be divided by policy issues. For instance, there are civilizational or cultural pulls that form an undercurrent between, say, Hindus and Muslims in India, Pakistan, Bangladesh, and between Indians, Nepalese and Sri Lankans in the subcontinent. There is a civilizational pull that draws together mainland Chinese, and Chinese élites and populations in Taiwan and Hong Kong. There is a pull between North and South Koreans who form two parts of the Korean nation. There is a cultural attraction as well between Japanese and Chinese societies. Samuel Huntington emphasizes the clash of civilization.[8] I emphasize cultural pulls even among regional rivals. Furthermore, I see cultural differences as a stimulus to nation-building and a motivation to engage the competing culture (e.g. Indians–Chinese/Hindu–Muslim) by modernizing science and technology, the economy and the political system. Here cultural competition and differences have a positive influence in bringing out the best in different spheres of a country's development. In other words, inter-state diplomatic and military strategies in the post-Cold War era are primarily regionally and culturally driven diplomatic and military encounters that require either strikes (war, intervention or economic and psychological warfare) and/or negotiation (settlement of disputes through compromise and compensation based on accommodation and adjustment of competing interest). This view is particularly relevant with reference to the five centres of gravity in Asia noted earlier.

Second, regional powers are tied increasingly to regional rivalries and to regional partners as well as international powers. All Asian geo-political pivots have a regional character, and regional great powers have horizontal links with regional players, and vertical ones with the international powers. At the same time if we take a top–down approach, all international powers must of necessity (not by choice) maintain links or points of engagement with regional strategic issues and with regional powers, that is, if they are to protect their interests and their prestige in the region(s).

Third, historically, international great powers have been tied to each other but as the number of great powers have shrunk since the 1940s, and the great powers have less wriggle space in managing international relations through concerted great power diplomacy, they must tie themselves more to regional great powers if they must of necessity do so either as rivals or as partners to regional powers. In the latter case, they are locked into bargaining relationships with the regional powers. The traditional paradigm of dominant–subordinate relationships no longer explains the pattern of relationships and the power structure in our five geo-political pivots or centres of gravity in Asia.

It is not implied in this book that regionalism is a step towards the development of a harmonious, conflict free international society. In my thinking, regionalism is not a step towards economic globalization, which is presumed to exist independent of regionalism. It does not carry the expectation that regional integration will be the result of regionalism. It is not a step towards the utopia of a world driven by the absence of war, fear, insecurity and inequality. In my view, regionalism can be a terminal condition where the evolution is from competitive nationalism and inward-looking thinking to the development of outward looking, albeit competitive, inter-state relationships. In one sense such relationships are coerced linkages that reflect an awareness of shared destiny as a matter of necessity among cultural and strategic rivals. In another sense regionalism means the existence of regional consciousness or a sense of community. This implies the existence of a shared belief in the value of development of informal or institutionalized methods of conflict management and conflict resolution. Rivalries are not deemed to be pathological in my view. As stated earlier, rivalries can stimulate the development of ideas, skills and strategies, and the mobilization of capabilities that help the process of nation-building and inter-state engagement with rivals. It is implied that regionalism is rooted in competitive nationalism, i.e. foreign policy is a bridge between domestic politics and regional politics; and competitive ethnic and religious sub-national (or transnational) forces may be present and interactive within a region. In this sense regionalism is a powerful and an elemental form of inter-state and inter-society interactions. It is elemental and basic because no individual nation or state can be truly isolated or independent of its external environment especially its regional neighbourhood. A country's external relationships have a distinct geographical scope; they are area specific because developments in the neighbourhood impact on a neighbour's future destiny. Thus, a Talibanized Afghanistan affects issues of Islamic fundamentalism in Pakistan, China's border areas and Indian Kashmir. The drug and the arms trade between Afghanistan and Pakistan and the neighbourhood affects social development in the subcontinent. Islamic terrorism from bases in Afghanistan and Pakistan has an impact on Central Asian states. Another example is that PRC's push into Myanmar impacts on Indian policy and social consciousness because China's activities have the potential to create a wedge between South and South East Asia. China's policy challenges the social and political tendency to build economic, political and social bridges for the well-being of the Bay of Bengal 'community' that includes Myanmar and Thailand. In the South China Seas, Chinese strategic activities impact on the well-being of a number of regional neighbours: ASEAN states, Taiwan, Japan and a number of extra-regional countries who depend on international commerce and maritime security. To take another example, military and diplomatic developments within the Korean peninsula impact on the economic, strategic and social peace of PRC, Japan, Russia and Taiwan (from within the region) and America from outside the region. These are a few examples of regional 'circles of states' which exist in Asia–Pacific and the Indian Ocean areas. In the 19th century, the great powers functioned in the terms of the 'sandwich system'. Now, as there are limits for the great powers' ability to club together (i.e. to act in concert) or to intervene unilaterally, the regional circle of states is the paradigm for great powers as well as regional states.

Regionalism is rooted in the reality of geographical links among countries. Another reality is the idea of a neighbourhood that may be either friendly or conflict-prone, more likely to be the latter in the case of Asian neighbourhoods. Table 5.1 offers the definitions and criteria for measuring regionalism. These perspectives are drawn from mainstream Western literature. They form the basis of development of my view of the increasing importance of regional security structures in Asia–Pacific and the Indian Ocean area.

Defined as coerced linkages or as voluntary community, regionalism is facilitated by the presence of a regional great power in two ways. The regional great power may seek regional cooperation to secure the consent of its smaller neighbours. Here regional cooperation tames the fear among the smaller neighbours about the danger of malign hegemony from the regional great power: unless it is addressed, such a fear may induce them to reach outside the region and to seek the help of an international power to balance the danger posed by the 'malign' regional hegemon. It is preferable for a regional great power to secure the consent of its neighbours rather than to encourage great power intervention in regional power politics. It is in the interest of the regional great power to encourage the growth of bandwagoning relationships on part of the neighbours rather than to encourage balancing activity.[9] Great power intervention in regional politics would raise the costs of defence and diplomacy in the policies of the regional great power.

Secondly, regionalism is also favoured by the smaller neighbours because benign protection and aid by a regional great power can be secured through bandwagoning. That is, they may be willing participants in bandwagoning activity in relation to the regional great power because their interests are better served that way.

In South Asia, Pakistan's choice was to seek balancing activity vis-à-vis India, first by seeking an alliance with the USA to balance India (1950s–1980s) and then with the PRC (1960s to present). India's other 'smaller' neighbours however, for the most part choose bandwagoning.[10] Taiwan sought balancing of mainland China by its alignment with the US. North Korea sought a bandwagoning relationship with the Soviet Union during the Cold War (and with China thereafter), and now it seeks to bargain with the US, China and Russia as a regional power.

The regional great power (e.g. India) is expected to pursue a dual strategy. First, it seeks a position of asymmetrical distribution of power in its favour within the region so that the combination of local power (e.g. Pakistan) and international power (e.g. USA and PRC) is not able to undermine the diplomatic and military policies of the regional great power. Secondly, it seeks to follow a policy of regional cooperation and mutually satisfactory bilateral relations. This is intended to secure the consent of its neighbours. Consent is

Table 5.2 Different criteria for measuring regionalism

Author	*Concepts*		*Exclusion*
	Core concepts	*General concept*	
Barry Buzan, *People, States and Fear: An Agenda for International Security in the Post-Cold War Era*, New York: Harvester Wheatsheaf, 1991	Security interdependence (pp. 188–94) and geographical proximity (p. 188–91)[a]	Regional rivalry (p. 194); economic interests – complementary or competitive (p. 202)	Cultural and racial ties are ignored.
Adda B. Bozeman, *Politics and Culture in International History*, New Brunswick, Transaction Publishers, 1994	Role of cultural conflict and international conflict (pp. xv 10)[b]	History, ideology, political systems, (pp. 10–11)	Regional military/security linkages are not stressed but are implicitly recognized.
S.B. Cohen, *Geography and Politics in a Divided World*, New York: Oxford University Press, 1973	Geo-politics and geo-strategy (pp. 64–5)[c]	Economics, politics (pp. 65–70); technology and ideology (p. xiv)	Cohen seems to embrace all the factors in regionalism, albeit with different emphasis.
Zbigniew Brzezinski, *The Grand Chessboard: American Primacy and its Geostrategic Imperatives*, New York, Basic Books, 1997	Geo-politics and and geo-strategy (pp. 37–40)[d]	Economics (pp. 165–6); Military, politics, technology (pp. 10–29); history, geography (pp. 164–6)	Culture is emphasized as a complementary factor for America's role as a global hegemon but not in regionalism especially in Asia.
Raimo Vayrynen, 'Regional Conflict Formations: An Intractable Problem of International Relations', *Journal of Peace Research*, 16/4 (1979)	Economic, military (pp. 349, 360) and political. These three factors coincide and reinforce each other (p. 365)	Geopolitics and national ideology (p. 355)	Regional powers and regional conflict formations are emphasized.
Raimo Vayrynen, 'Regional Conflict Formations: An Intractable Problem of International Relations', *Journal of Peace Research*, 21/4 (1984)	Economic (pp. (pp. 342–3); geographical proximity, political expediency (p. 340)[e]		Culture and national unity are treated as disruptive factors by economic disorganization (p. 345)

Table 5.2 – cont

Author	*Concepts*		*Exclusion*
	Core concepts	*General concept*	
Michael Antolik, *ASEAN and the Diplomacy of Accommodation*, New York: M.E. Inc., 1990	Secure external environment (pp. 9–10; 12; 14–17)[f]	History, economics and social realities (p. 140)	Culture (pp. 14–15) is not emphasized.
Ramses Amer, 'Conflict Management and Constructive Engagement in ASEAN's Expansion', *Third World Quarterly*, 20/5 (1999), 1031–8	Security (conflict management)[g] and politics[h] (pp. 1032–3; 1040–2)	Economics (pp. 1040; 1042–3)	Cultural?
Jose T. Almonte 'Ensuring Security the ASEAN Way', Survival, 39, 4. (Winter 1997–8, 80–92	Security (p. 81); Economic (p. 85)[i]	Geo-strategy – dealing with a rising China (pp. 83–5)	Culture (lack of overarching civilization) (p. 81)
Seyom Brown, *International Relations in a Changing Global System: Towards a Theory of the World Polity*, 2nd edn, Boulder, CO: Westview Press, 1996	Security, conflict prevention and conflict resolution (pp. 31–5)[j]	Economics (p. 31); influence of external powerful state (hegemonic stability (pp. 38–9)	Culture is ignored. Regionalism is deemed to be soft.

Notes:

a 'region means that a distinct and significant subsystem of security relations exists amount a set of states whose fate is that they have been locked into geographical proximity with each other' (p. 188).

b 'political systems are grounded in cultures . . . present day inter*national* relations are therefore by definition also inter*cultural* relations' (p. 5).
'the realities of world affairs probably were not rendered adequately when conveyed in the simple myth of the bipolar world; for between the poles of the contemporary may were numerous well-defined cultural and political entities as well as some that were just beginning to define themselves' (p. 5).
'the real affinities and differences between the various cultural and political systems of the present world society can be uncovered only after a thorough exploration of the historic sources of all significant patterns of political thought and behavior. Only when one knows what meanings a particular nations has traditionally attributed to such prominent words in the current international vocabulary as peace, war, unity, authority, and freedom, or what other values and institutions . . . can one test with any hope of accuracy the authenticity and worth of presently existing international arrangements and assumptions . . . if such records are to yield the insights into local value systems requisite for an understanding of present international conflicts and accords, they must be read in the context of region and the time in which they refer' (p. 10).

Table 5.2 – cont

c 'The geostrategic region is the expression of the interrelationship of a large part of the world in terms of location, movement, trade orientation, and cultural or ideological bounds' (p. 64).
d 'The exercise of . . . global primacy must be sensitive to the fact that political geography remains a critical consideration in international affairs' (p. 37).
'geographic location is still the point of departure for the definition of a nation-state's external priorities . . . geographic location still tends to determine the immediate priorities of a state – and the greater its military, economic, and political power, the greater the radius, beyond its immediate neighbors, of that state's vital geopolitical interests, influence, and involvement' (p. 38).
e 'A regional subsystem is . . . characterized by a certain distinctiveness and proximity, not only in the geographical, but also in the economic and political sense. Proximity is institutionalized by means of mutual interaction and common organizations' (p. 340).
f 'individual national interests and not ethnic magnetism were the reasons behind the membership' (p. 14).
g 'The documents aim to provide guidelines for managing inter-state relations in general, and existing and potential disputes in particular. (p. 1035).
'Successful conflict management creates conducive conditions for both economic and political co-operation and it contributes to enhance the security of the countries in the Southeast Asian region' (p. 1039).
h 'The political factor seems to have been crucial in creating the necessary basic conditions for an expansion of membership of ASEAN in the first place' (p. 1042).
i 'The ARF, the political forum, and APEC, the economic grouping, are the two main strands in the strategic framework within which most East Asian states now define national security' (p. 80).
j 'cooperative security regimes are fully consistent with and the most rational responses to the security dilemmas facing modern great powers under the anarchic nation-state system' (p. 34).

achieved in a number of ways: by developing regional relationships so that common diplomatic, economic and military interests of the players are served; by using the diplomatic principles of compromise and compensation to stabilize inter-state relationships, or regional conflicts; by using civilizational pulls or cultural traditions to foster bonding among the regional players despite the asymmetry in the distribution of power among states. These methods are meant to minimize polarity within the region.

Balancing activity *à la* Pakistan is appropriate when there is extreme polarity between the regional great power and the local power, and international allies are available who share a desire to contain the regional great power. On the other hand, bandwagoning is realistic if the smaller neighbours lack a choice because the international powers are not interested in supporting them; or the policy differences between the regional great power and the smaller neighbours do not merit balancing activity through international allies; and/or if the regional great power is supportive of the interests of the smaller neighbours and is able to offer diplomatic and economic solutions to pressing problems of the smaller neighbours. Absent extreme polarity, the smaller neighbours are likely to coopt the regional hegemon (e.g. Indonesia in South East Asia) into regional arrangements (e.g. ASEAN) so that the regional hegemon functions as a benign force. The origins of ASEAN show that Indonesia's neighbours recognized the danger of Indonesian hegemony but sought to tame the danger through ASEAN diplomacy.

This discussion shows the possibility of two kinds of regionalism in Asia–Pacific and the Indian Ocean areas today: soft and hard. Seyom Brown thinks of Asian regionalism as soft. To quote him.

> 1) Regional subsystems like regional empires of the past, can not be expected to be 'content with what they have and refrain from balance of power games against each other'. There is a 'profound *jealousy and suspicion' against regional hegemons*. 2) There are no longer 'universally acceptable definitions of *which peoples constitutes what regions*'. 3) Finally, '*If multipolar regional subsystems do temporarily emerge*, the ever-present prospect of the disintegration will present outside powers with temptation to cultivate local *clients* and, in the event of actual disintegration, to intervene competitively'.[11]

In my judgement Asian regionalism has acquired the qualities of hard regionalism. Here are the reasons. Soft regionalism exists when a local power seeks international alliance activity and active intervention – by itself and by its international partner – in regional strategic and economic affairs, and in the internal politics of the regional great power. Here the local–international alliance is irredentist and interventionist, the relationship between the regional players is one of conflict, and the distribution of power between the regional players (without the borrowed power of the international ally of the local power) is asymmetrical. In South Asia's international history since 1947 the strategies of Pakistan and USA (1950s to 1980s) and Pakistan and PRC (1960s to the present) were to balance Indian power and influence within the region and in the international sphere. India, bigger than Pakistan, was territorially satisfied and sought instead to check the intrusion of foreign alliances into subcontinental. affairs. Although the record is mixed in terms of Indian intentions and results, India sought consent in its relationships with the smaller neighbours. By way of example, Figure 5.2 outlines the pattern and the elements that defined soft regionalism in South Asia in the 1950s–1980s period when it was replaced by hard regionalism in the 1990s.

Figure 5.3 outlines the pattern and the elements of hard or hardening regionalism. This figure assumes that there is no change in Pakistan's approach. It strategies are based on polarity with India. It seeks balancing as before. There are, however, several salient differences in the context of Pakistan's strategies in the 21st century. First, it no longer enjoys the patronage of the USA, the pre-eminent international power. USA has shifted into a partnership mode with India, recognizing it as a stabilizing force in the region and in Asia. Second, the PRC has the capability and the motive to engage in dangerous meddling in subcontinental affairs and to raise the costs of Indian

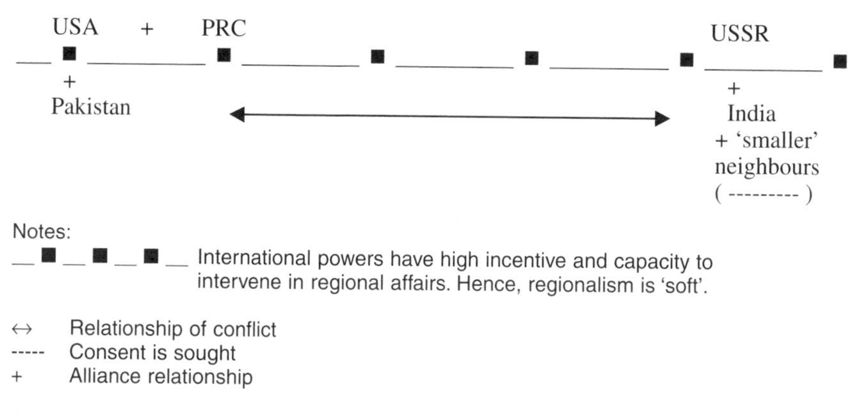

Strategies

- USA, PRC, Pakistan: contain or balance India.
- India: (i) Check or disrupt US, Pakistan, PRC alliance activity
  (ii) Seek a margin of safety by acquiring asymmetry in the distribution of power in the subcontinent.
- 'Smaller' neighbours of India (excluding Pakistan): bandwagoning with India is the preferred strategy.

Figure 5.2 Soft regionalism in South Asia 1950s–1980s

security and its economic well-being.[12] However, the PRC–Pakistan combination alone cannot alter the pattern of subcontinental international relations. It alone cannot disrupt Indian unity or to undermine Indian political will to challenge and counter the PRC–Pakistan combination's interventionary potential in the region. When the US–Pakistan combination was not able to contain India, the PRC–Pakistan combination is even less likely to do so. Third, India itself has demonstrated staying power and a commitment to its territorial unity, and the continuous development of its economic and military (including nuclear and missile) strength. The growth of Indian offensive capabilities demonstrates an Indian capacity to initiate and to manage regional conflict, and to raise the costs of defence or security of Pakistan's international partner, China. That is, China's policy towards India and Pakistan is not cost free in China's internal strategic planning and in its relationships with other international powers. The costs are tangible and growing. They require a commitment of additional resources (budgetary, military technology, military capability, military and political intelligence and development of policies and strategies) to deal with the India problem. China's policies towards India and Pakistan impact on international issues like missile and nuclear proliferation, maritime security and regional stability in parts of Asia. China's policies bring together America, Vietnam, Russia, India and other states because there is uncertainty about China's strategic orientation and future policies in Asia. As Sun Tzu would remind us, the aim of strategy is to disrupt enemy's alliances, not to create unfavourable ones against yourself. However, China is expected to disrupt Indo-Pakistani reconciliation negotiations by stimulating the hardliners on both sides as long as it has influence on its lobbyists in the two countries.

In sum, the case of the Indian subcontinent shows the shift from soft to hard regionalism. Interventionist policies by international powers prevent the growth of stabilizing regional relationships and the influence of the regional great power (Figure 5.2). On the other hand, when international power(s) encourage the build-up of the power and prestige of the regional great power within and outside the region, the prospects of hard regionalism increase (Figure 5.3). Here the international powers recognize the regional great power as a benign hegemon. These circumstances reflect the shift in the policies of the international power(s). Another set of circumstances concern the expansion of the capacities, skills and ideas of the regional great power. When a regional great power demonstrates its staying power in the strategic, economic and political spheres, the evidence of its skills in war, peace and intervention require that it be taken seriously as a major regional and an international player. India has demonstrated staying power by its ability to manage South Asian military conflicts, by its ability to break up Pakistan by force against a hostile international coalition in 1971, by the demonstration of its nuclear and missile power and by its ability to withstand international sanctions. At the same time it shows an ability to maintain coerced linkages as well as a measure of consent in subcontinental relationships.

In soft regionalism regional relationships are vulnerable to external intervention and international vetoes. In hard or hardening regionalism the regional great power is able to function as a regional cop; it is in the driver's seat. Its policies shape the regional strategic agenda. Its behaviour is not vulnerable to successful external intervention even when it frontally challenges global norms such as non-proliferation and anti-missile proliferation. It has staying power, and furthermore, its power and influence has been factored into the strategic calculations of the international powers. The geographical sphere of its strategic interests is growing visibly.

Hard regionalism is defined by the emergence of a regional great power and by the development of stable regional relationships with elements of polarity as well as friendship within the region. Three major processes exist within the region. First, power consolidates around the rise of the regional great power (i.e. regional power formation exists). Secondly, the emergence of stable and predictable parameters in the regional relationships along the lines indicated in Figures 5.2 and 5.3 indicate regional conflict formation. Finally, the structure is multipolar and the international players cannot dominate regional politics as they could during the Cold War and bipolar eras. The international powers must continue to participate in regional affairs because their interests and their prestige is involved in regional issues and the costs of non-involvement are higher than the costs of involvement.

Hard regionalism implies the existence of a stable set of regional relationships that revolves around the primacy of regional power and regional conflict formations. It is not necessarily a point of equilibrium because

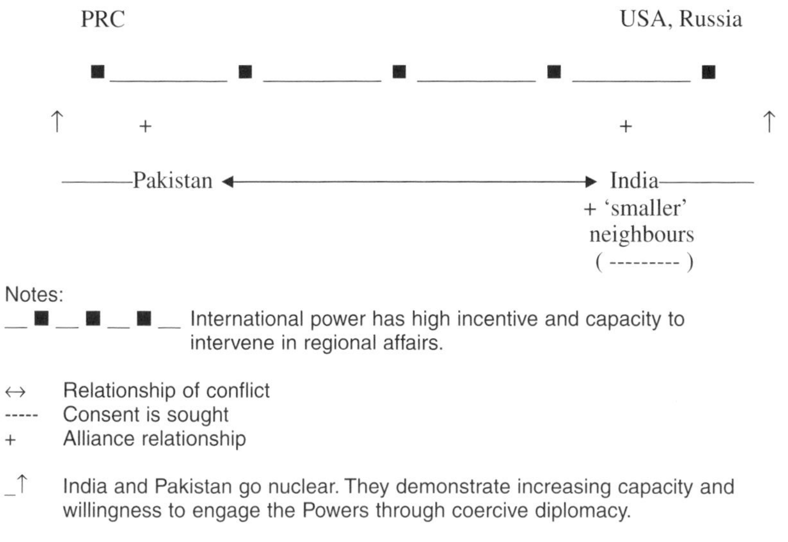

Strategies

- PRC & Pakistan: contain and balance India
- USA & Russia: support India's positive role in regional and international affairs
- India:
  - (i) Check of disrupt Pakistan–PRC alliance activity
  - (ii) Seek a margin of safety by acquiring asymmetry in the distribution of power in the subcontinent.
  - (iii) Challenge the non-proliferation and anti-missile proliferation regimes by going nuclear openly.
  - (iv) Seek security dialogues and partnerships with USA, Russia, China and Pakistan.

Figure 5.3 Hardened regionalism in South Asia 1990s–2000

regional conflict exists, the relationships are dynamic, not static, and the region is managed by the regional great power in concert with selected international power(s). It implies a condition of manageable instability, not of harmony and peace (meaning the absence of conflicts among states). Hard regionalism is neither imperialism nor is it equilibrium. As Figure 5.1 shows, it is an intermediate condition between local nationalism and globalism. It is not necessarily a stepping stone to globalism; it may be viewed as a terminal condition in the world today. It may be viewed as a suitable alternative to globalism, given the widespread belief that economic globalization is dominated by the corporate agenda and is insensitive about to local and regional social/cultural context as well as consequences of economic liberalization policies. However, hard regionalism is compatible with capitalism.

Hard regionalism rests on a fundamental distinction between 'interdependence' and 'pattern of relations'.[13] The first requires a political peace settlement so that the expectation of the danger of armed conflict is taken out of the relationship. An example of interdependence is the Canada/USA relationship. There are policy disputes in this relationship but there is no expectation of a danger of war. There are extensive economic, military, diplomatic, people to people and communication linkages. Mechanisms exist to manage the disagreements; there are rules of the road and there is a road map. On the other hand, the India–China and the India–Pakistan relationships show a changing pattern of relationships that reflect the effect of changing regional and international circumstances. Note that these relationships are stable, i.e. the structure of conflict has defined parameters which show the limits about the escalatory potential of conflicting issues, but there is no political peace settlement in the picture. They are like Barry Buzan's 'regional security complexes', i.e. they are tied together by geography, territorial disputes, policy disagreements, status differences and historical memories but they are not regional interdependencies. There is a pattern of alignment between these pairs but it is changeable. Hence Martin Wight's view about the 'pattern of power' is more applicable to the India–China and India–Pakistan cases than Barry Buzan's regional 'interdependencies'.

Regionalism showcases the major difference in the functions or roles of middle and regional great powers. Canada is a middle power by virtue of its advocacy of important international issues such as disarmament, human rights, trade liberalization in the international arena. The influence it enjoys in world affairs does not correspond to its military and economic weight but it reveals the force of ideas and the skill of presentation. On the other hand India is a regional great power by virtue of its ability – its capabilities, skills in war and peace making, and ideas – to shape the pattern of relationships within the Indian subcontinent, and to project power and influence into the neighbourhood and in the international sphere. Canada pursues its international relationships with likeminded countries like Australia and those in Europe. Canada can largely choose its strategic and negotiating partners (or adversaries) with one exception: it cannot avoid sharing the bed with its continental neighbour, USA. India on the other hand cannot choose its strategic and negotiating partners or adversaries. It is preoccupied by critical and subcritical issues in its geographical neighbourhood; and it is located in a region of military and social conflicts that Canada is not. So regional great powers occupy an important place in conflict zones and they gain their power and their status by their ability to manage and/or resolve regional conflicts and by their ability to shape the international agenda as well. Middle powers on the other hand do not possess regional roots of power or influence in the sense that they are not necessarily located in regions of military and social conflict and they have neither the inclination nor the capacity to function as regional cops. As a middle power, Canada is a junior partner of the USA in international regime building activities, or it participates in coalitions of likeminded countries, but its international influence is circumscribed by what the USA, the senior partner, will tolerate or accept. Middle powers are committed to international causes and agendas; they are forward-looking. However, they are not involved in costly and risky neighbourhood quarrels. In Asia, regional great powers function in crowded and dangerous neighbourhoods.

Regionalism is pursued in an environment of deadly quarrels and ritual confrontations. Regional élites preside over fragile domestic coalitions; there are few rules of the road. Their world is one of jungles not roads. The challenge is to maintain and to extend the cease-fires, to discover and develop the wriggle space and the envelope of negotiations, and maintain a situation of manageable instability. Regionalism requires active war and peace diplomacy, i.e. a commitment to both military and political security. Regionalism requires leaders who can fight wars, who know when to fight and/or to negotiate, who can organize regional and international relationships, and locate mutual interests in an unruly neighbourhood, who can create disincentives against war and incentives towards negotiated settlements and create regional and international stakeholders in peace making. At the same time a regional leader must mobilize domestic as well as regional and international opinion so that a public identification exists with the agenda and strategies adopted. Because of the high incidence of nationalism in Asia, regional great powers require an ability to channel local nationalism into constructive channels. Middle powers are disdainful of local nationalism because they do not need to deal with it, and they do not believe that local nationalism is desirable. On the other hand, regional leaders recognize the importance of local/national cultures and nationalism because cultural conflicts are tied to international and regional conflicts, as Bozeman correctly notes in her seminal work.[14]

Regionalism is tied intimately to cultural conflicts and to regional conflicts. It is tied to power politics. Successful regional leaders are adept in pursuing cultural-military-geopolitical strategies. They have to know when to strike and when to negotiate if they are to survive and thrive in deadly domestic, regional and international environments.

6 Multipolarity in Asian regions 1940s–2000

An overview

Introduction

Multipolarity has a history in Asia. It has evolved in the context of rapid change in the distribution (re-distribution) of power at two levels. The first concerns the development of power as well as relationships among the continental powers in Asia. Table 6.1 outlines the rapid changes since the 1940s.

The second concerns the period following decolonization when regional power and regional relationships crystallized and changed rapidly. This chapter examines the major trends in Asia since 1945. The general argument is that the strategic and diplomatic space in Asia has been taken by Asian powers. The Western powers enjoyed spheres of influence from the 19th century up to the mid-20th century. These spheres have been reconstituted. There are no longer any power vacuums in Asia. Asia is still out of Western control, as Lattimore indicated in 1949, but now there are many centres of regional power in Asia which have redistributed the power in Asia in their own favour.

Robert Gilpin predicts the importance of war as an institution that revises the hierarchy of powers. He sees war as the method to deal with the disequilibrium created by redistribution. In his scheme war is inevitable. It is a necessary method to deal with international power changes because the hierarchy of winners and losers is recreated after a major war. Hence international change and war are twinned together in a dynamic international environment.[1]

In my conception war is neither inevitable nor necessary, nor is great power imperialism or intervention the logical consequence or condition of modern international relations. Equilibrium (defined as total peace or harmony) is also ruled out because of the scope and the intensity of ongoing rivalries in the Asian strategic landscape. In other words, neither the expectations that a general war will occur, nor the likelihood of great power imperialism, nor the likelihood of equilibrium (as distinct from balancing activities to manage rivalries and to maintain a pattern of manageable instability among major and minor powers), forms the context in which continental and regional multipolarities have emerged in Asia since 1945. In my scheme continental and regional multipolarities are based on an expectation that states are tied

Table 6.1 Changing distribution of power in Asia

	India	*USA*	*Japan*	*Britain*	*Other Europeans*	*Russia*	*China*
	India	USA	Japan	Britain	Other	Russia	China
1940s	0	↑	↑	↑	↓	↑	0
1945	0	↑	↓	↓	↓	↑	0
1950s–80s	∪	↑	∪	↓	↓	↑	↑
1990s	↑	↑	∪	↓	↓	↓	↑
2000	↑	↑	∪	↓	↓	∪	↑

Notes
↑ upwardly mobile
↓ downward mobile
↔ moving sideways
0 zero international power
∪ down and up
tentative upwardly mobile

together, either through the politics of repulsion or that of attraction, and international great powers as well as regional great powers are repositioning themselves in relation to each other on this basis. They do so by *increasing* their military, organizational and economic *capabilities*, by the development of diplomatic *alignments*, by the skills they employ in their *strategies* to advance their interests, and by the articulation of *indigenous philosophies* and ideas that challenge the methods employed by the great empire builders in Asia (the Europeans, Russia and America).

Multipolarity, not unipolarity or bipolarity, is our theme about the character of Asian security structures. These structures are expressed by the shaded areas in Map 5.1. These are the geo-political pivots, the centres of gravity where high impact developments are taking place. At the continental and the regional levels they are explained by the changing patterns of strategic thinking and strategic relationships among the growing list of major and minor powers in Asia. The number and capacities of Asian powers has grown and their ambition is supported by their ability to project their agenda and their power into the geo-political pivots. In addition, the centres of gravity of strategic action have shifted southwards in Asia. From the traditional focus on East Asia, it has broadened now towards an awareness of the importance of links between the issue of maritime security in the Pacific and the Indian Oceans, between seapower and landpower in the geo-political pivots, and in the policies of the major and the minor powers in Eurasia.

Asian multipolarity should not be confused with multilateralism because Asia is different from Europe and North America. Unlike Europe there is no security architecture or a tradition of multilateral discourse and conflict resolution among competing nations. Arms control arrangements do not seem to work in Asia. Asia is a geo-political jungle. There are many deadly quarrels, unresolved territorial and prestige disputes, civilizational and power rivalries. The policy challenges are to manage conflicts, extend cease-fires, develop negotiation envelopes and to create strategic dialogue among leaders who preside over fragile domestic coalitions of power and internal competition. Asia has many nasty and crowded neighbourhoods. Western arms control specialists maintain that the future lies with arms control agreements. This is not necessarily true in Asia because there is no entrenched tradition of a multilateral discourse in the area. ASEAN and ARF are modest beginnings in this direction but in the absence of widely accepted rules of the game or even roads or pathways of strategic discourse in the Asian jungles, warmaking is easier than peace making. Even states' territorial boundaries are porous, for example, between Afghanistan and Pakistan, India and Pakistan, India and Bangladesh, Chinese Yunnan and Myanmar and so on. So Asian multipolarity is located in a context more of coerced linkages among neighbours and among regional great powers and the international powers than voluntary communities or associations. ASEAN is an example of the latter but, as the International Institute for Strategic Studies notes:

> The greater diversity of identities and interests now included in ASEAN and its unwillingness to bend its cardinal rule of non-interference in domestic affairs has left the association unable to address its structural weaknesses. It is now, to an even greater extent than before, tied to the lowest common denominator in managing consensus. In addition, the authority vacuum in Indonesia in the face of its continuing troubles has deprived ASEAN of a locus of leadership and has diminished its international standing.[2]

How do coerced linkages shape hard regionalism and multipolarities in the geo-political pivots in Asia? The answer lies in the awareness among many practitioners in many Asian states that the costs of war, and intervention by the international powers, are high. At the same time, the costs of disequilibrium are also high. Hence, the need to develop strategies to manage and to resolve regional conflicts. In this sense coerced linkages and multipolarities in the geo-political pivots facilitate the protracted process of searching for negotiated solutions to transform deadly quarrels into ritual confrontations, and the latter into negotiated peace settlements, by the use of carrots and sticks diplomacy in regions of conflict. War is no longer a realistic option in a crowded neighbourhood of coerced linkages because of its unpredictable consequences such as the danger of the Third World War in the Korean War (1950–3), the danger of the US–USSR–PRC interventions in Indo-Pakistani Wars, and the danger of military escalation in China–Taiwan confrontations, in the late 1990s. So the value of war and great power military intervention in geo-political pivots has broken down. The presence of multipolar centres of power, albeit of varying degree and effectiveness, creates opportunities for players who are locked into coerced linkages to find the necessary wriggle space to manage the disequilibrium, and to move towards a pattern of manageable instability and eventual peace settlement. Asia is important in this respect compared to Africa, Middle East, Latin America and the Caribbean worlds because it is the centres of gravity of conflict and strategic action in the world today. Asian geo-political pivots possess the ability to produce high probability and high impact events and developments compared to the other areas. Note also that major challenges to Western authority have come from dissatisfied Asian powers – from Japan (pre-1945 period), from China (1949 onward), from North Korea (1990s onward), from Iran (1979 onward), from India (1947 onward) and from Vietnam (1950s onward). Despite the high moral ground the Nelson Mandelas of the world occupy, they are actually no threat to Western diplomatic and military authority. They are respectable but weak, hence manageable.

In addition to the fear of the escalatory potential of war-like situations, the USA, particularly the Bush administration, is aware that its hegemony in Eurasian affairs is temporary. Ground realities rather than notional or subjective realities are now in play in US thinking. Brzezinski notes

> In the long run, global politics are bound to become increasingly uncongenial to the concentration of hegemonic power in the hands of a single state. Hence, America is not only the first, as well as the only, truly global superpower, but it is also likely to be the very last.[3]

Kissinger is more explicit about the emerging structure of international relations in the 21st century. To quote:

> The end of the Cold War has created what some observers have called a 'unipolar' or 'one-superpower' world. But the United States is actually in no better position to dictate the global agenda unilaterally than it was at the beginning of the Cold War. America is more preponderant than it was ten years ago, yet, ironically, power has also become more diffuse. Thus, America's ability to employ it to shape the rest of the world has actually decreased.
>
> As the twenty-first century approaches, vast global forces are at work that, over the course of time, will render the United States less exceptional. American military power will remain unrivaled for the foreseeable future. Yet America's desire to project that power into the myriad small-scale conflicts which the world is likely to witness in the coming decades – Bosnia, Somalia, and Haiti – is a key conceptual challenge for American foreign policy. The United States will likely have the world's most powerful economy well into the next century. Yet wealth will become more widely spread, as will the technology for generating wealth. The United States will face economic competition of a kind it never experienced during the Cold War.
>
> America will be the greatest and most powerful nation, but a nation with peers; the *primus inter pares* but nonetheless a nation like others. The

> American exceptionalism that is the indispensable basis for a Wilson-ian foreign policy is therefore likely to be less relevant in the coming century.
>
> 'The international system of the twenty-first century will be marked by a seeming contraction: on the one hand, fragmentation; on the other, growing globalization. On the level of the relations among states, the new order will be more like the European state system of the 18th and 19th centuries than the rigid patterns of the Cold War. It will contain at least six major powers – the United States, Europe, China, Japan, Russia, and probably India – as well as a multiplicity of medium-sized and smaller countries.[4]

Heeding the views of Brzezinski and Kissinger, we turn to a discussion of the major trends which underpin multipolarity in Asia.

Trends in Asia

These points require a close inspection of the significant trends that shape Asian multipolarities at the continental and regional levels. Generally speaking, many powers in Asia are repositioning themselves in relation to strategic issues and the policies of other players. The US has repositioned itself in two ways. (1) It is revising its defence policy along the lines indicated previously. (2) It is seeking new strategic partners in Asia, e.g. India, Vietnam and Iran are being courted. Asian states are also repositioning themselves. India is cultivating USA, Russia, Japan, Australia, ASEAN countries, Pakistan and Taiwan. Australia is cultivating Indonesia and India. Japan is cultivating India and it is revising and publicizing changes in its defence policy. Its quest for refuelling aircraft and satellite technology indicates a desire to upgrade its intelligence acquisition and force projection capabilities in the direction of the South China Seas. Russia under Putin is re-engaging China and India on a geo-political basis. The possibility of a Russia–China–India alignment, albeit a remote one, exercises American diplomacy into looking at India in a geopolitical fashion rather than in terms of the Cold War view of Indo-Pakistani parity.

These changing alignments are a response to a major undercurrent in Asian international relations today. It runs through East Asia, South East Asia and the Indian subcontinent. It is focused on the China question and it shows an awareness that USA and China now provide the overlay in regional Asian relationships. China is a potential world power and it has geographical proximity to three major regions (sub-regions) in Asia. Many Asian countries have China on their mind in the context of the future of Taiwan, and the future of sea lanes security which extend from Japan to the Persian Gulf. The futures of Taiwan and of the sea lanes are tied because the assertion of China's sovereignty in Taiwan could imply that the Taiwan straits and the South China seas are Chinese lakes. This would have serious negative implications for Japanese as well as American maritime security. Furthermore, political, economic and social developments within China also concern the Asian states. A powerful China is likely to be expansionist and hence dangerous. A weakened China is also dangerous because it is likely to export social problems (like refugees and activities of criminal syndicates) and political problems (like external adventurist policies which reflect internal power politics). In China's case the line between domestic and foreign is getting blurred. Uncertainty about its strategic intentions and policies vis-à-vis its Asian neighbours and the international powers explain, in part, the military build-ups by most Asian states after the Cold War ended.

The sustained pattern of military modernization in Asia after the Cold War ended indicates that the expectation of a peace dividend was a false one. It was based on the mistaken belief that military modernization in the world was the consequence of the Cold War; and once the Soviet Russian Empire had collapsed, the cause for military modernization would disappear. By tying the arms build-up phenomenon to the Russian question, Western analysts failed to recognize that in Asia it was tied to the China question and to the need to maintain the internal power of leaders of fragile coalitions.

There are several high impact and high probability trends in the Asian strategic scene that underpin my discussion of multipolarity at the continental and the regional levels in Asia–Pacific and the Indian Ocean areas. They also explain the repositioning outlined above. There is a slow and steady proliferation of weapons of mass destruction in Asia. China, India, Pakistan, North Korea and Iran either possess such weapons or have the ambition to acquire them and are developing such capabilities. Japan has all the capabilities to display such weapons should its strategic circumstances so require; in other words, Japan is not a convinced non-proliferator and the nuclear question in Japan should be studied in the context of rapid change in its defence posture. As a result of the trend by several Asian states to acquire nuclear and missile capability, it follows that the non-proliferation game is over in Asia; and the future of arms control as well as unilateral nuclear restraint is dim. This trend appears to be irreversible. Being realistic, the US government is likely to accept selective nuclear and missile proliferation as it seeks to develop non-traditional partnerships with, say, India. This trend shows that geo-politics is strong in Asian international relations and arms control is struggling to retain its value.

The centres of gravity of strategic action are shifting and broadening in Asia, from North Asia (the traditional centre from 1945 to the end of the Cold War), towards South Asia and the Persian Gulf in the 1990s. The southward shift passes through the Taiwan straits, the South China Seas and the choke points in the straits of Malacca and Hormuz – strategic gateways for major and minor powers in Asia. This strategic loop was central in the extension of European empires into Asia. (The other loop defined the Russian sphere of interest.) In both loops the idea of discrete sub-regions was not relevant. Thus, British imperial thought and behaviour recognized the unity between the Persian Gulf, the Indian subcontinent and British interests in

South East Asia and the Far East. The requirements of military communications and its commercial interests (e.g. tea, opium and spice trade) provided the linkages between the sub-regions. For instance, for the purpose of free trade in opium, British India, the source of the opium supply, was integrated with the China market; and Indian manpower under British command was meant to service British war efforts in the Middle East. During the Cold War, however, discrete sub-regions became the accepted norms. The work of a number of Foreign Offices was organized into divisions dealing with the Middle East, South Asia, South East Asia and East Asia. These divisions were not simply organizational and notional realities; they represented the boundaries of the pattern of interactions that were intense within each region. Thus, Myanmar was truly the boundary where South East Asia ended and South Asia started; and Afghanistan and Iran represented the dividing line between South Asia and the Middle East. Following the end of the Cold War, the idea of discrete sub-regions is no longer valid because now strategic issues have an inter-regional character. North Korean and Chinese missile aid flows from North Asia to Pakistan and Iran and it impacts on the international relations of South Asia (India–Pakistan), the Gulf (Iran–Israel) and the Middle East. The channels of international commerce and military movement reveal the heightened importance of the sea route from Japan to Israel. The politics of development of oil pipelines in Central Asia makes it a centre of the oil trade in the 21st century that could reach Europe, Middle East and the Indian subcontinent. Islamic activities involving the Taliban, the Saudi Wahabbis and Pakistani authorities show the impact of religious ideas across borders. Central Asia, the Indian subcontinent and China are now part of a vortex, or a point of friction and engagement between Islamic Jihad ideology, the Chinese opposition to minority rights, its emphasis on the primacy of the Hans in its border areas, the Indian opposition to fanaticism as the basis of statecraft and terrorism, and the Russian as well as American opposition to Talibanization of regional politics. A sign that the US government recognizes the irrelevance of traditional sub-regions is revealed by the decision to change the sphere of responsibilities of the US Central Command. It is no longer limited to Pakistan, Iran and Afghanistan. Its responsibility includes Central Asia. This brings the command in touch with China. Now the commanders-in-chief of the U.S. Central and the Pacific Commands need to coordinate their planning vis-à-vis the two extremities of Asia, with China in the middle. In other words, the idea of sub-regional boundaries or divisions was limited to Cold War scholarship and governmental practices; it is not the pattern in Asian history. Inter-regional linkages were the norm in the 1500–1940s period, and after 1990.

Another trend is that basing rights that are currently available to the US in Okinawa, South Korea and the Gulf have an uncertain future. So it is likely that the US will rely more on offshore power projection capabilities and advanced technologies, e.g. stealth, precision guided munitions, satellite imaging, anti missile technologies. Historically it has been shown that America is an island nation; it is insular in its thinking and strategic orientation. As noted earlier, it finds it difficult to form long-term rewarding ties with nationalistic friends and foes. Reliance on military power and military technology is easier for America. This approach is deeply rooted in American military history and its political culture.

To recap, the rate of change and volatility are the highest in Asia compared to other continents in terms of nation building policies, growing energy requirements, changing defence orientations, increasing pace of economic reforms, sustained acquisition of military power projection capabilities and, finally, consolidation of the strategic ambitions of major and minor Asian powers. Europeans are satisfied; Asians are not. Peace studies have a future in Europe but not in Asia because Asians are currently preoccupied with the development of culturally motivated military strategies in the context of regional (or inter-regional) rivalries. China, Japan and India among others will continue to build their military and economic strength to secure their economic and their strategic spheres and to find the means to engage their rivals from a position of some strength. Asian powers now are into the development of military and economic capabilities, strategies, skills and ideas that enable them to engage regional as well as international rivals. Gunner Myrdal had described the *Asian Drama* as a problem of underdevelopment. Now the drama is in the realm of geo-politics as well as economics. The two are no longer compartmentalized endeavours.

Finally, most Asian states are active participants in the world economy. Globalisation is a double-edged sword. It tames armed conflict if the economic and diplomatic costs of fighting are higher than the costs of not fighting, but if the social and diplomatic costs of not fighting are higher than the costs of fighting, economic growth creates an opportunity to increase the availability of resources for military modernization. These calculations are in play in the policies of major and minor Asian powers.

These trends reveal the fundamental nature of change in Asia's strategic landscape. The innovative policies of several major and minor Asian powers have shaped these trends. Here is a short list of the players and their policies.

Taiwan

The rise of Taiwan's Democratic Progressive Party (DPP) led to the emergence of democracy in Taiwan from 1996. This development fosters pressure to build pluralistic institutions within China. A belief in the value of a league of democratic countries in the post-Cold War era is indicated by the spread of democracy in Asia since 1945. The DPP's rise meant the defeat of the KMT, an authoritarian regime which had ruled Taiwan since the late 1940s. The DPP's rise points to the role of 'Taiwanese democracy' and native 'Taiwanese' public opinion (as distinct from the imported KMT) in relation to KMT as well as the mainland. As a result, Taiwan's new government now talks with confidence in cross-straits relations, and the PRC is on the defensive in dealing with Taiwan internationally and with the Taiwan issue in its domestic politics. The pro-democracy forces now occupy centre stage in Taipei. Moreover, the US government is committed through the Taiwan Relations Act to provide advanced defensive military equipment to Taiwan and to support Taiwanese democracy. The Bush administration did just that in 2001. Consequently, the importance of the 1972 Shanghai communiqué declined following the end of the Cold War. That agreement had signalled a Nixon–Mao strategy to contain Moscow. However, the Cold War's end eliminated the American need to use the China card in its relations with Russia. Thus, changing international relations give Taiwan more international space as long as it does not go nuclear or declare independence. Taiwanese democracy is a challenge to Beijing's authoritarianism, and Taiwan's increasing military capability is a sign that the PRC can rain missiles into Taiwan but it cannot take it by force. The PRC is thus currently a regional great power but it is not the natural or sole leader in Asia. Its pre-eminence is not a foregone conclusion in the light of major changes in Asia.

China and her neighbours

Many Asian states have China on their mind because it is a geographical neighbour and they fear China's hegemony. It physically touches East Asia, Taiwan straits, South East and South Asia and its diplomatic attitudes and growing military capacities impact on the maritime security of Japan, Taiwan, USA and other Asian states who rely on the Pacific and the Indian Oceans for peace-time commerce and military movement. China has special ties with Pakistan, Iran, Nepal, Myanmar and it appears to have a plan to create a wedge between South East and South Asia through Myanmar, and to maintain access to the Arabian sea through the Karakoram Highway and a new port, Gwador, being built in Pakistan under Chinese auspices. China has different policies for its neighbours. It strengthens Pakistan militarily to contain India and seeks to do the same through its activities in Nepal, Myanmar, Bangladesh and its missiles cover all major Indian cities. It has a policy of developing naval bases for its use in Myanmar and in Pakistan, so its India-related policy has a naval dimension which eventually also affects South East Asian countries and America and its allies in Asia. With the Koreas, however, its policy is to facilitate inter-Korean dialogue. Its long-term aim is to replace the US as the primary influence in the peninsula and as the security guarantor in the area. But here China is being hemmed in. South Korea and the US continue to emphasize the ongoing need for US military presence in the Korean peninsula, and the North Korean leadership implicitly accepts this idea. The US–North Korean dialogue is a step towards a strategic bargain that would likely extend American strategic and commercial influence into North Korea, across the Yalu. This will hem China in the north.

Japan's defence posture is changing rapidly in response to the concern about PRC's ascendance and the possibility that Bush administration will alter its defence posture in Asia, either by reducing its troop commitments or by relying more on modern technological measures like National and Theatre Missile Defence. Japan already possesses a fine military machine. It has submarines, modern military aircraft with offensive warfare capability, surface naval vessels, a standing army. Its military officers are now training to fight in an area that is away from the Japanese islands using power projection equipment. It is acquiring air and naval capability that will enable it to project power 3000 miles away from Japan, and it is seeking satellite intelligence acquisition capability as well. The historic China–Japan rivalry is resurfacing and Beijing must factor this into its calculations along with American and Indian missiles and other means and strategic intentions.

The internal politics of China

The third element is that, as China is being hemmed in by alert neighbours militarily and diplomatically, its internal situation is deteriorating significantly and the difference between internal politics and external policies is losing meaning for the Chinese leaders. International developments in China's environment have an impact on internal Chinese power struggles. By creating situations in China's areas of interests, outside forces can 'mess with the Chinese mind' and interfere with China's decision making process and the inputs into its decision loop. Even as China flexes its military muscle through exercises against Taiwan, American intelligence notes that it is not showing a capacity to take Taiwan by force. The military exercises have political significance because, presently, the political leadership is divided between hawks (Li Peng) and moderates (the current president and the prime minister), and then there is a further division between the political leaders and the PLA who do not want an end to lucrative military enterprises and who seek more funds for the military services. There is also a significant challenge to Party's authority from a group like Falun Gong whose members belong to the Party and the security service. Furthermore, about seven million Chinese are unemployed because of economic reforms and layoffs from inefficient state enterprises. So economic reforms in China are leading to social and economic dissatisfaction and the problems are likely to grow. Entry into World Trade Organization is likely to produce more layoffs. To manage the negative impact Beijing is investing in its internal riot police. It also needs to pump billions of yuan into agriculture banks to keep the peasants happy with loans. In other words, the PRC does not have a glorious domestic future. Growth of corruption and criminal activity adds to a picture of social and political decay. This means that Beijing must find diversionary activity to mobilize nationalism and to manage the growing costs of internal reforms and internal power politics as well as pressures in its external relationships.

US assessment of China and India

The fourth element which is medium to long term is that the US government assesses that India and China are likely to be major players in the world economy. They will move ahead of Europeans by 2025 if present trends continue, and India and China maintain their current growth rates, Javed Burki, former senior World Bank official, sees India's economy at 12 trillion dollars, 40% greater than the US in 2000, and the estimates are that Japan and Germany will fall behind China and India in the future. India also has some political and social advantages over China. It favours pluralism in state and society and it has a legal system that protects property and contracts, which are the foundations of modern commerce.

The changing US defence policy and the role of modern technology

The fifth significant element concerns the Bush administration plan to develop and deploy NMD and TMD. In part, the moves represent a response to PRC's military build-up against Taiwan and the North Korean missile threat against Japan and the US. The international debate centres on the effect of the NMD on Russia and the ABM Treaty rather than Japan and China and the Outer Space Treaty. Also the discussion focuses on the military requirements and the technical problems in mounting a credible defence. There is a view that NMD is no good technically and politically, and that the world community should not accept it. This view appears to be wrong and shortsighted. A broader political view shows that the issue for Russia requires attention to its international prestige, and a negotiated termination of the ABM Treaty is possible. NMD is less of a military problem for Russia than it is for China because Russia can manage to maintain a capacity for both nuclear deterrence and missile defence. It wants to be taken seriously as an international partner of the US. This need is being satisfied by Bush–Putin summits. China's political concerns are different. TMD stimulates Japanese militarization, and it encourages Taiwanese autonomy. It signals the US determination to be the pre-eminent space cop and a hegemon in Asia. TMD will degrade PRC's offensive missile capability and hence its military security. TMD also plays into the already intense internal power struggles in Beijing. Further, China calculates that, even if it increases the size of its nuclear and missile arsenal against India, Japan and the US, these countries can match the increases.

Indian and Pakistani nuclear and missile proliferation

The sixth major element is that India's and Pakistan's entry into the nuclear and missile clubs fractured the non-proliferation and the missile control regimes. Both countries showed a determination to stay the course in their nuclear and missile policies in the face of international sanctions and pressures. Both were also able to avoid drifting into a nuclear war over Kargil (1999), much to the surprise of critics in the developed world who thought that the South Asian natives were not capable of pursuing coercive diplomacy with restraint. At the same time, both sought to engage each other and the world community as autonomous players, and not as clients of proxies of the international powers.

The repositioning by India and America vis-à-vis each other is particularly significant. It has both a deep and a broad Asian geo-political and modern military technological framework. The repositioning is not a passing flirtation, rather it is grounded in new geo-political and economic realities. The radical Indo-US realignment rests on a number of concrete factors which make India important for American interests and strategies. This is a good example because it provides the background to similar changes in the policies of USA's other Asian partners.

Foremost, there is a triangular rivalry between the US, Russia and China in Eurasia. The US is presently the sole superpower because it alone can project power globally but at the same time, it is aware that its hegemony is temporary. As noted earlier, experts like Z. Brzezinski and Henry Kissinger acknowledge this but our criteria in grading powers suggest that Russia, China and India are presently regional great powers. There is a possibility that India is encouraged by Russia to join a coalition with China and Russia. America would like to pre-empt this possibility. The other alternative rests on the Sino-Indian rivalry. This rivalry is reinforced by China's policy of special support for Pakistan. So as US–Pakistan relations cool over the growing influence of Taliban and Islamic forces in the region which Pakistan supports, and China is seen as a long-term problem for America, there is a natural affinity between the US and India in the strategic and other spheres. The attraction of the Indian economy is an additional element. The Indo-US repositioning has a positive effect on Japan's and Australia's attitude to India as well.

Secondly, there is asymmetry between Russian and American roles in India. Moscow is interested in selling arms to India for hard currency but it cannot provide credits. Its military technology while useful in subcontinental conditions nevertheless has a technological plateau compared to American military technology. Moreover, Putin's Russia has a China card. It has the option to transfer military technology to China which can be used against India, i.e. Moscow does not have a strong incentive to build up India militarily against China and hence its usefulness as an Indian strategic partner is diminished.

Lastly, Indian and American interests in the Indian Ocean are complementary. The US has the pre-eminent navy in the Pacific and the Indian Oceans. India is the second (by a big gap) strongest navy in the Indian Ocean but it is stronger than the Australian navy. The US has major interests in the Gulf area because of oil and the safety of its partners in the region, and because of the politics of Iran and its international relations. The US also must keep the sea lanes open in war and peace for the commerce and military movement of itself and its allies; and it must ensure the safety of the choke points, the Malacca Straits and the Hormuz area. India has major interests in guarding its coastal and economic zones. The PRC is building ports in Pakistan and in Myanmar, hence India must factor in the impact of Pakistani and Chinese naval activity, including submarine activity, on its interests. So Indian naval development is reacting to concrete developments in the Indian Ocean area, and a loose Indo-US naval link-up is mutually beneficial. Indian naval diplomacy also converges with Australian and Japanese interests in the area. In this context, an Indian Ocean trading community with Indian naval backing is a feasible proposition, and it likely has American support. Here, strategic as well as economic arrangements are beginning to converge in Indo-American diplomacy in the Indian Ocean area. Two outward-looking, non-expansionist democracies are coming together and the language of hegemony, intervention and pressure no longer makes sense to either in their bilateral relations.

These trends and events have significant characteristics. The broadening of the centre of gravity of strategic action and its southern shift compels the major and minor Asian powers to reposition their economic and military policies to engage the changing geo-political scene in Asia. In motive and method China is the most active as a result of its activities in Pakistan, India, Iran, Myanmar, Nepal, Bangladesh, South China Seas, the Central Asian area and the Korean peninsula as well as the Indian Ocean. It has an aggressive and well thought out policy to contain the spread of Indian power and influence in the region and in the international sphere and this is disguised in a deceptive mask of 'peace diplomacy'. The greatest opportunities for expansion of China's influence and prestige lie in its activities in the Indian subcontinent, the Indian Ocean and the South China Sea. If successful, it could create a wedge between South and South East Asia through its activities in Myanmar and the Bay of Bengal. It could establish a gateway to the Arabian Sea and the Persian Gulf through its activities in Pakistan. The expansion of the Silk Route, the development of a rail link in Tibet, and its access to the strategic Karakoram Highway along with future access to ports in Myanmar and Pakistan shows the pattern of China's communication expansion.

However, despite its activism in the post-Cold War period, China is not seen in this book as a success story in either its international or its internal affairs. The Shanghai communiqué (1972) was the high point of Chinese diplomacy because it was able to pursue triangular diplomacy where China and America were aligned in a common cause to contain Soviet Russia. With the collapse of the Soviet regime, this rationale was lost. In the post-Cold War era, Asian multipolarities have grown, as have the complications in the development of Chinese leverage in strategic neighbourhoods that are crowded by multiple major and minor powers in the five major geo-political pivots noted earlier. China has often proclaimed the value of multipolarity rather than unipolarity. However, it values a particular type of multipolarity, one which favours triangular great powers manœuvres as in the Shanghai communiqué days rather than the regional multipolarities which dot the Asian landscape today. China is hemmed in by other regional great powers who are its neighbours and its wriggle space in regional multipolarities is limited.

American policy under the Bush administration also has a distinctive southerly character. The US government is better able to deal with both continental and regional multipolarities because its strategic interests are specific and limited, its capacity to act militarily is extensive, its technological prowess is undiminished in the military and the economic sphere, and it has a tradition of proactive coalition-building in the international sphere which stems from its domestic political culture. My discussion of the major events and developments which define the Asian geo-political landscape in 2001 shows that American strategy recognizes the importance of India, the nature of the China problem, the importance of the sea lanes, and the connection between Eurasian continental rivalries and its policies towards Japan and other Asian states. America has wriggle space in shaping the pattern of relationships in continental as well as regional multipolarities. America cannot dominate the regions because its hegemony is temporary – as both the US and the regional great powers understand. However, America is a powerful pole of attraction and it remains the reference point for Asian states.

Japan's changing defence posture shows the remarkable impact of the changing Asian geo-politics on an almost pacifist island nation since its defeat in 1945 and imposition of a peace constitution and a peace treaty thereafter. Today, Japan's defence policy has a distinctive southerly direction, towards the South China Seas and the area up to the Persian Gulf is its sphere of strategic interest because of oil, commerce and prestige. Also, Japan has major economic investments in Indonesia. So there are extensive economic stakes and growing military stakes for Japan in the southern part of Asia–Pacific in the 21st century.

Since Stalin's discovery of the Third World as a strategic opportunity to enlarge Moscow's international presence beyond the Western arena, Moscow has retained its interest (with ebbs and flows during the Gorbachev, Yeltsin and Putin eras) in Middle Eastern and South Asian affairs. It is reviving its naval presence in Asia–Pacific and developing a modern high technology fleet. In 2001, Russia deployed its naval forces in the Pacific Ocean in 'show the flag' missions.

Moscow's southerly strategic direction is also evident in other ways. It is preoccupied with the spread of Islamic influences into Central Asia from Talibanized Afghanistan. It is interested in developing a strategic partnership with India, and it is building its influence as a naval player in the Asia–Pacific and the Indian Ocean area. Putin's Russia thus seeks to be an active participant in the organization of continental multipolar relationships (Russia–America–China–India–Japan) and in regional multipolarities which are the primary centres of gravity in Asia today.

Finally, Indian diplomacy and military strategy has since 1947 had a southern orientation with the subcontinent as its primary focus. Since 1998, India under the BJP coalition government has broadened the southern orientation of its naval and political diplomacy by its 'Look East policy' which makes the South China Seas its area of strategic interest. Thus India is integrating its economic and military interests in the Bay of Bengal, Myanmar, Bangladesh, South East Asian nations (particularly Vietnam) and the Persian Gulf area. A broadened and a vigorous southern strategic orientation is the new element in Indian diplomacy and strategy.

7 Multipolarity during the Cold War

Asia is a fertile ground for the study of regional multipolarity during the Cold War and following its end. Three examples illustrate the point.

1. Multipolarity existed during the Korean War, 1950–53.
2. Multipolarity was the basis of Indian foreign policy, from 1947 onwards. The distribution of power as well as the pattern of relationships in the Indian subcontinent since the end of the British India Empire have been shaped in a multipolar context.
3. Following the retreat of European empires from South East Asia, the rise of Vietnam, and the militarization of conflict in Indo-China during the 1950s and the 1960s, the region became a point of engagement between American, Chinese, Russian and Vietnamese power.

In each case multipolarity existed because of the continuous and organized framework of interaction between the international and the regional powers. The scholarly literature widely and erroneously thought that the bipolar international system was the framework of diplomatic and military action in Asia. The literature also erroneously implies that asymmetry in the distribution of power is the basis of the pattern of relationships in Asia. The emphasis is often on the military balance rather than on relationships. Ability to wage war from a position of military inferiority, and ability to shape the power relationships in a region, however, show that multipolarity often emerges in a situation of asymmetrical distribution of power. Furthermore, regional multipolarity is sensitive to local and regional situations rather than the distribution of power in the international system. This work indicates that in each case bipolarity and Cold War were not sufficient bases for explanation of the diplomatic and military policies of the players in Asian regions (sub-regions). Multipolarity, not bipolarity, was the defining element of the international structure that formed the external context and the basis of diplomatic and military policies of the Asian states.

Of the three regions (sub-regions), South and South East Asia had been key parts of the Asiatic buffer belt during the colonial and imperial eras. During the Cold War era the former colonial/imperial territories gained political independence and developed policies and capacities to mobilize their internal resources, to build strength, to mobilize the international environment and to engage it. By developing the means and the political will to initiate and to escalate armed struggle in regional conflicts, the former members of the Asiatic buffer belt have emerged as regional great powers. Countries like China, India, Vietnam here led the process of regional power and regional conflict formation since the 1950s. India made its mark in 1971 when it successfully opposed the Pakistan–USA–PRC coalition and broke up Pakistan by force. Vietnam made its mark by defeating American military power in the region and by successfully resisting Chinese military action against Vietnam in a border war. In these cases, multipolarity is revealed by the growth of regional powers who are able to engage the international powers, who function as autonomous centres of power and authority, and whose policies affect the distribution of power and the pattern of relationships in a defined geographical area which in turn affects international relations. The test of multipolarity is not simply the intent to be independent. Rather it lies in the ability of regional states to achieve multipolarity through a strategy of engagement of competitive regional and international forces. It is shown by a demonstrated ability to shape power relationships. Multipolarity exists at the regional level when the actions of a regional power tie the regional as well as international players to the policies of the regional great power. Tight regional multipolarity takes root when a regional great power emerges, it demonstrates a capacity to escalate the level of conflict which raises the costs of great power policies in regional affairs, and it is able to reduce the great power ability and willingness to intervene or club together in regional affairs. Tight regionalism exists when a regional great power can pursue a carrot and sticks policy based on its strategic agenda. In other words, multipolarity is the result of regional power formation as well as regional conflict formation (i.e. the emergence of a stable paradigm or structure of conflict which is not pure or total conflict, where regional conflict has limits or policy boundaries which are shared and respected by the practitioners within the region).

The rest of this chapter illustrates the theme of regional multipolarity in three zones of conflict in Asia during the Cold War era. The discussion illustrates the origins of multipolarity in Asia. The claim is that multipolarity today is entrenched in Asian international relations. Multipolarity is the dominant and the durable theme in Asian relationships since the end of the Second World War, whereas bipolarity and the Cold War were passing phenomena. To sum up: during the Cold War the popular view was that Asia was neatly divided into a bipolar world; this contention was wrong. The evidence suggests that there was multipolarity in Asia in the early 1950s in Asia. Multipolarity is not an abstraction. It is the ability and willingness to act together (or independently). Evidence of this derives from three factors.

- Availability of resources and capability to act independently, to initiate and escalate conflict by coercive means, and to function as a major or minor power.
- Possess the skills and the will to use the resources; skill in fighting war and negotiating peace (diplomacy) must be evident.
- A set of ideas or beliefs that shape competing strategies must be evident.

These factors form the spectrum of power and beliefs. Each is necessary but none is sufficient. One without the other is useless.

Multipolarity in Asia: the Korean War, 1950–1953

The new documentary evidence from the Russian archives suggests that all three supreme leaders of the USSR, PRC and the DPRK – Stalin, Mao Tse-tung, and Kim Il Sung – were personally and intimately involved in the prosecution of the Korean War. Notwithstanding this, their will often failed to prevail, for the war policies of these states were also shaped by the pressures of intra-alliance bargaining, domestic politics, bureaucratic outputs and personal preferences of people in charge of the implementation of leaders' decisions, not to mention circumstances created by enemy and external forces.[1] However, the evidence shows that the centres of power and decision were not simply the US and USSR as would be expected in a bipolar system. In the Korean War, the sources of decision and military action included China and North Korea. Their interests, attitudes, perceptions and behaviour varied as Table 7.1 shows.

Multipolarity in the Indian subcontinent, 1950–1980s

The Indian subcontinent is an important region. It holds a quarter of all humanity. It has two nuclear powers, religion and politics play an instrumental role and the economy is growing rapidly. The Indian economy has an appeal for the West because of the large Indian middle class, estimated between 160 and 250 million people and a diversified productive base. It sits astride the strategic sea lane between Japan and the Persian Gulf. The region is also a prosperous route for the drug trade from Afghanistan and Burma (Myanmar). Such trade, combined with arms trade and terrorism, criminalizes the domestic and external politics of the region and this has had a negative impact on regional security. Since the days of the Afghanistan War in the 1980s, there has also been a lively arms trade. It is so pervasive that Kalashnikov rifles can be easily *rented* in the Karachi and Peshawar bazaars.

When the world was dominated by the Cold War and biolarity, practitioners in the Indian subcontinent were essentially functioning in a multipolar world. At that time, there were three outside powers (the United States, the Soviet Union, China); two regional ones (India, Pakistan); and a number of smaller states who were active in subcontinental affairs. Thus, the mental

Table 7.1 Multipolarity in Asia during the Korean War

Event	*Players (major and minor)*	*Interests, attitudes perceptions*	*Behaviour*
Korean War	USSR	To achieve a reunification of the south with North Korea through military means (p. 87). To prevent the US from taking over ROK (p. 95) and thus getting to the Soviet border in the Far East (p. 100). To avoid direct confrontation with US (p. 98) even if it meant abandoning N. Korea (p. 100). Russia was unwilling to enter into a large-scale war in the aftermath of 2nd World War (p. 102).	Stalin changed his hesitation to support the reunification by military means because of victory of communists in China; Soviet acquisition of the atomic bomb; establishment of NATO and perceived weakness of Washington. Curtailment of Soviet presence in Korea and encouragement of greater Chinese role in the crisis (p. 100). China was not consulted in advance of the decision to reunite the south with N. Korea because Stalin wanted to avoid interference and objections from China (p. 87).
	China	To protect China's vital domestic and international interests (p. 41). The threat of mortal danger to the Chinese revolution should the US occupy Korea (p. 89).	CPP leadership undertook intensive deliberations in order to make a judgement about how China's security interests had been challenged during the Korean War (p. 41).
		China believed that the outcome of the Korean crisis was closely related	Strong influence of CPP's domestic policy on Party's

Table 7.1 – cont

Event	*Players (major and minor)*	*Interests, attitudes perceptions*	*Behaviour*
		to China's vital domestic and international interests (p. 85).	foreign policy behaviour (p. 41).
		To prevent the US from taking over Korea and and thus be within proximity of China's north-east border with Korea (pp. 105, 118). At the same time, China wanted to avoid Sino-American confrontation and hence drag the Soviet Union into war due to the Sino-Soviet Alliance Treaty (p. 100).	CPP leadership's perception of the outside world and China's position in it; escalating conflict between CCP and the United States in 1949 and early 1950; Mao's influence. China was careful not to stumble into the Korean War, merely on the prodding of Stalin (pp10, 89). (China rejected initial Soviet request to enter the war, p. 100.) China agreed to enter the conflict only if Moscow will provide military aid and air cover (pp. 89, 103).
	North Korea	To reunite the South with the North by military means; believed that the Korean people wanted liberation and would not understand if the chance for unification has been missed (pp. 54, 87).	Kim Il Sung in consultation with Stalin to get the blessing to undertake the invasion (pp. 59, 87). North Korea relied on USSR for direct support and military advice and on getting China to enter the conflict (p. 88).

Table 7.1 – cont

Event	*Players (major and minor)*	*Interests, attitudes perceptions*	*Behaviour*
			Note: During the war Kim Il Sung occasionally ignored Stalin's tactical advice e.g. Kim Il Sung did not heed Stalin's initial advice on approaching the war by redeploying four KPA divisions from the Naktong River from to the vicinity of Seoul (pp. 95–6).

framework from the very beginning was multipolar, and the South Asians never bought into the notion of bipolarity. It is important to recognize that this belief was maintained throughout the Cold War and its end.

In this context, the Indian élite believed that weaker powers such as India could develop niches in the international system and could develop regional spheres of influence. Despite the Indo-Pakistani partition and the ensuing bitterness and divisiveness, India sought a pre-eminent position in the region as a territorially non-expansionist and a mature internationalist force. This indicated an ambition to seek a position of a regional great power or a 'benign' regional hegemon. However, this notion of hegemony bumped straight into American policy. In now declassified Department of Defense documents written in 1949, the US government appeared very uncomfortable with the idea of regional powers not friendly to the US. The US argument was framed in terms of containing the Russians, but a few other states were mentioned – China, Japan, India. In other words, the Indian notion of benign hegemony constantly ran into American disquiet over regional hegemons during the Cold War.

India was also at odds with the US in another way. In conversations between former Indian Prime Minister Nehru and American ambassadors, Nehru expressed the belief that nationalism was a more elemental force than communism. In the early 1950s, Nehru wanted to discover the cracks in the Sino-Soviet system. The point here was to find contradictions in the Communist world that revealed the vitality of competitive nationalism among Communist states. These Indian points collided with standard

Western beliefs, especially the belief that the choice for India and other developing countries was between Western capitalism and democracy or Soviet socialism. This was not a real choice for Indian practitioners. Another belief was that the West was superior for its ability to master nature and modern technology, and the vitality of the Western marketplace indicated that Western values and methods were better. This crass message did not sit well in the Indian subcontinent. It stoked nationalism.

Multipolarity was revealed in the pattern of relationships in the region in this period. During the Cold War three major conflicted relationships were prominent in the Indian subcontinent. The most obvious one was India and Pakistan; the second, India and China; the third, India and the US. Even through India and the US are both democracies, strategic controversies existed. Hence, my choice of the worked 'conflicted' to describe these relationships. However, each of these relationships have acquired a multidimensional focus over the years. The first dimension was rivalry. Rivalry led to intervention, military pressure and military modernization. This dimension is still very prominent in Indo-Pakistan and Sino-Indian relations, and it was present in Indo-US relations until recently.

The second dimension is that, despite the hostilities, wars, conflicts, pressures and controversies, these countries are now or have in recent years engaged in security dialogues with each other. Furthermore, this is becoming institutionalized. The Sino-Indian security dialogue took shape in the mid-1980s, before the Cold War ended. It was built on two concepts: (1) neither side could change borders through military means, thus accepting the current military situation was realistic; and (2) the two countries should put border concerns on the back burner and start developing common ground on technology, science, economic linkages, border trades, military confidence-building measures (CBMs) and general cooperation. This dialogue has been pursued through the development of working groups, thus giving it an institutional face. There is now serious debate, although it remains inconclusive and a political settlement remains elusive.

Moreover, there are some side effects of this process. For instance, China no longer publicly promotes self-determination in Kashmir, a sea change in the Chinese approach. (However, Beijing does not mind if Indian forces bleed in Kashmir.) Although they take this position because they did not want the Indians supporting Tibetan self-determination, it is significant nevertheless. Another element is that the Chinese are becoming concerned about Islamic influences from Pakistan creeping into Xinjiang province.

It would be foolhardy, however, to suggest that the trend has gone towards agreement and away from rivalries. It has not. There are three major unresolved controversies in the China–India relationship which took shape during the Cold War. One is the purpose and intent of Chinese nuclear and missile assistance to Pakistan. The other issue, a development of the late 1980s, is the emergence of a Chinese presence in Burma. This too took shape during the Cold War era. This is an interesting development because of its dual commercial and military orientation. The Chinese have provided loans of approximately US$1.2 billion for military modernization. There is also the problem of two agreements between the Chinese and the Burmese on the Cocoa islands, 15 miles from the Bay of Bengal. One is to establish a radar facility, as well as a low frequency communications facility. This has been implemented. Another agreement, signed but not yet implemented, will allow Chinese submarines access to berthing facilities in the Bay of Bengal, a critical part of India's strategic backyard. These are the kinds of things which create strategic uncertainties in the relationship and they fuel military modernization. Continuous military modernization of the Chinese and Indian armed forces is the third dimension of the conflicted relationships.

The India–Pakistan relationship is quite different from the Sino-Indian relationship. The fundamental difference is that the latter relationship is quite predictable and steady, more traditional than impetuous. The India–Pakistan relationship is very volatile because it is heavily connected to domestic politics. Since 1947, the temperature of the India–Pakistan relationship has fluctuated more than the Sino-Indian relationship. I should emphasize, however, that the range of conflict between India and Pakistan is within fairly defined parameters – low-level intervention, nuclearization, military development and political controversies. India and Pakistan have also decided to establish a high level political dialogue as expressed by the July 2001 summit between Indian Prime Minister Vajpayee and President Musharraf in Agra.

The third conflicted relationship is the India–US relationship. There were two common elements here. One is that both states are democracies. I do not, however, rate this characteristic except in a very general sense. This democratic factor did not bring the two countries together during the Cold War. One factor that did is that American and Indian business interests converged. Linking the countries economically had a positive effect on cooperation. However, there was also a long list of strategic disagreements between the two countries, e.g. the Non-Proliferation Treaty (NPT), and the Comprehensive Test Ban Treaty (CTBT). The new Bush administration, however, is not inclined to pursue these issues and instead it seeks a strategic relationship with India.

A number of elements have fostered multipolarity in the Indian subcontinent. First, the subcontinent was the most imperialist of all regions.[2] It was a central part of the British Empire. The Indian political class was exposed to British political ideas as well as British rule in India. Indian soldiers were widely used in the service of the empire in the Middle East, Asia and Africa. Indian traders had commercial links with the British and in the Indian Ocean area. Indian migration was fostered in different parts of the empire and migrants kept their links with India. Through British imperialism Indian society acquired an extensive exposure to the thought processes and strategic behaviour of their imperial master. Furthermore, Indians had been exposed constantly to international influences since ancient times – Greek, Persian, Mughal and the Europeans and they learned the value of cultural synthesis as well as the importance of active engagement of the foreigners. India was one of the most internationalist regions in the world. Historically, since the 1500s India has been at the crossroads of all major international cultural (including religious) and strategic influences. Both the strategic loops discussed earlier went through the Indian subcontinent. The first touched India's land frontier in the Afghanistan area. The second loop touched India's sea frontier across the Indian Ocean. Thus, Indian history had prepared the Indian political class to deal with multiple international, regional and local influences, and to exploit them to their advantage.

Second, ancient Indian statecraft as outlined in Kautilya's *Arthasastra* insisted on the centrality of the 'circle of states'. This view was built on the premise and promise of multipolarity and regional geo-politics as the basis of statecraft in the Indian subcontinent. That is, a key theme in Indian political thought rejected utopianism and embraced the idea of regional geo-politics (or continuous attention to neighbourly ambitions, power and quarrels) and the importance of expansion and alliance building. Kautilya's approach was akin to the modern Western balance of power activity where the emphasis was to manage friction and to manage instabilities and threats to one's power and interests. Although modern Indian practitioners do not refer to Kautilya as the basis of their thought process and policies there is a clear affinity between Kautilyan principles and India's development as a regional great power since 1947.

Third, international politics after 1947 revealed the presence of a multipolar international structure in the Asian continent. This created opportunities for the advancement of the interests of a materially weak but diplomatically ambitious India. With the onset of the Cold War in 1947, the Communism/anti-Communism and the US–USSR divide became the basis of America's involvement in subcontinental affairs. America needed support of moderate anti-Communist states that occupied the southern underbelly of the USSR. Turkey, Iran and Pakistan were inducted as the moderate Muslim and anti-Communist states to contain the spread of Soviet influence into the Middle East and the oil-rich Gulf region. American interests in the Middle East attracted America's interest in an alignment with Pakistan. Thus the Cold War was introduced into the subcontinent by American policy. As India was tied to Pakistan by the legacy of Partition, and as America tied itself to Pakistan by its Cold War interests and the rivalry with Soviet Russia, India also became tied to American policy; it had no influence in shaping it but it was tied to its consequences in the region. Here international and regional politics were joined because Pakistan too had an active interest in securing outside help to balance India and to reduce India's advantage in size and potential. The joining of international and regional politics reinforced the India–Pakistan, Hindu–Muslim polarity. It also produced a new polarity between two democratic polities, India and America, because of the pre-eminence of Cold War politics. So even before India built relations with its Communist neighbours, the subcontinent was multipolarized by America's diplomatic and military involvement in Indo-Pakistan relations.

International politics were to sharpen multipolarity in the subcontinent in another big way in the 1950s. The obvious element in the international situation was the American–Soviet Cold War. For Indian practitioners however, two other Cold Wars – between Soviet Russia and China, and between America and China – created diplomatic opportunities for Indian statecraft. There were cracks in the Sino-Soviet front that were rooted in nationalist rivalry and the mistrust between Stalin and Mao that went back to 1927; the national interests of the two sides varied significantly. The Indian leadership under Nehru calculated that they were bound to create a schism between the two that could be exploited to India's advantage. The Indian expectation, outlined in the early 1950s, was sound. Three Cold Wars at the international plane (America-Soviet, Sino-Soviet and Sino-American), one at the regional level (Indo-US) and one hot/cold war relationship at the regional level (Indo-Pakistani) meant that the international and the regional structures as they affected India were fragmented and multipolar from the early 1950s. The structures had a trend towards fragmentation and multipolarity, and it was in the Indian interest to foster this to its advantage provided it did not lead to war. Hence a peaceful (no war) environment was deemed to be necessary to exploit the multipolarities and to build Indian strength and stature through a policy of diplomatic activism and nation-building.

Morris Jones offers a perspective about the position of the Indian subcontinent in an essay written in the 1990s:

> Furthermore, the emergence of the USA as the surviving great power – China has for its own reasons turned inwards and come to focus on matters in its own vicinity – at once revealed and underlined the presence in the Soviet Union of more than a collapse of a doctrine: an economy in ruins. The effect was at once to make more salient than ever the economic relations of States. There are still three great powers, but they are a different three – the USA, an integrating Europe of uncertain scope, and Japan – and their greatness is economic. Their interest will be in trade and investment, anywhere opportunity beckons. At least one possibility could be the further marginalization and dependence of the Third World.

Given that scenario, South Asia may be less easily marginalized than Africa but less well equipped than much of South East Asia.[3]

Alastair Buchan too saw India as a marginal force in international politics:

> But though India is Asia's second largest state, she possesses little external influence there (except with her immediate neighbours); she is a static power in diplomatic terms at present, and the evolution of local relationships elsewhere in Asia is unlikely to be greatly affected by her conceptions or initiatives.[4]

Both assessments miss the point that despite changes in India's external fortunes – Nehru's international messages were ignored because of India's military defeat at China's hands in 1962, because India lacked staying power in the strategic and economic arenas until the 1990s, and because the end of the Cold War ended the special relationship with Moscow – still India was never completely out of the regional and the international game of power politics.

In my assessment, the Indian subcontinent is a major geo-political pivot because of the gradual rise of India as a regional great power and because of the failure of Pakistani, Chinese and American policies to create a situation so that Indian and Pakistani activities effectively cancelled each other's influence and power. From the Cold War era, the subcontinent incrementally acquired the qualities of hard regionalism and multipolarity. India, a regional great power, and Pakistan, a regional state that occupies important strategic space, have tied the world community to their future as a result of several important issues: the Soviet invasion of Afghanistan, China's push into Tibet, the Kashmir insurgency, nuclear and missile proliferation, Islamic terrorism in the arc from Chechniya to the Philippines, the security of the sea lanes from Japan to the Gulf, and the danger to regional security if Pakistan should fail as a state. The 1970s and the 1980s seem in hindsight to have been a lull in the vital process of repositioning of subcontinental relationships with the major powers. It was a temporary lull but the framework of multipolarity was never lost in the subcontinent. There are a number of reasons for this assessment. The international powers could not club together vis-à-vis the subcontinent and continue the imperial strategy to maintain the subcontinent as a critical part of the Asiatic buffer belt where all major powers could compete on a non-exclusive basis. Nor could they contain the rise of India as a regional great power. Nor could they act with indifference towards Indian and Pakistan strategic interests. Nor could they marginalize the two in world affairs. Mutlipolarity was never lost because, despite the ebb and flow of Indian and Pakistani fortunes, the five players – America, Soviet Russia, China, India and Pakistan – were continuously engaged in the region with varying degrees of intensity (that was explained by differences in interests, power and skill) but it was never indifference.

During the Cold War, multipolarity in the subcontinent revolved around two central conflicts: Sino-Indian and Indo-Pakistani. The third conflict – American–Soviet – was actually less central in the subcontinent because, despite the ideological and military rivalry between the two, they discovered common ground in subcontinental affairs. In 1962 the superpowers came out on India's side, offering aid and diplomatic support against Chinese expansion. In the 1965 Indo-Pakistan War, both helped promote Soviet mediation of the Tashkant agreement. In the mid-1960s both agreed on the importance of non-proliferation which was meant to contain Indian nuclear power. On the other hand, the two central rivalries have remained undiminished in scope and intensity. India and Pakistan recently fought a nasty war in Kargil in 1999. China and India are locked in a bitter strategic rivalry in the Himalayas, in the Bay of Bengal, in the international diplomatic arena where China still seeks Indian nuclear and missile disarmament, and in regional affairs where China seeks to continually develop Pakistan as a line of military pressure against India. At the same time there were three central alignments during the Cold War: Sino-Pakistan, US–Pakistan and India–USSR. So subcontinental multipolarity revolved around a structure of five relationships. Two (Sino-Indian, Indo-Pakistani) were negative or relationships of strategic conflict (either because of war, expectation of war or fundamental differences of strategic interests); and three were positive (noted above). These alignments were constant and they were organized. Hence the claim that the subcontinent was multipolar from the 1950s to the 1980s, and beyond.

Multipolarity in the Vietnam War

Multipolarity was clearly evident in the Vietnam War as a result of interaction among four major players. The Table 7.2 shows the conflicting interests and strategies of the four powers. Multipolarity was indicated by a high degree of polarity in these relationships and a high degree of engagement in a secondary zone of international conflict.

Summing up

These were three major examples of multipolarity during the Cold War. They indicate that regional powers cast their diplomatic and military policies not in a US–USSR framework but rather, from the early part of the Cold War, there was an awareness of multipolarity – measured in terms of the distribution of power, multiple relationships, varied strategic interests and policies, and shifting pattern of alignments that did not indicate bloc discipline as in Europe in the 1950s.

Table 7.2 Multipolarity in Asia during the Vietnam War

Event	*Players (major and minor)*	*Interests, attitudes perceptions*	*Behaviour*
Vietnam War 1964–73	China	Fear that increasing American involvement in Vietnam posed a serious threat to China's security especially at the southern border.[a] Desire to form a broad international united front against both the United States and the Soviet Union. China recognized national liberation movements in the Third World as the most important potential allies in the coalition against the US and the Soviet Union.[b] To prevent any disruption to the Chinese Communist revolution. Mao's fear of a derailment of his life's handicraft US presence in Indo-China was perceived as a threat to the Chinese revolution.[c] Following the Soviet-American Nuclear Test Ban Treaty in July 1963, the Beijing leadership publicly denounced any suggestion that China was subject to any degree of Soviet protection.[d] Desire to avoid a major confrontation (a Korea-style war) with the US. This attitude was changed in 1962 when Mao switched to a more militant attitude against the US.[e]	Perceived threats were met with several domestic measures notably massive Third Front project – a major strategic action designed to provide an alternative industrial base that would enable China continue production in the event of an attack on its large urban centres.[f] Beijing wooed Hanoi to take sides in the Sino-Soviet ideological dispute– e.g. China extended massive aid to Vietnam with the intent to draw Hanoi into China's orbit.[g] Disagreed with the Soviet Union on strategies to reunify Vietnam in accordance with the Geneva accords and encouraged North Vietnam to prepare for a protracted struggle.[h] Encouraged North Vietnam to emphasize on a combination of political and military struggle in the South.[i] Between 1954 and 1963 China supplied Hanoi 270,000 guns, over 10,000 pieces of

Table 7.2 – cont

Event	*Players (major and minor)*	*Interests, attitudes perceptions*	*Behaviour*
			artillery, nearly 200 million bullets, 2.02 million artillery shells, 15,000 wire transmitters, 15 aircraft, 28 warships and 1.18 million sets of uniform.[j]
	Soviet Union	In the spirit of proletarian internationalism the Soviet Union sought to uphold what she perceived be a just cause by North Vietnam.[k] Apprehensive of a radical pro-Chinese orientation by the North Vietnamese.l Unwilling especially after October 1964 under Brezhnev to lose influence in the region.[m] Following the 1962 Cuban Missile Crisis the Kremlin sought to avoid a direct clash with the US.[n] Vietnam provided an opportunity to test Soviet military hardware and a chance to update on US weapons advancement by inspecting the war booty captured by DRV.[o]	Provided massive economic and military aid (e.g. Soviet made artillery shelling systems) as well as moral and political support to North Vietnam.[p] Favoured a more peaceful resolution of the conflict. In fact the Soviet Union became the primary mediator favoured by the US.[q] From 1964, with the election of Lyndon B. Johnson, who favoured greater right-wing influence in American politics, Soviet policy shifted to public denunciation of US aggressiveness and increased contact with North Vietnam, e.g. in 1964 opening of permanent mission of NFLSV.[r]
	United States	Support of anti-Communist South Vietnamese regime of Ngo Dinh and	US dispatched 100 advisers and 400 special forces to train South

Table 7.2 – cont

Event	*Players (major and minor)*	*Interests, attitudes perceptions*	*Behaviour*
		determination to prevent the spread of Communism to the S. Vietnam from the North.[s] After January 1969 the US sought a diplomatic solution to the conflict and increasingly relied on the USSR to play the role of mediator.[t]	Vietnamese in the event of war with North Vietnam. Increased assistance in 1962 – MAC v.[u] Dropping anti-Communist leaflets in Hanoi.[v] From 1969 pushed the USSR to mediate and was ready to play the 'Chinese card' if the USSR was not forthcoming.w
	Vietnam	Determined to fight perceived US imperialism with active support from China and USSR, whichever was convenient at each stage.[x] Keen to end the war on her terms.[y]	WPV Central Committee was keen to exploit it friendship with both China and USSR – tried to rid North Vietnam of excessive Chinese wardship and to avoid any kind of dependence on the Soviet Union.[z] Minimized the influence of the USSR on her policy options, e.g. in 1967 the Soviets failed to convince the Vietnamese leaders to hold talks on a peaceful settlement.*

a Quiang Zhai, 'Beijing and the Vietnam Conflict, 1964–1965: New Chinese Evidence', *The Cold War in Asia*, 6–7 (Winter 1955/96, Woodrow Wilson Center for Scholars, Washington, DC), 237.
b Ibid., p. 239.
c Ibid., p. 241.
d Ibid., p. 240.
e Ibid., pp. 234–5.
f Ibid., pp. 237–8.
g Ibid., p. 240.
h Ibid., p. 233.
i Ibid., p. 234.

Table 7.2 – cont

j Ibid., p. 235.
k Ilya V. Gaiduk, 'The Vietnam War and Soviet-American Relations, 1964–1973: New Russian Evidence', *The Cold War in Asia*, 6-7 (Winter 1995/96), 252.
l Ibid., p. 250.
m Ibid.
n Ibid.
o Ibid., p. 253.
p Ibid., pp. 251–2.
q Ibid., p. 253.
r Ibid., pp. 250–1.
s Quiang Zhai, 'Beijing and the Vietnam Conflict', 237.
t Ilya V. Gaiduk, 'The Vietnam War and Soviet-American Relations', p. 253.
u Ibid., p. 235.
v Ibid.
w Ibid.
x Ibid., p. 250.
y Ibid., pp. 254–5.
z Ibid., p. 251.
* Ibid.

8 Regional multipolarity after the end of the Cold War

To recap, there are five nodal points or geo-political pivots in Asia today. These centres developed from the foundation of regional multipolarity that emerged during the Cold War era and they crystallized following its end. The nodal points express local and regional power rivalries that interact with international power politics. However, the conflicts are structured and organized. Their parameters are defined and predictable. They are grounded in regional and sub-regional politics and must therefore be understood by a 'bottoms–up' rather than a 'top–down' approach. They have Asian roots. Their existence and stability are affected by the relations among the powers outside Asia but the outside powers too are affected by developments within each geo-political pivot.

This section sets out the criteria for measuring multipolarity in Asian regions (sub-regions) and then it outlines the patterns of polarity and amity in each region (sub-region).

Coerced linkages between states exist

With multipolarity, the major and the minor players find that they are tied together on a number of issues of social and practical importance. The linkages are unavoidable because of geo-political proximity. They find that disengagement either is not possible or counter-productive and costly for their interests and well being. Regionalism is thus deemed to be hard. It is entrenched. The players are tied together by history, culture, issues, consciousness about the neighbourhood, awareness of their stakes in the future of the region and a recognition of the costs to them of non-involvement.

Regional great power exists in each nodal point

This is a significant development that stimulated the development of regional security structures. A regional great power is able to engage the great powers and to shape the character of the regional neighbourhood as well as its strategic agenda and its institutional framework. A regional great power is a hub or a pole of attraction in a region; and it can insulate the region from interference outside the region.

Great powers' dominance of the Asian regions (sub-regions) is no longer possible by 'clubbing together' or intervention

Nor is indifference a viable option for the great powers because decoupling between the international system and regional politics is not feasible in Asia today. The great powers must be continuously engaged to guard their interests in Asian regions (sub-regions). For this they must pay a price in securing a negotiated solution. Even America, the global hegemon after the end of the Cold War, finds it necessary to reposition itself in relation to other power centres in Asia. The entrenchment of regional multipolarities in Asia increases the challenges before American diplomacy.

War is not inevitable in each region (sub-region) but conflict is

However, modalities exist to contain it and to establish parameters of controlled or limiting conflict. That is, the system in each region (sub-region) has shifted from the hypothetical 'chaoistic' situation to one of regional power formation (in the form of emergence of Asian regional great powers) and regional conflict formation (in the form of emergence of stable conflict systems in each region (sub-region)).

A basis exists for the development of regional initiatives for conflict resolution

Peace constituencies have regional roots and regional appeal. They are 'made in Asia' proposals. In other words, prospects of regional peace-making in Asia exist probably more so than in the Middle East today. This application is in play in Asian regions and is the basis of the pattern of amity (public and secret friendships based on common interests) and polarity (based on public and secret enmities based on conflicting interests) in each region (sub-region). Figures 8.1–5 illustrate the patterns.

US–PRC

Public enmity

There is a widespread belief in China that US policy is aimed at preventing China from emerging as a great power in the 21st century able to challenge American interests regionally and globally. US policies that support this objective, according to many Chinese experts, include: strengthening the US–Japan defence alliance; developing a theatre missile defence system that may provide coverage not only to US allies, but also to Taiwan; continuing

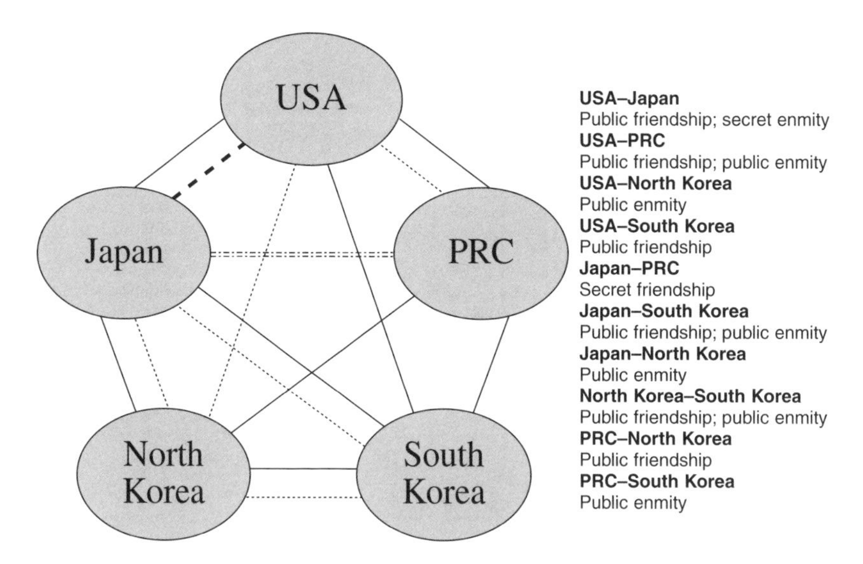

Figure 8.1 Regional relationships: USA–Japan–PRC–North Korea–South Korea

arms sales to Taiwan; and resuming sponsorship of a motion criticizing China's human rights record in the United Nations Human Rights Commission after a one-year hiatus.

Public friendship

This friendship is shown by economic means. US grants China MFN status, reducing number of sensitive goods and technologies covered by export controls, allowing Chinese companies to operate relatively freely in the US and facilitating Chinese entry into international economic organizations such as the WTO.

US–Japan

Public friendship

US–Japan Security Alliance (1952) stipulates America's commitment to defend Japan. This agreement was elaborated in 1996 from the narrower 'Far East' to a wider 'Asia–Pacific'.

Secret enmity

Japan is nobody's ally. According to Owen Lattimore, US reliance on Japan as a staunch ally in Asia is based a chain of assumptions: that Japan can be

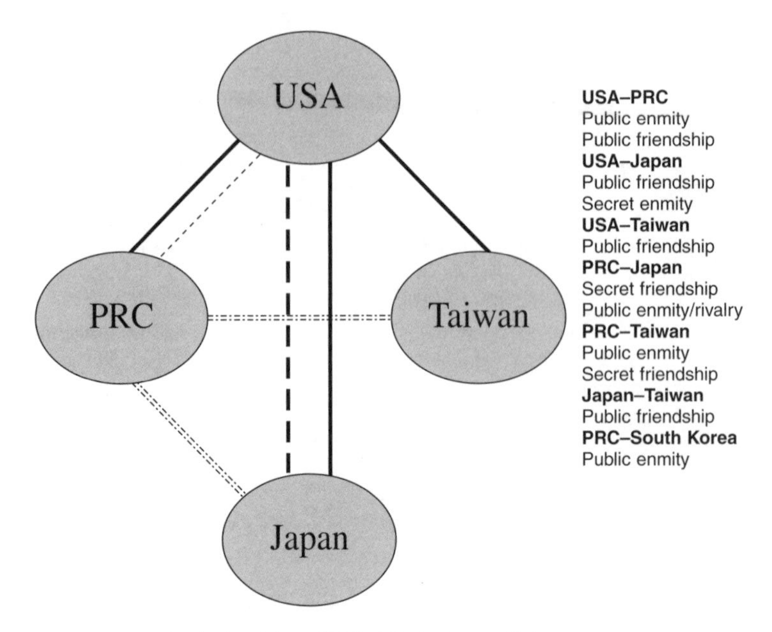

Figure 8.2 Regional relationships: USA–PRC–Japan–Taiwan

made not only into a workshop, but a workshop that controls Asia; that Japan can be made into a politically reliable bulwark against Russia; that there is only one Japan, a solid, internally indivisible unit. Unfortunately these assumptions are illusory. Lattimore contends that the present 'realistic' policy in Japan is going to fail because it is not realistic but pseudo-realistic. The real Japan is unstable in its internal composition. No necessity ties Japan down to be America's permanent ally in Asia. A Japan made strong enough by American subsidy to hold an economic ascendancy over the rest of Asia, and strong enough to be an American ally against Russia if it wants to be, is automatically a Japan strong enough to double-cross America and make its own deals both with Russia and the rest of Asia. Lattimore concludes that given Japan's past and in view of a possible reconfiguration of power in Asia, it is inadvisable for the USA to rely absolutely on Japan's friendship. The possibilities of Japan aligning with Russia or China should not be overlooked.

Japan is developing its ties with Russia, including the conduct of naval operations with Russia.

There is also growing discomfort from the Japanese, especially those residents in Okinawa where the US bases are located. Okinawans detest the encroachment on their society in terms of noise, accidents, crimes by military personnel (e.g. rape) and the distasteful reminder of the tragic Battle of

Okinawa in 1945. As a result, the governor of Okinawa is reported to have demanded the closure of all the island's bases by 2015.

Japanese practitioners continue to debate the pros and cons of US–Japan security ties.

Pros

- The alliance has a defensive and deterrent role in the region.
- It helps to contain potentially destabilizing effects of economic and trade friction between the US and Japan.
- Others think that it is simply the best available post-Cold War security arrangement. There is no better alternative.

Cons

- Some Japanese think US policy in Japan as elsewhere around the world is increasingly driven by economic imperialism.
- Others detest the huge host nation support Japan is undertaking. Japanese are reluctant to engage in wars in other parts of the region simply in the interest of the US.

PRC–Japan

Secret friendship

Japan provides ODA support to China.

Public enmity

This rests on a history of Japanese conquest and occupation of parts of China in the 19th century and particularly because of Japan's active alliance with the US.

Japan's rapidly evolving military posture challenges China's strategic position in the region.

They are economic rivals. Both seek to be the pre-eminent Asian economic power in the region.

China will not allow Japan a permanent seat in the UN Security Council as it will diminish China's pre-eminence position as the Asian voice and veto.

PRC–Taiwan

Public enmity

One China policy and China's desire for political subjugation and control of Taiwan is the major cause of enmity. This is exacerbated by Taiwan's democracy and its strong ties with the USA and others. Cross-strait relations continue to struggle and the turnover of Macao to China seems to have stoked the flames. Reports of a Chinese missile build-up across the straits since the 1990s added to the tensions, as did the possibility of Taiwan developing a counter-missile capability. Beijing also continues to strongly protest any potential Taiwan participation in US-led theatre missile defence (TMD).

Secret friendship

Despite rising political and military tensions, and the absence of formal political and economic relations, China and Taiwan have formed significant trade and investment ties (which occur indirectly through Hong Kong and other countries) over the past few years. Between 1990 and 1995, total trade between the two economies grew from $5.2 billion to $21 billion (according to Taiwanese data). Taiwan exports to China over this period rose from $4.4 billion to $17.9 billion, making China the second largest destination (after the United States) for Taiwanese exports (1995).

Japan–South Korea

Public friendship

Despite minor friction (predictably over Tokto/Takeshima), Seoul–Tokyo relations saw overall improvement, staying in line with the Kim Dae-jung–Keizo Obuchi vision of a new era of cooperation enunciated in 1998.

The highlight in formal terms was the half-day summit meeting between Kim Dae-jung and Japanese Premier Yoshiro Mori (29 May), but the substantive improvements took place at lower levels in the realms of military cooperation and culture exchanges. Meetings between ROK Defense Minister Cho Seong-tae and Japanese counterpart Tsutomu Kawara (20–4 May 1998) produced important agreements to expand bilateral military exchanges. The two components of this are annual reciprocal visits by the chairs of the ROK Joint Chiefs of Staff (JCS) and Japan's Joint Staff Council. The other is a student exchange program, involving cadets from each branch of the South Korean and Japanese Academies for full programs of study beginning in 2001. The latter program, following the precedent of academy exchange programs in the US (at West Point), builds for the future by facilitating familiarity and interchange among the best and brightest of future military leadership in the two countries. Regularization of JCS visits, while almost a formality given the recent frequency of dialogue, is no small accomplishment as it rounds out the institutionalization of the whole range of bilateral defence dialogue over the past few years from working-level officials up to the level of defence minister. Indeed, given the recent volume of leadership interaction and joint exercises, some argue that the military has been the most active in terms of fulfilling the Kim–Obuchi 21st-century vision, ahead of the curve and more practised in bilateral cooperation efforts than the politicians or general public.

Japan and South Korea have significant economic and diplomatic ties.

Japan–North Korea

Public enmity

North Korea's demand for compensation from Japan's colonial control, N. Korea's nuclear weapons' threat to Japan, its treatment of Japanese held hostages in North Korea, alleged North Korean smuggling of drugs and counterfeit currency into Japan are major irritants.

Public friendship

Japan participates in KEDO and is interested in the peaceful development of North Korea as well as South Korea. The Korean peninsula is Japan's strategic and economic backyard.

US–South Korea

Public friendship

Close security and economic ties express the friendship since 1945.

US–North Korea

Public enmity

This goes back to the Korean War and the military confrontation in the DMZ. Since the armistice in 1953, acquisition of nuclear weapons or long-range missiles threatens the peace in the region. North Korea is aligned to Communist PRC.

Public friendship

The US and North Korea both seek a bilateral relationship that has strategic as well as commercial consequences for the bilateral as well as regional relationships.

Pakistan–Afghanistan

Public enmity

Two areas – Pashtunistan and Baluchistan – have long complicated Afghanistan's relations with Pakistan. Controversies involving these areas date

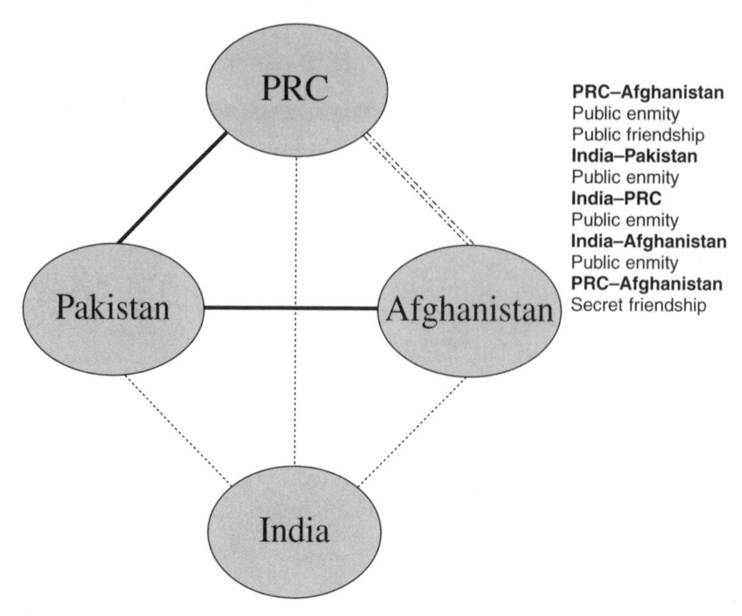

Figure 8.3 Regional relationships: PRC–Pakistan–Afghanistan–India

back to the establishment of the Durand Line in 1893, dividing Pashtun and Baluch tribes living in Afghanistan from those living in what later became Pakistan. Afghanistan vigorously protested the inclusion of Pashtun and Baluch areas within Pakistan without providing the inhabitants with an opportunity for self-determination. Since 1947, this problem has led to incidents along the border, with extensive disruption of normal trade patterns. The most serious crisis lasted from September 1961 to June 1963, when diplomatic, trade, transit and consular relations between the countries were suspended.

Public friendship

There was a deep friendship between Pakistan's military intelligence agency and Islamic groups in Pakistan and the Taliban/Al Qaeda regime in Afghanistan, 1994–2001.

India–Pakistan

Public enmity

A history of war and the bitter controversy about Kashmir shows the enmity.

Secret friendship

Non-governmental constituencies – business, academic, press, citizens' groups – and a desire for peace in some sections of the Indian and Pakistani political establishments show the possibility of a friendship between the two enemy states.

PRC–India

Public enmity

This centres on boundary disputes in the Himalayan region and China's concern about India's support for Tibet separatism.

Pakistan in Sino-Indian Relations

Since 1990, the PRC has adopted a more equidistant stance on Kashmir. After India's nuclear tests, in an apparent effort to exert pressure on India, the PRC briefly floated the idea of a multilateral meeting to help resolve the Kashmir dispute.

The PRC's military, nuclear and missile relationship with Pakistan, however, remains profoundly problematic for Sino-Indian relations. In July 2000, President Narayanan again requested clarification that China's Pakistan relationship is not aimed at India. Foreign Minister Tang duly obliged during his visit to the subcontinent. Indians are unconvinced. Throughout 2000 there was evidence of missile transfers by the PRC to Pakistan. Indians are convinced that China uses Pakistan to 'contain' India in South Asia, preventing India's emergence as a possible challenge to China. Combined with the rapid growth of China's economic and military strength and its revived relations with Russia, Indians have become extremely anxious about the Sino-Pakistan relationship. India regards Pakistan as China's most important link in a chain of strategic encirclement. China, on the other hand, regards Pakistan as a major partner (even reportedly suggesting that it is on par with the US relationship with Israel) with which it has a normal, legitimate 'state-to-state' relationship. Untying this complicated knot will be extremely difficult.

India–Afghanistan

Public enmity

There are Al-Qaeda activities in Kashmir supported by Pakistan, e.g. the reported training of guerrillas in camps to battle Indian forces in Kashmir with Pakistan's support, religious fanaticism and drug trade.

PRC–Afghanistan

Secret/public friendship

Joint communiqué on the establishment of diplomatic relations between PRC and Afghanistan.

Secret enmity

The involvement of Afghan and Pakistani groups in the struggle between Muslim separatists who want to see the creation of an independent Uyghur state has long been hinted at. In recent years, these groups have been responsible for a number of incidents, including three bomb attacks in Urumchi in February 1997, two more bus-bomb attacks in Beijing a month later and the explosion of a military vehicle in the Xinjiang region in September 2000. Reports suggesting that Uyghur militants from Xinjiang have undergone training in Afghanistan have been around since the early 1990s.

Chinese officials have started to suggest in private that the Taliban have been directly involved in fomenting trouble in Xinjiang. Equally common are tales of weapons being smuggled along the Karakoran Highway from Pakistan into China, and allegations that Uyghur nationalists have established ties with fundamentalist parties in Pakistan.

Beijing fears that Xinjiang will become another Kashmir. More broadly, China is worried about the Taliban's potential to influence developments in the other Central Asian republics, thereby impacting negatively on its security, particularly in Xinjiang.

China's growing willingness to speak out on the challenge posed by Afghanistan to its own and regional security indicates that Beijing is starting to adopt a more hands-on approach to events. China's traditional approach to Afghanistan has been to use well-established links with Pakistan, allegedly closely involved in the Taliban's rise, to try to influence and build links with the Taliban.

China explored the possibility of providing military aid to the Northern Alliance. Such a policy, as well growing Chinese concern at the spread and influence of Muslim groups inside Pakistan, hads the potential to influence relations between Beijing and Islamabad. China decided after President Jiang Zemin's visit to India in December 1997 not to support Pakistan's claim over Indian Kashmir. Instead, it called for a peaceful settlement. This is indicative of a growing divergence of views between these two old allies. Similarly, China failed to publicly back its ally Pakistan during the Kargil crisis. This incident fuelled private concerns in Beijing about Islamabad's ability to exercise control over many of the Muslim groups operating within its borders.

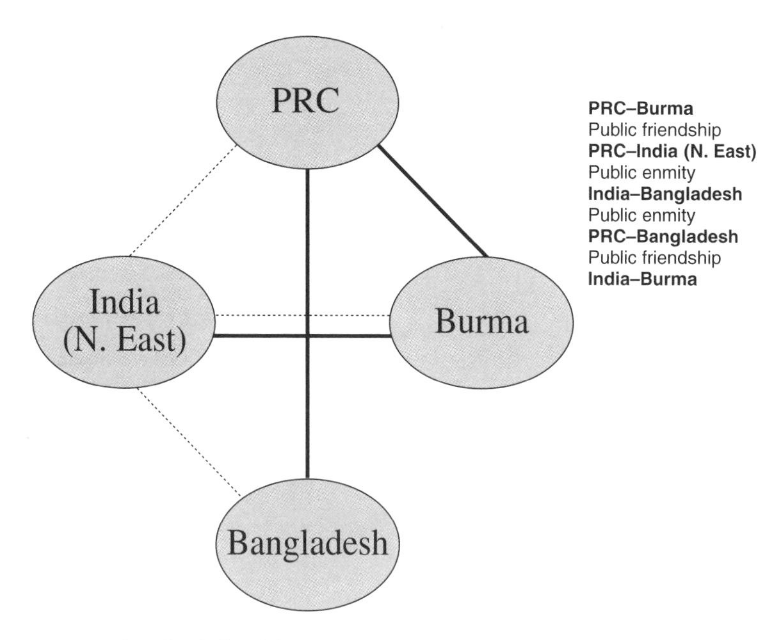

Figure 8.4 Regional relationships: PRC–India (N. East)–Burma–Bay of Bengal (Bangladesh)

India–Bangladesh

Public enmity

Border disputes include a 6.5 km disputed piece of land called Muhurirchar claimed by both countries. There are three types of disputed lands – enclaves, lands under 'adverse possession' and undemarcated lands. However, according to a published report in the Dhaka press, Bangladesh has in its possession 'over 111 disputed lands covering around 700 acres' likely to be handed over to India as per the 1974 agreement. Similarly, over fifty-one such lands are under Indian possession covering over 10,000 acres and should come to Bangladesh.

Public friendship

India was instrumental in the creation of an independent Bangladesh.

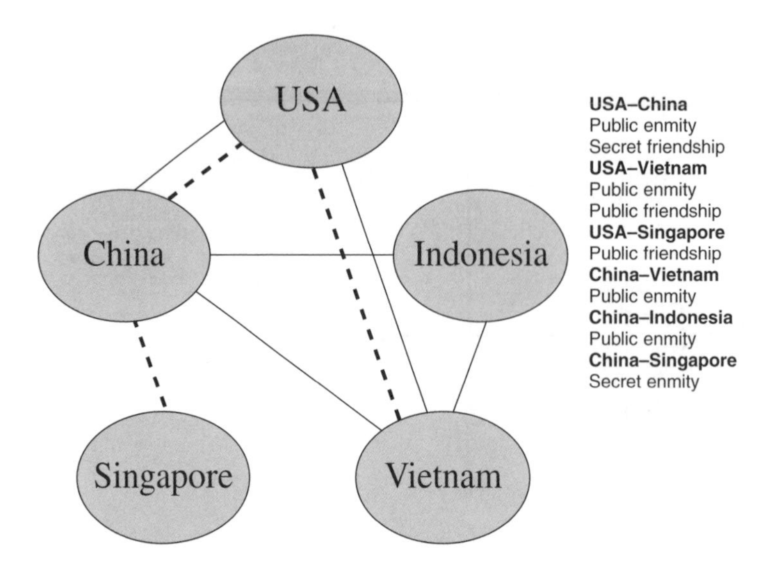

Figure 8.5 Regional relationships: China–Indonesian archipelago–Singapore–Vietnam–USA

China–Burma

Public friendship

China holds most of the keys to a resolution of the Burmese crisis. It supplies the Burmese military with most of its modern weapons, though smaller quantities of arms arrive from Singapore. It is Burma's major trading partner, taking and trans-shipping large quantities of Burma's illicit opium and heroin exports, and supplying consumer goods in return. In 1998, Burma also exported to India, Singapore and Thailand, and imported from Singapore, Japan, Thailand and Malaysia, but the products listed did not include narcotics and weapons, which dwarf all other commodities.

India–Burma

Secret enmity

Burma's close economic and military ties with China challenge Indian security interests.

Public friendship

Burma is open to Indian overtures to build Indo-Burmese economic and military links to balance Sino-Burmese ties.

US–PRC

See Figures 8.1 and 8.2.

US–Vietnam

The public enmity was indicated by the Vietnam War.

The public friendship is revealed by Clinton and Bush administration efforts to build economic and diplomatic links with Vietnam and to build the weight of Vietnam as a lever vis-à-vis China, given historical rivalry between China and Vietnam.

US–Singapore

Singapore is important as a financial centre in Asia, and its independent stance in diplomatic and strategic affairs makes it a valuable player in South East Asian diplomatic affairs. Singapore is developing as a major military power in South East Asia, with a potential to project its military power into the South China Seas.

China–Vietnam

The two are historical rivals. Vietnam is on guard against the danger of Chinese hegemony. China and Vietnam have fought a border war that China lost in 1997.

China–Indonesia

The Indonesia Army and the Suharto regime was responsible for the slaughter on a mass scale of ethnic Chinese in Indonesia because they were alleged to have pro-China sympathies. Indonesia has been on guard against China since Indonesia gained independence.

China–Singapore

Despite its significant Chinese make-up, Singaporean diplomatic and military policy as well as its democratic activity reveals fear of China.

Summing up

This chapter indicates that a pattern of strategic relationships has developed in the five nodal points in Asia. These are the centres of gravity of strategic action which occupy the attention of major and minor powers who are active in Asian international relations. Each nodal point has a structured pattern of multipolar (not unipolar, not bipolar) relationships and the distribution of military and economic power in each nodal point is asymmetrical. The countries involved in each nodal point are tied together, but now the tie up involves major and minor powers. The contrast is with the 19th century up to the second half of the 20th century when the great powers were tied up with each other. Clubbing together and using compensatory arrangements for themselves along with buffers were then the basis of Asian international relations. This is no longer a sufficient method to organize international relations in Asia. Once the natives have successfully drawn blood in deadly quarrels with superior force, then it is a matter of practical necessity to grant them a seat at the table.

The existence of regional security structures in these nodal points rules out the prospect of a general war but it does not rule out friction and rivalries. The study is based on ongoing competition in each nodal point but the coerced linkages facilitate a search for wriggle space that leads to 'conflict formation' and eventually 'conflict resolution'. To a discussion of the process lending to conflict resolution we turn to Chapter 10.

9 The future of geo-politics in Asia

Introduction

The end of the Cold War did not produce the widely expected peace dividend; in fact, the 1990s and the beginning of the 21st century have seen tremendous turbulence in the international system. Two major events are noteworthy. First, the Indo-Pakistani nuclear and missile tests (1998 and thereafter) shattered the Western smugness and overconfidence in the belief that the problem of nuclear and missile proliferation had been laid to rest; and that it could be controlled by the development of an international coalition and international treaty arrangements or international regimes against further proliferation. It is significant that Asia has emerged as the centre of further nuclear proliferation, and this made nonsense of Washington-led efforts to prevent further proliferation since the 1960s. It would be a mistake to conclude that the problem has been laid to rest by the emergence of India and Pakistan as the new members of the nuclear club. A reason for the strong Western condemnation of the Indian bomb was that it opened the way to the Pakistan bomb, and it may have stimulated proliferation activity in Iran and Iraq, among others. But, as Martin Wight wisely pointed out, the great powers usually fail in their cry to halt the arms race, and once unleashed technological innovation cannot be eliminated in the absence of a political settlement.[1]

Indian and Pakistani nuclear bomb programs attacked Western policies which believed that it was morally right as well as diplomatically practical to institute discriminatory international arrangements in pursuit of their security interests. The Indo-Pakistani challenge was an argument that was carried out within the framework of the system of sovereign states. It was conducted in terms of the traditional principles and methods of statecraft. Both sides employed the language of power, the one from a position of privilege, the other from the position of under-privilege; the one sought to freeze the status quo, the other sought to alter it. For the West, the argument was in terms of international rules and road maps; for the South Asians, the argument was in terms of regional geo-politics and the unwillingness of the existing great powers to accept a redistribution of power and a change in the pattern of alignments peacefully. This argument showed the limits of American power and the need to accommodate the challenger. Owen Lattimore was right although he wrote without specific reference to the nuclear question:

> the limits of American power and the degree to which Asia is passing out of control mean that American policy must team up with the policies of some countries and come to the understanding with other countries that is far short of hostility in one direction, but far short of alliance in the other.[2]

The Al Qaeda attack on the World Trade Center and the Pentagon on 11 September 2001 was the second major event which shattered the smugness and the over-confidence of the US, the centre of world capitalism and military might. It showed that the issue had the appearance of a contest between 'Jihad versus McWorld'.[3] It was, of course, more complex than that. 'McWorld' is shorthand for globalization, the taming of nationalism, the end of anti-Western ideology, the emphasis on better productivity and more consumption (i.e. the virtue of greed), the rejection of culture and identity as decisive elements in politics, the acknowledgement that economics was king, but geo-politics was not. McWorld also implied that globalization and modernization would be followed by Westernisation; and that would mean the end of ideology as well as cultural conflicts. 'McWorld' offered a paradign which was the exact opposite of the analysis of A.B. Bozeman and others. She stresses the central relationship between cultural conflict and international politics, and maintains that this conflict had intensified historically.[4] 'McWorld' was challenged by S. Huntington's *Clash of Civilizations* which sees a prolonged – over 1400 years – contention between Islam and the West. The soothing messages by Presidents Bill Clinton and George W. Bush that 11 September 2001 and its aftermath is not a fight between Islam and the West has no factual or historical basis.[5]

In sum, the Indo-Pakistani nuclear behaviour shattered the belief that world order could be secured through international pressures and international arrangements without the consent of the weak. Before 1998, the language of Western power had prevailed. It showed extraordinary faith in the ability of the West and its international coalition to manipulate and contain the rogues who refused to accept Western norms. It did not work for two reasons. It did not rest on a sound knowledge about the decision processes of the objects of containment and the principle of consent as the basis of international treaty-making among sovereign states was ignored. In this second aspect America failed to appreciate the power of the Islamic faith, and the fault lines in the 'McWorld' thesis. In the Middle East, modernization did not mean acceptance of Westernization – and there are historical-territorial and prestige type – grievances in the Muslim world which need to be addressed. Although the Taliban is on the run in Afghanistan, Al Qaeda still exists, as do the issues of injustice in US policies in the Middle East. The forces supporting Islamic Jihad have not bought into the Western strategic agenda. To appreciate the future of geo-politics in Asia, let us remind ourselves of the constants and variables in Asian international relations today.

Recapping the dynamics of Asian international relations

There are four constants and four variables in Asian international relations. We need to recall them as they form the context for our assessment of the Asian situation after 11 September 2001. These dynamics help us evaluate whether or not the strengthening of American military position in the axis from Central Asia to the Arabian Sea (via Afghanistan and Pakistan) signals the onset of American unipolarity in Asian affairs. Another question merits examination. What are the consequences of America's strengthened military position in Asia (post-September 2001) for the geo-political interests of other Asian (major and minor) powers?

The *constants* are as follows.

1. *Nationalism in Asia is strong and it is modern*; it favours and facilitates modernization. It points also to the importance of the cultural imperative in the formulation of the policies of Asian powers. It is the antithesis of imperialism or hegemonism (domination). The friction between nationalism and empire in Asia in the past century is now a friction between nationalism and great power hegemonism (domination, real or perceived or feared) in the world today. Nationalism is the basis of a country's search for autonomy in its strategic neighbourhood and in the international sphere. It remains a vital force in the politics of major and minor Asian countries. The USA's international coalition partners in Asia are still nationalistic.

2. *Asian powers have continuously given full weight to the importance of power politics and geo-politics in the pursuit of their interests.* Their policies show an awareness of being tied to forces which repel and attract in their respective strategic neighbourhoods. Hence Asian power politics are invariably expressed in the form of regionalized geo-politics. Asian military and diplomatic experiences have fostered the growth of regionalism in Asia. The experience of being tied together has increased the awareness of the limits of power – one's own and that of outside forces.

3. *Asia has been an international arena since 1945 – a centre of conflict as well as regional power development and conflict formation.* This led to the growth of latent multipolarity within the context of Cold War bipolarity in Asia (1947–90), i.e. changes in external relationships and internal policies of Asian states since 1945 led to the growth of multipolarity and stability in regional structures in Asia. Previous chapters have shown that this trend is irreversible.

4. *Even though America is the strongest power on earth now there are limits to its power and influence, as well as those of other great powers.* The two events highlighted earlier demonstrate the limits of American power.

The variables too point to the importance of geo-politics in Asia.

1. *The strategic and political fortunes of the first tier countries – the great powers – show an ebb and flow.* Upward and downward mobility is demonstrated. It appears that great powers have short shelf lives because their ambitions may, at times, exceed their capabilities, and the jealousies of rivals are likely to bring them down. The Italian philosopher, Botero, made the point convincingly in 1589:

> But 'middle-sized states (*i mediocri*) are the most lasting, since they are exposed neither to violence by their weakness nor to envy by their greatness, and their wealth and power being moderate, passions are less violent, ambition finds less support and licence less provocation than in large states. Fear of their neighbours restrains them, and even if feelings are roused to anger they are more easily quieted and tranquillity restored . . . Thus some middle-sized powers (*alcune potenze mediocre*) have lasted far longer than the greatest (*grandissime*), as we see in the case of Sparta, Carthage and above all Venice, for there has never been an empire (*dominio*) in which mediocrity of power went with such stability and strength.[6]

The great powers are vulnerable to external pressures from other great powers as well as second-tiered countries who seek a revised and improved status for themselves.

2. *The diplomatic and strategic space or influence of second-tiered countries varies*; it is situational and it is relative to the power and influence and the skill at power politics by others. The wriggle space was limited during the Cold War era but it was not insignificant. Lately, in the post-Cold War period, it has increased for these countries.

3. *The intensity of revolutionary violence (or Jihad or liberation) has varied in international history.*[7] And this pattern continues.

4. *The distribution of power at the international and the regional levels as well as the pattern of relationships (polarities/friendships/difficult relations/indifference) are changeable as a result of internal policies and external circumstances*; and depending on the issues and interests in play, lines of stress are formed and dealt with by states. The junction where countervailing forces meet/collide are the points of friction or points of decision. When the points of friction are static (as in the case of the Berlin Wall and the DMZ in Korea), the relationship of conflict produces a stalemate. When the points of friction are dynamic, then the relationship of conflict produces uncertainty (which neither markets nor generals nor politicians like) and then the challenge is to achieve manageable instability or a controlled outcome. In either case, equilibrium is not the expected outcome in the system of states.

Unquestionably, modern Asian international relations are in a state of disequilibrium – there is obviously no Asian order, and at best, there is a situation of manageable instability even in the aftermath of the retreat of the Taliban in 2001. But what is the nature of the problem, and what is the nature of the policies of the powers in Asia today in relation to the constant and the variable factors in Asian international relations?

Two important fault lines have emerged clearly in Asian geo-politics since 11 September 2001. Despite the terrible destruction wrought on innocent civilians in America on that day the situation in Afghanistan and Pakistan provided 'good' information in the sense that it helped clarify the two important fault lines. The bad news provided good insights into the nature of conflict in Asia and its geo-political consequences. My argument is that 11 September did not alter the constant elements in Asian international relations but it defined clearly the nature of the problem and the nature of the policies of the main powers. This definition is now likely to be the basic context in which the variable elements will be shaped in the foreseeable future of Asian international relations.

The first fault line is expressed by the distinction between the theory of Just War and that of Holy War. Martin Wight helps us better understand the distinction:

> The institution of the Holy War seems to have originated with the Jews, and to have reached its highest development in the Islamic *jihad*, whence it passed (though the matter is controversial) to the West as the crusade. It is distinct, in theory and practice, from other kinds of war. One is tempted to say that the Just War is the norm within the states-system, the Holy War the norm between states-systems. In the notion of the Just War, the premise is that all parties *have* their due rights, and war is the means of penalizing violation of right and ensuring restoration and restitution. It is a juridical conception, of war as the instrument of law. In the notion of the Holy War, the premise is that the true believers *are* right, and that infidels are to be converted or exterminated . . . It is religious conception, of war as the instrument of God's will, or of history.[8]

This is the real divide or the central debate of the moment in international relations. President G.W. Bush's rhetoric that 'you are either with us or against us', or that you are for terrorism or against terrorism, is a distraction in this debate. The Bush line is good public relations vis-à-vis the American public. It whips up patriotism and meets the American political standard of 'doing something'. But it does not facilitate understanding of the nature of the problem and the nature of the players and their interests. The international debate ought to focus on the dividing line between Just War and Holy War theories and practices. This is a legal as well as a cultural or a philosophical divide, and it has practical implications. The USA has a good case against Al Qaeda if it is based clearly on the Just War/Holy War distinction. However, President Bush himself muddied the American case by referring at one point to the Crusades. Bush implied that America was fighting a Holy War, though he retracted this later. This undermined the legal basis of American military action because the US acted militarily against the Taliban on the ground that it harboured Al Qaeda which had attacked America and its citizens on the basis of Jihad; and US military action was justified by the principle of Just War, not Holy War. It was also bad politics because the West lost the Crusades. The Bush administration employed brute force to confront the Jihadis when it had a better case asserting the language of the Just War and right of states under international law and the system of states. This provides for military action in defence of the state's rights whereas the system of states does not recognize the right of believers to coerce or convert Non-believers.

The American military campaign as well as the media campaign projects primarily the role of brute force. The message is that America is the number one military power in the world today and its authority must not be challenged. This language is accompanied by the language of greed. The long-term American interest is to develop its oil interests in the Central Asia/Caucasian region, and to develop its advantages in the strategic and the commercial spheres through an extended military campaign in Afghanistan and internationally against shadowy Al Qaeda enemies. Although American policy implicitly makes a distinction between Just War and Holy War doctrines, this is clouded by its political culture that stresses the importance of power, and its oil interests that stress the importance of greed. President Bush's 'axis of evil' speech in 2002 made a contrived connection between three 'rogue' nations: Iraq, Iran and North Korea; two of them, Iran and Iraq, are enemies. The connection between these three countries and Al Qaeda and terrorism, however, is not obvious.

The America-led international coalition is based on a number of pillars. First, the coalition has an implicit Just War doctrinal base, although this has not been expressed in a convincing way. Secondly, the international coalition against Al Qaeda came together on the basis of convergent interests or bargains that included blandishments or payoffs. This shows the power of expediency in inter-state relations. For example, Russia saw value in joining the US in the fight against terrorism because of its problem in Chechniya; and India saw a value in joining the US coalition because it induced America to curb Pakistani support for insurgency in Kashmir. Pakistan opted to support the US coalition because of US pressure and blandishments: it received generous aid for its support. Because expedient interests are in play, American practitioners have to maintain the points of convergence among the key coalition members.

China's case is interesting in relation to both Just War and Holy War doctrines. China selectively offers conditional support to both. China's public stance favours the importance of principles of the states' system; China is a beneficiary of the states' system, for example, its international prestige is tied to its permanent seat at the UN Security Council. It is through the states' system that China pursues its strategic and commercial interests. China also repeatedly advertises its 'principled stands' on international and regional issues. But the pattern of its strategic and economic behaviour and interests shows the importance of the language of power, greed and expediency. China's foreign policy is innovative because it adheres to both the Just War and Holy War traditions. The former because China assets its rights as a member of the states' system. The latter is evident in China's military, economic and diplomatic support of countries that promote Holy War such as Iran, Syria and Pakistan. Huntington points to the history of China–Islamic states links; he calls this the Confucian–Islamic linkage.[9] There is a pattern in Chinese foreign policy supporting Islamic regimes in South Asia and the Middle East and in giving the relationship a significant strategic and political content through missile and nuclear trade.[10] By its military supply policies, China has aided the military capabilities of groups and countries that promote Holy War in the secondary zones of international conflict, provided they are removed from China's border areas. China pursues this path in a calculated manner. It is not interested in simulating its Muslim minorities but it favours the support of Muslim countries including those like Pakistan and Afghanistan (pre-11 September) whose internal policies, military and intelligence organizations and external policies favoured the Jihad. Note here that the connection between the forces of atheism and Communism reflects an alliance of calculated strategic expediency.[11]

Before 11 September, the contradictions between the two doctrines did not affect international relations in Asia. America tolerated Islamic Jihad as long as it did not affect its physical security and strategic interests. Indeed, the American language of greed (Caucasian oil) created an incentive to seek relations with the Taliban in Afghanistan so as to facilitate American oil interests and pipeline development in the Caucasian region and Central Asia, Afghanistan-Pakistan region.[12]

America won the Cold War, so the application of American military power was not required in Afghanistan after the USSR's withdrawal from Afghanistan. However, the politics of greed was in play in the 1990s because of oil. The distinction between the Just War and Holy War doctrines was inoperative in American diplomacy in Asia at the time. However, Saudi Arabia (an American ally) was busy promoting Islamic fundamentalism in Afghanistan and Central Asia. It was working against Russian interests in Chechniya and it supported Pakistani promotion of Holy War in Afghanistan, Chechniya, Kashmir and elsewhere. Pakistan, ex-military ally of the US, was most active in promoting Holy War. It used vital parts of its state apparatus – i.e. its military and intelligence machinery – to support the cause of Islam in its liberation policies outside Pakistan. China formed the outer circle of support for the Islamic forces in the region by its support of Pakistan, Afghanistan and key Middle Eastern countries. China had a strategic plan of creating a wedge between South Asia and the Middle East. By forming a special relationship with Pakistan, it expected access to Pakistani naval bases in the Arabian Sea and the strategic coastline. Thus China sought to develop a channel for the flow of its diplomatic, economic and military influence from Tibet through Pakistan into the Arabian Sea. (It also sought to develop Myanmar as a strategic gateway that linked Yunnan to the Bay of Bengal.) This way China could outflank India through the growth of China's presence in Pakistan and Myanmar and, secondly, it could engage America as well in the Indian Ocean if China developed its naval power and projected it into the South China Seas, the Indonesia archipelago and the Bay of Bengal. From China's support for the development of submarine facilities in Gwador (in Pakistan's strategic Arabian Sea coastline) and in Myanmar's coastline, one can surmise a role for Chinese submarines in the Indian Ocean area.

11 September and the American military response changed Asian geopolitical configurations of the major and minor Asian powers. It also brought to the fore the contradictions between the Just War and the Holy War doctrines and highlighted the nature of the problem as well as the nature of the policies of the Asian states. To a discussion of these aspects I now turn.

2001 was a year of major turbulence but it is significant that, in dealing with the problem, the decision-making processes of a number of key players have produced significant shifts in Asian alignments. This demonstrates the vitality of geo-politics in the strategic behaviour of the major and the minor powers in Asia. Two standards of state behaviour are in play. The first one rejects the doctrine of the Holy War where the aim is to defeat or convert the infidel and where the world is divided between believers and non-believers; the second one validates the central position of geo-politics and national interest as the basis of state behaviour. Both standards acknowledge the value of the traditional system of states. Utopianism defined as the love of humanity or the unity of mankind stand rejected in this process. Pacifism too is irrelevant. Economic globalism and modernization are still important but international economics is no longer king; it is now tempered by a consideration of geo-politics in the thinking of even the central banks of the industrial democracies.

What was the nature of the players and the nature of the problem which led to 11 September and what has changed in the pattern of Asian alignments since then? 11 September was the result of the development of a powerful and a destructive linkage between a non-governmental organization (Al Qaeda) which had a territorial base (Afghanistan) and two powerful state sponsors – Pakistan's military and intelligence services. They had policies of intervention in Afghanistan, Central Asian and Indian affairs. The combination was inspired by the fundamentalism of the Wahabbi faith in Saudi Arabia. 11 September conveyed three messages. (1) The heart of American capitalism and American military power could be attacked successfully. (2) Holy War or Jihad was the alternative answer to the modern states' system and its conventions which legitimized corrupt Muslim regimes in the Middle East and which enabled the Western governments to sanction the oppressive and unjust policies of Israel. The modern states' system was impeding a just settlement of Muslim concerns in the Middle East. (3) Finally, the centre of gravity of Islamic politics had shifted to the Afghanistan–Pakistan–Saudi Arabian arena, away from the Mediterranean zone (Israel–Arab states).

The Bush administration's response to 11 September showed its capacity to consolidate its military presence in Central Asia (including Russia's backyard, Georgia), Afghanistan, Pakistan and the Arabian Sea. America showed an ability and a determination to integrate these hitherto separate regions (or sub-regions) into a single integrated military front. Here American political and military authority flowed under American leadership in such a way that American land power was now in synch with its sea power. The flow of power was from both ends: land to sea and sea to land. Z. Brzezinski had written in 1997 in terms of making Europe a bridgehead to Russia and Russia a bridgehead to Central Asia.[13] The dream was being realized, and more.

After 11 September, Afghanistan and Pakistan emerged as the bridgeheads in a chain of American military and diplomatic influence which extended from the Atlantic to the Indian Ocean through Central Asia. This front is expected to outlive the defeat of the Taliban and the reconstruction of Afghanistan because the war is against a shadowy organization (Al Qaeda), and terrorism is a shadowy problem. Here intelligence is the queen, military power is the king, the game is one of continuous chess that does not have a single front but there are opportunities to make different moves in different directions. Just as American forces did not leave the Gulf region after Desert Storm (1991), they are unlikely to leave the Central Asian–Afghanistan–Pakistan areas after the defeat of the Taliban in Afghanistan. The new American messages which are conveyed by its military actions and press releases, are as follows. (1) Despite the psychological blow of 11 September, America is still powerful; it has staying power. (2) Holy War is not acceptable to America and the anti-terrorism campaign which includes Muslim countries. (3) The centre of geo-political gravity is Central Asia–Afghanistan–Pakistan but now America and its allies are in the driver's seat.

The aftermath of 11 September altered the pattern of relationships in Asia. The changes affected external as well as internal relationships. That is, the effects concerned the domestic politics as well as the foreign policy of several players, and it changed the nature of the problem. Before 11 September, there was a contention between two global tendencies: economics driven globalization which supposedly tamed nationalism and military conflicts and which created the basis of human security; and fundamentalist politics which militarized social conflicts. Globalization marginalized the issue of regional and international geo-politics and was carried away by fanciful declarations about the end of the Cold War, the end of ideology, the growth of capitalism, modernization and Westernization; it also marginalized the issue of politics based on faith. Now the contention is between the doctrines of Just and Holy War. The former is located in the states' system and it is based on an expectation that fear and hatred are an inevitable part of international politics. On the other hand, the doctrine of the Holy War is a war between the believers and the non-believers. After 11 September, economic globalization is no longer the opposite of geo-politics in Western thinking. It is noteworthy that even central bankers with their fondness for market sentiment, consumer confidence and economic fundamentals publicly acknowledge the role of geo-politics in the marketplace. Realpolitik rules.

Let us summarize the main changes in the pattern of alignments post-11 September.

1. America's military campaign and its diplomatic strategy was to defeat the Taliban in Afghanistan, establish a superior military presence on the ground in Central Asia, Afghanistan and Pakistan and in the Arabian Sea, and develop an effective coalition in support of its policy to change the domestic politics and the foreign policy of the 'rogue players'. There are two tests of this proposition. The first is that Afghanistan now has a weak, manageable and legitimate political regime in the form of an administration headed by an articulate man, Hamid Karzai; and the policy aim is to reconstruct Afghanistan into a modern Muslim state and society which conceivably could function as a role model for the Middle East. The second is even more significant. Following September 11th, the military regime in Pakistan has been under relentless American pressure (aided by Indian diplomatic and military pressure) to shut down the operation of the Pakistani intelligence organization which was the 'state within the state' and the agency to promote terrorism in Afghanistan and Indian border areas including Kashmir. There is compelling evidence to show the complicity of the Pakistani Inter-Services organization (ISI) as the premier supporter of terrorism in the region. In this context, it is significant that President Musharraf agreed in a public address on 12 January 2002 to roll back the Pakistani government's support of Jihad. These changes were achieved between September 2001 and February 2002.[14] It is significant that such monumental changes were achieved in a short time span as a result of US efforts.

2. The second set of changes lies in the transformation of US–India strategic relationship. India made important intelligence inputs into American decision-making after September 11th and these showed the links between Pakistani-based Al Qaeda operatives who were active in Afghanistan, Kashmir and Central Asia. Here the two events – Indian nuclear and missile tests and 11 September – facilitated the institutional development of a dialogue and linkages between the American and the Indian armed forces. Now the scale of military cooperation is significant.[15] Three developments – a major change in Indian strategic behaviour (the nuclear and missile tests), a major change in the international environment (the 11 September attack) and the Bush administration concern about China's strategic capabilities and intentions – facilitated the strategic convergence of interests between the two countries. These developments showed that, even though America was the No. 1 power in the world, the strategic and the diplomatic space of

middle-tiered countries like India had also increased. The Indo-US strategic dialogue recognizes that India sits astride the lines of sea communications in a critical part of the Indian Ocean, that it has an influence and an ability to manage China's military pressures and diplomatic push in the Himalayan region, as well as in India's strategic flanks (Pakistan, Myanmar), and in South East Asia; and that India along with the US can exert pressure on the military regime in Pakistan to reform itself and make Pakistan a stable society and a partner of democracy and regional security. Pakistan has an importance of its own in American and Indian strategic thinking and policy because Afghanistan is expected to remain internally divided and weak due to the pattern of warlordism in its history and current politics; and the interim government is not likely to develop its authority over Afghanistan outside Kabul (which itself is problematic). Both the US and India have a stake in President Musharraf's ability to reform Pakistani state and society and to create conditions for Pakistani internal stability and growth.

3. The third change was a result of the strengthened American position in the region and the changing pattern of alignments. The realignment of relations among the US, Russia and India on the basis of a common course against international terrorism affected China's position in Asia. America has been acting in a geo-political way since 11 September. It has strengthened its military presence on the ground and now the geographical reach of its military power extends from the Arabian Sea to Pakistan, Afghanistan and key Central Asian republics (where America has acquired military bases and diplomatic support). Its anti-terrorism fight has been extended to Georgia (a Russian sphere). Simultaneously, America developed its strategic policies in three spheres. Its decision to scrap the ABM Treaty is firm, as is the decision to mount a missile defence and to scrap the dependence on mutual assured destruction and deterrence. It will store, not scrap, its nuclear arsenal and thus it will maintain its margin of nuclear safety through storage. Recently America and Russia negotiated reductions in the US and Russian nuclear capabilities, and Russia is now a NATO partner. Finally, a first-strike policy involving nuclear weapons against non-nuclear targets has been accepted. America clearly seeks to shape the international balance by maintaining a margin of strength in conventional and nuclear/missile/space armaments. However, this does not constitute unipolarity because the desire for a margin of strength implies that the US no longer has a monopoly over weaponry and it cannot function in a detached way vis-à-vis major and minor powers in Asia. With a number of major and minor powers in the strategic picture, America needs a strategy to maintain a pattern of relationships with friends and rivals in the Asian sphere. While anti-terrorism is an obvious point of convergence in the US-led international coalition, other strategies are being formed to build links with non-traditional partners such as India. There is a strong move to build a partnership with India and Japan on the issue of sea lane security; this involves joint patrolling of the seas, especially in the crowded sea lanes from the South China Seas to the Persian Gulf. This

reflects a concern with China's naval development and its military intentions.

The strengthened US position in the region is most evident in the dominance of the US in Afghanistani and Pakistani politics and external policies. President Musharraf is now under a clear obligation to dismantle the Jihadi infrastructure within Pakistan and to abandon the freedom struggle in Kashmir. In effect, President Musharraf's Pakistan rented its airspace for American dollars (a replaceable commodity) because of the fear of American punishment (and secondarily, because of the fear of Indian punishment). As a result, Pakistan's space in Afghanistan and Indian affairs has shrunk considerably, America's has grown significantly, and India along with Japan and several Asian countries have discovered opportunities to enlarge their strategic space in Asian international relations. Australia and South Korea sent forces to the region in response to 11 September. The Japanese Diet has been busy changing Japanese laws. It passed the Anti-Terrorism Special Measures Act, SDF Amendment Act, Maritime Security Agency Amendment Act, and now Japanese military forces can legitimately go into the Indian Ocean in aid of the anti-terrorism international coalition. During the Second World War, the geographical reach of the Japanese Army extended to the Burma jungles. Now the Japanese navy is in the Indian Ocean along with the American and other allied navies. 11 September and its aftermath were 'good' in expanding the space of middle-tiered countries in Asia and the Indian Ocean area.

The changes have significant implications for the international position and the pattern of relationships among Asian countries and for defining the structure of power. That is, the distribution of power as well as the pattern of relations has been recast along geo-political lines. The expansion of China's strategic and commercial influence into Central Asian areas has been halted by the American ascendancy and cooperation with Russia in these areas. Now China's manœuvrability is limited to the Korean peninsula, South East Asia where China is promoting a free trade zone, the Taiwan straits and the South China Seas (where China competes with the American and Taiwan navies and other influences and where Japanese and Indian interests are engaged). China still has significant influence in South Asia. It is dumping economic goods into the Indian market via Nepal and it continues to develop a military, commercial and cultural presence in Myanmar. Should it succeed, it will be able to develop a wedge between South and South East Asia with itself as the premier external power. China still seeks to promote an American interest in an Indo-Pakistani balance but this appears to be a losing battle because the idea no longer appeals to the American political establishment. Moreover, China's special position within Pakistan has been degraded. Musharraf now turns to America, not China for material and moral support. Chinese assets in Pakistan – Chinese conventional armament, and its nuclear and missile supplies – are frozen assets; they are not usable in the present crisis. There is little that Beijing can offer Pakistan other than platitudes about regional peace and peace through dialogue. China's dream to acquire a deep water port in Gwador, in the strategic coastline between the Arabian Sea and the Persian Gulf, is in tatters because major Pakistani military facilities are now under effective American control – physical and/or diplomatic. Hence, the importance of the Karakoram Highway as the Chinese gateway to the Arabian Sea has been degraded by post-11 September developments. Furthermore, India retains its capacity to escalate the level of violence against Pakistan, but China cannot realistically expect to do so with India. Pakistan can continue its support of insurgency and civil violence in India but it cannot alter the balance of power (an imbalance) between the two. Moreover, it is debatable if the American political establishment sees China as a factor for regional stability in the volatile Afghanistan–Pakistan area. The mainstream Indian political establishment does not because China is for Chinese interests only, which require that India be kept on edge by Pakistan and others.

Asia now has reached a defining moment that revolves around three central propositions and questions. First, was 11 September, a manifestation of a divide between Just War and Holy War doctrines? My view is that the divide is deep-seated, it has not been resolved even by the defeat of the Taliban in Afghanistan and the division still exists. 11 September brought the issue into the open and showed that it is rooted in international history and cultural–political conflicts. It showed that it has a military manifestation that engages the attention and the strategies of major as well as minor powers in the primary as well as the secondary zones of international conflict. (Asia including Russia and Central Asia, the US and Middle East are the primary zones; and Europe is the secondary zone.) This great divide surfaced following the end of the Cold War – when the major controversies of international relations were presumed to have been settled. Islamic Jihad in Middle East and Asia is at serious odds with globalization, democracy, Westernization, modernization and US policies in the Middle East. The proposition is that the debate between these approaches and constituencies is unsettled. It is important because the constituencies are well entrenched – like Forbidden Cities in Imperial China where each such city had its internal hierarchy, rules, decision-making process and political culture.

Secondly, within Asia, the issue of democracy and autonomy divides China from the rest of Asia. Democracy and regional autonomy should be on the Chinese agenda for several reasons. (1) Following the collapse of the one-party state in a large area like Soviet Russia, Chinese politics ought to recognize the impermanence of one-party or Communist-Party-dominated political system. *Cultural forces* exist within China, such as the demand for political and religious freedom. They require an acknowledgement of the importance of political pluralism and policies that accommodate diversity. Here conflict of social and political ideas and interests is expected. (2) *Economic development* of regions in China will inevitably generate linkages between the prosperous regions and their international partners. Such linkages affect the agendas of the different Chinese constituencies: economic, political and social reformers seek modernization and peaceful internal change within China; the military planners seek military preparations to deal with external and internal problems; and finally, the Party commissars seek ideological 'top to bottom' controls and purity. (3) Most Asian countries have embraced the idea of representative government, they either follow it or aspire to do so. (4) Finally, there is now an emergent view that Middle Eastern states too need to embrace the principles and process of democracy as the way to manage internal controversies and to build internal legitimacy. My question is: will democracy become the basis for the development of a league of democracies that extend from Israel to Japan and will such a league emerge as the long-term solution to the problem of international conflict? The proposition is that this remains a realistic possibility but that a time frame cannot be specified for its consummation.

Thirdly and finally, the staples or the constants of modern Asian international relations – Asian nationalism, regionalism, geo-politics and multipolarity – are entrenched and they provide the framework for the distribution of power and the pattern of relationships in Asia. As Owen Lattimore wisely pointed out in 1949, America will have to negotiate with the Asians. Lattimore's prediction has been proven true because now America negotiates with the major and the minor powers in Asia – from Russia to China, India, Japan, North Korea among others. It does so as a pragmatist; it recognizes the realities and it does not have ideological fixations. Samual Huntington defined his work as a 'Clash of Civilizations', and by projecting the theme 'West and the Rest',[16] he appeared to show his pessimism about the future of American power. America's ability to negotiate realistically with major and minor Asian powers shows its willingness to acknowledge the sensitivities of lesser but nonetheless essential powers and its determination to induce them to recognize American sensitivities as well. In the current phase of Asian international relations, the issue is no longer 'America, West and the Rest'. Judging by the military and diplomatic policies of the Asian major powers, the issue appears to be cast in terms of 'China and the Rest in Asia Now'. This is a theme, it is not my prediction or preference. The suggestion is that it is very much in China's interest to abandon its Middle Kingdom mentality and shun the search for a China-centric Asian international system which puts China at odds with the rest of Asia.

10 From conflict to conflict resolution

An outline of the process

Introduction

Asian history and politics offer a thick inventory of conflicts and instability in practically all their parts. At the same time, durable coerced and/or voluntary linkages in regional politics in North East, South and South East Asia have emerged, and there is both 'regional power formation' (around regional great powers) and 'conflict formation' as well within regions. As a result of the entrenchment of these developments since 1945, Asians are now exploring ways to facilitate conflict resolution in regions of conflict. The two Koreas are engaged in a serious multidimensional dialogue. In 2001, India and Pakistan started a thorough dialogue and even though the two governments failed to reach a breakthrough in the first summit, consultations among Indian and Pakistani experts in the fields of security studies, business, press and citizens' groups were able to identify numerous areas of commonality where significance linkages could reduce the legacy of bitterness, hatred and mistrust.[1] These dialogues are stimulated and sustained by regional players and are conducted with an awareness of a number of salient regional circumstances. (1) Leaders preside over fragile domestic coalitions with deep divisions among local hawks, doves and herds; hence there are ever-present internal vetoes and spoilers who have a strong and historically entrenched interest in instability rather than peace-making. (2) The issues are complex and the challenge is to establish domestic as well as inter-state bargains that facilitate peace-making. (3) The challenge is to convert war situations into military truces, to extend the cease-fires in time as well as geographical scope and, finally, to convert cease-fires into negotiated political settlements. The negotiations about the future of the Korean peninsula as well as the Indian subcontinent are being pursued along these lines although the case histories vary. The test that Asian regions (sub-regions) are developing along these lines lies not simply in the formal agreements that are made. Agreements beg the question whether or not they are being implemented. So an agreement is a useful sign of inter-state cooperation but it is not a sufficient sign. The actual pattern of behaviour, whether it is aggressive or restrained, and whether shared norms exist to regulate inter-state behaviour, is significant.

The pattern of behaviour reveals the scope and nature of the relationship. However, written agreements are significant because they create public commitments which are costly to break.

Essential steps in rapprochement

My study of past successful rapprochement agreements between bitter enemies indicates that rapprochement is a process which requires imagination, planning and courage.[2] Melting ice between the enemy states is not easy. The question is how do enemies come together? How do they overcome distrust, fear, anger and bitterness? How do they overcome war, military tension and propaganda? My assumption is that political will is not enough. Will can not overcome obstacles, rather strategies have to be developed to do so.

In devising the strategies, four elements must be considered. The leadership must agree that confrontation is costly and counter-productive. They must agree that there can be mutual gain through cooperation. They must agree the geo-political realities cannot be changed by coercive means. The other three elements deal with non-geo-political issues. They emphasize the importance of facilitating the flow of people, ideas and economic goods and reducing the flow of coercive action and military movement across the borders. With the rapprochement efforts, the idea is to facilitate the positive flows and to create a framework to deal with the fundamental clash of objectives in certain areas. So the strategy should be to de-link the hard core problem(s) from other issues and to realize that a military stalemate and a catalytic event is important to convince the military practitioners about the futility of a war. Only when consciousness of stalemate and growing costs sinks in the mind of the leaders do they develop the mood to negotiate.

There are several key elements that make for success in a rapprochement process. The first is to break up a big issue into smaller parts. Second, for success it is important at all times to maintain a high level political control over the process and to have few participants in the decision-making cycle. Third, it is very important *initially* to minimize the role of bureaucracy. Bureaucracies have entrenched points of view that reflect the culture of the service and the history of the organization. Also bureaucracies have particular mandates and by training and inclination bureaucrats will perform their duties according to these mandates. A bureaucracy can live with manageable conflicts or manageable instability and as long as it is manageable it is not necessary to end it. So the political settlement must be pushed by the top leadership and by social forces. Otherwise the negotiations can get mired in bureaucratic politics. Bureaucracy functions within defined parameters and the paradigm shift has to come from outside the bureaucratic world. However, bureaucracies are important later in the negotiations as they have the training as diplomatic technicians to formulate the political agreement in legal and diplomatic terms. Fourthly, in successful negotiations in the past back door channels have been an important method of communication to explore new ideas, to formulate alternative proposals that may originate from non-governmental sources and that may be projected into inter-governmental negotiations. Fifthly, unilateral moves with or without expectation of reciprocity can be helpful. They are signs of intent to seek rapprochement. Even if there is no formal agreement, they create a norm and if there is a reciprocal agreement, they create a mutual commitment. Such commitments are valuable because there are costs attached to breaking a norm or an agreement. So creating a network of agreements on specific issues adds value in creating a web which can be broken at a cost. At the same time in addition to the psychological values of unilateral moves, they can achieve cooperation on specific issues if they deal with smaller significant steps. Sixthly, it is not helpful to practise ambiguity. Let the other side know what is do-able, what requires further study, and what is absolutely non-negotiable. It is better to be up front rather than to be vague. In modern international negotiations, especially in the West, silence can mean consent. So it is better not to be silent even if this means a disagreement.

Figure 10.1 outlines the mix of structural factors which favour war-making, and then the factors which facilitate peace-making. It is based on the premise that the initiative for war-making comes from the dissatisfied state which possesses both motivation and the means to fight if its demands are not satisfied peacefully. Stage I outlines the factors which promote war if Stage I military encounter is inconclusive. It produces an intermediate condition which alters the cohesiveness of the four structural factors in Stage I but the alteration is not a turning point from war-making to peace-making. It represents a change but it is not sufficient to produce peace-making. In Stage II, structural factors favour initiation of peace-making process. In Stage III, a peace settlement is negotiated and it takes effect.

This combination (A + B + C + D) results in war (e.g. Indo–Pakistani Wars; Korean War). If war results in a military stalemate, i.e. there is no clear winner or loser, and structural factors remain unchanged, Stage I is likely to repeat itself. However, if any of the structural factors change then the process is described as the ‘intermediate condition’.

Intermediate condition between Stage I and Stage II

Even if war ends in stalemate (i.e. no clear winners/losers) the military stalemate may induce domestic changes, as follows.

Polarity emerges within state and society about the validity of ideologies (causes) in conflict. The polarity is between (A) the hawks, whose beliefs in the role of war for liberation are reinforced by the military stalemate; (B) the doves, who think that the method of war in the cause of liberation requires rethinking; (C) the herds, who are passive observers, are indifferent to the ideological cause and the war method, or who will eventually follow the winning faction. Here the local ‘hawks’ and the silent ‘herds’ constitute the significant majority that controls the state’s policy agenda as well as its resources. The

Stage I: Structural Factors Favouring War-Making						
(A)	+	(B)	+	(C)	+	(D)
When conflictual ideologies, beliefs, grievances, passions are entrenched, there is high motivation towards irredentism and war.		When domestic coalitions are fragile with limited legitimacy war-making helps strengthen internal legitimacy, and there is an incentive to engage in war-making.		If the local state has limited military strength and international alliance support is available to achieve a regional military balance, and the external powers support local irredentism, then opportunity to wage war exists because of favourable international circumstances.		When distribution of military strength is unclear, and there is expectation of military victory, that increases the weight of the war faction in domestic policies.

Figure 10.1 From war-making to peace-making

'doves' may be located in the policy establishment and/or it may be a non-governmental citizen group. Either way, it represents the minority point of view in the internal balance of power. Its importance lies in the emergence of a 'peace' constituency in a war-like state/societal set-up, and its interface with international forces that favour peace-making. The 'peace' constituency functions in a set of two-dimensional relationships. The first, is a relationship of polarity or conflict with the 'hawks' within its own state and society. The second is a relationship of affinity vis-à-vis the 'peace' constituency in the international sphere. However, the structure of all relationships is more than these relationships. Figure 10.2 shows the interface between the international allies of the hawks and the international opponents of the domestic hawks. Shifts in international alignments usually take shape in the intermediate condition and they affect the internal balance of power. This shift is the basis of Stages II and III. The intermediate condition facilitates Stage II (peace-making) to the extent it weakens the public identification with the war constituency in a country. It is a necessary condition for Stage II but it is not sufficient. Changes in the structural factors are required to move a relationship of conflict into the second stage.

Stage II requires two major changes to facilitate the initiation of a peace-making dialogue. First, there must be a clear winner/loser following war, and an awareness that war is counter-productive, it is costly, it is unwinnable and that the political aim cannot be achieved by military means. Such an awareness and an intense and a public internal debate reinforces the hawks–doves–herds polarity within a country's system of conflict. Stage II

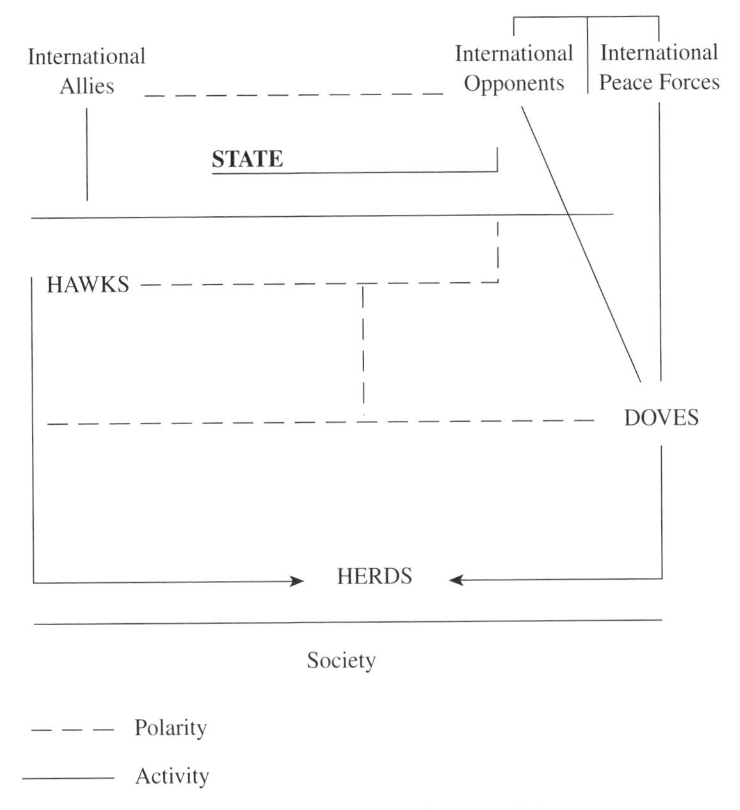

Figure 10.2 Inconclusive shifts in the intermediate condition

becomes possible when the internal balance of power begins to shift in favour of the doves and the herds, and asymmetry in the distribution of regional military power is clearly established in favour of the benign regional hegemon or regional great power. The latter eliminates an expectation of gain through war.

Second, there must be a significant adjustment in the international alliance(s) of a regional warrior or the irredentist state, so that it cannot borrow usable external power to balance the power of a regional great power or the opposing alliance. Critical here is the actual ability and willingness of the external power to balance the regional great power in a military crisis. The structural matrix has changed if such a commitment or ability is not clearly evident in a crisis.

However, State II is still not enough for a negotiated peace settlement. Note that significant changes have occurred in structural factors (A), (C) and (D) in comparing stages I and II but, until the peace-making constituency becomes dominant on *all* sides of a regional conflict, the internal vetoes will be in a position to sabotage the agreement and its implementation.

This road map applies generally to all major regional conflicts in Asia today. It applies to the major conflict systems in Asia (e.g. India–Pakistan, Sino-Indian, the Korean peninsula, and Sino-Taiwan). However, creative diplomacy is required to convert this general plan into negotiating opportunities for peace-making in Asia.

This negotiating process is relevant in the context of structural factors which represent the case history of a regional conflict. Figure 10.1 is in three stages. The first state is a general representation of structural factors which induce or favour war-making. There is an intermediate condition between the first and the second stage. The second stage is a general representation of structural factors which favour the initiation of the peace-making process. Stage III, however, is critical to achieve peace, i.e. an equilibrium that is measured by the existence of a permanent and a negotiated peace settlement.

Notes

1 Introduction

1 Gunnar Myrdal, *An Approach to the Asian Drama*, New York: Vintage Book Edition, 1970, pp. 12–13.
2 Richard Wright, *White Man Listen!*, New York: Doubleday and Co., 1957, p. 64.
3 R. Vayrynen, 'Economic and Military Position of the Regional Power Centres', *Journal of Peace Research*, 16/4 (1979), 349–69, and 'Regional Conflict Formations: An Intractable Problem of International Relations', *Journal of Conflict* Research, 21/4 (1984), 337–58.
4 On subordinate and sub-systemic regions and regionalism see the following: William I. Zartman, 'Africa as a Subordinate State System in International Relations', *International Organization*, 21 (Summer 1967), 545–64; Larry W. Bowman, 'The Subordinate State System of Southern Africa', *International Studies Quarterly*, 12 (September 1968), 231–62; Leonard Binder, 'The Middle East as a Subordinate International System', *World Politics*, 10 (April 1958), 408–29; Michael Brecher, 'International Relations and Asian Studies: The Subordinate System of Southern Asia', *World Politics*, 15 (January 1963), 213–35; George Modelski, 'International Relations and Area Studies; the Case of South East Asia', *International Relations*, 2 (April 1961), 143-55; Thomas Hodgkin, 'The New West African State System', *University of Toronto Quarterly*, 31 (October 1961), 74–82; Bruce M. Russet, *International Regions and International System,* Chicago: Rand, McNally, 1967; Joseph S. Nye, Jr., *International Regionalism,* Boston: Little, Brown, 1968; Raimo Vayrynen, 'Regional Conflict Formations: An Intractable Problem of International Relations', *Journal of Peace Research*, 21/4 (1984), 337–60.
5 Martin Wight, *Power Politics,* New York: Penguin Books, 1979, ch. 15, pp. 157–67.
6 Barry Buzan, *People, States and Fear*, 2nd edn, Boulder: Lynne Rienner, 1991, ch. 5.
7 International Strategic Studies, CIISS, Beijing, December 1994.
8 See SIPRI Yearbook, 1994–5, and the work of the Carnegie Endowment of International Peace, the Monterrey Institute of International Studies, the Mountbatten Centre at the University of Southampton, the *Non-Proliferation Brief*, and the now defunct Canadian Centre for Global Security. Also see 'CIA Special Cell to Monitor South Asia', New York,: *India Abroad*, (23 March 2001), 10.
9 P. Dibb, *Towards a New Balance of Power in Asia*, Adelphi Paper No. 295, IISS, Oxford: OUP, 1995.
10 Cited in T.H. Etzold and J.L. Lewis, eds., *Containment: Documents on American Policy and Strategy, 1945-50*, New York: Columbia University Press 1978, pp. 252–3.

11 D.S. Zagoria, 'The Changing US Role in Asian Security in the 1990''s, in S.W. Simon, ed., *East Asia Security in the Post-Cold War Era*, New York: M.E. Sharpe, 1993, pp. 46–54 and 23.
12 P.H.B. Goodwin, 'China's Asian Policy in the 1900s', in Simon, *East Asia Security*, pp. 119, 129, 142–3.
13 Wight, *Power Politics*, pp. 42–43.
14 M. Yahuda, *The International Politics of the Asia–Pacific*, 1945–1995, London: Routledge, 1996, preface, and pp. 5–6.
15 Wight, *Power Politics*, pp. 257–8.
16 Ibid., ch. 16.
17 Dibb, 'Towards a New Balance of Power', p. 4.
18 Barry Buzan, *People, States, Fear*, 2nd edn, Boulder: Lynne Rienner, 1991, ch. 5.
19 Owen Lattimore, *The Situation in Asia*, Boston: Little Brown & Co., 1949, pp. 3–4, 36.
20 In L. Freedman, ed., *War*, Oxford University Press, 1994, 102–103. My emphasis. These points are from S. Brown, *The Causes and Prevention of War*, New York: St Martin's Press, 1987, 1st edn. The third problem is not mentioned in *The Causes and Prevention of War*, New York: St Martin's Press, 2nd edn, 1994.
21 *The Cold War in Asia*, Cold War International history Project Bulletin, Woodrow Wilson International Centre for Scholars, Washington DC (Winter 1995–6, issues 6–7.
22 Great powers usually define their relations by compromise and compensation when threat or intervention fails. See Wight, *Power Politics*, chs. 17–18.
23 See n. 4.
24 For recent examples, see S. Harris, 'The Economic Aspects of Security in the Asia–Pacific Regions', in D. Ball, ed., *The Transformation of Security in the Asia–Pacific Region*, London: Frank Cass, 1996, pp. 32–51; and S. Chan, 'Regime Transition in the Asia/Pacific Region', in D. Ball, pp. 52–67. For dismissals of international economics as a challenge to the autonomy and primary of international politics in international history, see Wight, *Power Politics*, 2nd edn, Harmondsworth: Penguin Books, 1986., pp. 16–17. Also, there is a realist view of inter-dependence. While noting its impact, D. Ball also notes that in Asia–Pacific (1) countries are dependent on sea lanes for commerce (hence the value of maritime security), (2) economic growth offers more resources for military modernization, and (3) interdependence can spread security problems. See Ball's introduction, in Ball, *Transformation of Security*, 1–2.

2 The meaning and importance of 'Asia' in international history and international politics

1 A geo-strategic region has globe-influencing characteristics and functions. See S.B. Cohen, *Geography and Politics in a World Divided*, 2nd edn, New York: Oxford University Press, 1973. Eurasia deals with the international politics of Russia, China, the Far East, Central Asia, the Indian subcontinent, the Persian Gulf, South East Asia and the islands in the Pacific including Japan and Australia. 'Eurasia' is still in usage, e.g. in the recent writings of Z. Brzezinski.
2 For Russia's historical expansionism, see Louis J. Halle, *The Cold War as History*, New York: Harper and Row, 1967, ch. 2; and Owen Lattimore, *The Situation in Asia*, Boston: Little Brown, 1949, ch. 5. For the 'great game' in the 19th century (British–Russian rivalry), see Martin Wight, *Power Politics*, New York: Viking Penguin, 1979, 1986, ch 15. Wight also explains the relational aspect of policies and interests of the powers, ibid., ch. 15, p. 157. For the distinction between 'land' and 'sea power', ibid., ch. 6. Cohen, *Geography and Politics*, explains the fundamental differences in the orientations of the 'continental' and the 'maritime' worlds.

3 Geoffrey Fairbairns offers an insightful discussion of the principles of the British Empire in *Revolutionary Guerrilla Warfare*, Harmondsworth: Penguin Books, 1974, ch. 1, esp. pp. 46–64. See also K.M. Panniker, *Asia and Western Dominance*, London: George Allen Unwin, 1953, 1959.
4 Theodore Geiger, *The Conflicted Relationship*, New York: McGraw Hill, 1967.
5 For instance, Michael Yahuda asserts coupling and 'de-coupling' between the international powers and Asian regions in *The International Politics of the Asia–Pacific, 1945–95*, London: Routledge, 1996. This book, however, explains why 'coupling' is unavoidable in contemporary international relations since 1945.
6 See Adda B. Bozeman, *Politics and Culture in International History*, Princeton, NJ: Princeton University Press, 1960. Also see F.S.C. Northrop, *The Meeting of East and West*, New York: Macmillan Co., 1946. Samuel Huntington's *The Clash of Civilizations and the Remaking of World Order*, New York: Simon & Schuster, 1996, points to the role of civilizational differences in international conflict. A.B. Bozeman and K.L. Holsti take Chinese and Indian foreign policy experiences seriously but they are the exception in Western literature. For instance, in his seminal work *The Systems of States*, Leicester: Leicester University Press, 1977, Martin Wight ignores Asian experiences and influences in his study of states' system and international society.
7 See G.H. Jansen, *Militant Islam*, London: Pan Books, 1974: Peter Mansfield, *The Arabs*, New York: Penguin, 1981.
8 Pannikar, *Asia and Western Dominance*.
9 Fairbairns, *Revolutionary Guerrilla Warfare*. See Appendix I on Lawrence of Arabia; also Mansfield, *The Arabs*. For the British methods and altitudes that led to the conquest of India, see Phillip Mason, *Men Who Rule India*, London: Pan Books, 1985, abridged edn).
10 Northrop, *Meeting of East and West*, p. 1.
11 For Asian Nationalism and multipolarity, see Lattimore, *Situation in Asia*, ch. 4 and 6.
12 Northrop, *Meeting of East and West*, p. 2.
13 Ibid., p. 3.
14 Selig S. Harrison, *The Widening Gulf: Asian Nationalism and American Policy*, New York: Free Press, 1978.
15 Northrop, *Meeting of East and West*, p. 434.
16 Cited ibid., p. 413.
17 This point draws on Bozeman, *Politics and Culture*.
18 Lattimore, *Situation in Asia*, pp. 29–30.
19 Fairbairns, *Revolutionary Guerrilla Warfare*, ch. 2 and Wight, *Power Politics*, Ch. 7, p. 81.
20 The discussion about the Western African, Leninist and Islamic worlds draws heavily on Bozeman, *Politics and Culture*, introduction to 2nd edn.

3 Evolving international structures in Asia–Pacific and the Indian Ocean areas

1 'Rogues' play an important role in US foreign affairs. Today, Iran, Iraq, Libya, Cuba (and until recently North Korea) are all-purpose public rogues. During the Cold War, the Communist states, especially the USSR, were the main rogues. A rogue refuses to follow accepted standards of behaviour or an international norm, e.g. non-proliferation. By this definition, India, Pakistan and Israel are also rogues. For an examination of the use and misuse of 'anti-rogue diplomacy', see my article 'Rogue States and the International Nuclear Order', *International Journal* (Canadian Institute of International Affairs, Toronto, Summer 1996).
2 IISS, *Strategic Survey* 1994/95 (Oxford, Oxford University Press for IISS, May

1995), p. 5, expresses a concern about drift in US policy.

3 R. Vayrynen and M. Wight are two prominent writers who take this category of 'power' seriously. See Wight, *Power Politics*, ed. Hedley Bull and C. Holbraad, Harmondsworth: Penguin, 1979, ch. 5 and appendix 1; and R. Vayrynen, 'Economic and Military Position of the Regional Power Centers', *Journal of Peach Research*, 16/4 (1979), 349–69.
4 Wight, *Power Politics*, especially chs. 7–8, 11–13 and 17–18; and his *Systems of States,* Leicester: Leicester University Press, 1977, introduction by Hedley Bull.
5 Wight, *Power Politics*, p. 27.
6 Ibid., pp. 34–37.
7 Ibid., p. 41.
8 Ibid., pp. 50–2.
9 Ibid., pp. 63–6 and 298–9.
10 Ibid., p. 48.
11 Ibid.
12 Ibid., p. 53.
13 IISS, *Strategic Survey 1994/95*, pp. 5–8 and 63.
14 H. Williams Brands, *The United States in the World*, vol. 2, Boston, MA: Houghton Mifflin, 1994, p. 404.
15 Vice Chairman Shi Xia and Senior Research Fellow Zhu Chun, 'Retrospects and Prospects of the situation in the Asia–Pacific Region and the World', *International Strategic Studies* (CIISS, Beijing), 1 (March 1995), 2–3.
16 Wight, *Power Politics*, pp. 42–3.
17 Hugh Tinker, *Men who Overturned Empires*, London: Macmillan, 1987, ch. 1. F.S. Northedge and M.J. Grieve, *A Hundred Years of International Relations*, London: Duckworth, 1971, is a reliable source.
18 F.S. Northedge, T*he Foreign Policies of the Powers*, London: Faber & Faber, 1968, ch. 5.
19 Lattimore, *Situation in Asia*, p. 123, talks about Japan double-crossing the USA.
20 See especially recent publications by the IISS (London) and the CIIS (Beijing).
21 Dibb, 'Towards a New Balance of Power', p 3.
22 Ibid., pp. 10, 11, 15, 23–38.
23 Ibid., p. 70.
24 Wight, *Power Politics*, ch. 16.
25 Dibb, 'Towards a New Balance of Power', p. 53.
26 Ibid., p. 41.
27 'Can the Chinese Army Win the Next War', and a commentary by Ross Munro, 'Eavesdropping on the Chinese Military', *Orbis*, 38/3 (summer 1994), 355–72; and M.B. Zinger, 'The development of Indian Naval Strategy since 1972', *Contemporary South Asia*, 2/3 (1993), 351–5 assess Chinese thinking and strategies.
28 I have outlined the importance of consent in A. Kapur, 'The Indian Subcontinent: The Contemporary Structure of Power and the Development of Power Relations', *Asian Survey*, 28/7 (July 1988), 693–710; and A. Kapur with A.J. Wilson, *The Foreign Policies of India and her Neighbours*, London: Macmillan, 1996.

4 Tied together by power politics and notional realities: the great powers in Asia in the 19th and 20th centuries

1 Cohen, *Geography and Politics*, pp.208–9.
2 Ibid.
3 R.H. Jackson and A. James, eds, *States in a Changing World*, Oxford: Clarendon Press, 1993.
4 Wight, *Power Politics*, pp. 160–1.

5 Lamb, *Asian Frontiers, Studies in a Continuing Problem*, pp. 4–6.
6 Wight, *Power Politics*, p. 157.
7 Ibid.
8 Ibid., p. 158.
9 Mason, *Men who Ruled India*.
10 Wight, *Power Politics*, pp. 159–60.
11 Ibid., p. 68.
12 Ibid., p. 27.
13 Fairbairns, *Revolutionary Guerrilla Warfare*, p. 16.
14 Wight, *Power Politics*, esp. ch. 21.
15 Lattimore, *Situation in Asia*, p. 217, and generally ch. 10.
16 L.J. Halle, *Cold War as History*, p. 160.
17 Bozeman, *Politics and Culture*, p. xxxv.
18 Ibid., p. xxxii.
19 Henry Kissinger, *Diplomacy*, New York: Simon & Schuster, 1994, pp. 23, 26, 805, 808–9, 826–8.
20 Bozeman, *Politics and Culture*, p. xxxvii.
21 On strategic loops, see Lattimore, *Situation in Asia*, p. 45.
22 This section draws heavily on Lattimore, *Situation in Asia* and *Solution in Asia*, London: Cresset Press, 1945, ch. 7.

5 The situation in America and Asia and the growth of regionalism in Asia: an overview

1 Zbrigniew Brzezinski, *The Grand Chessboard*, New York: Basic Books, 1997, ch. 2.
2 Ibid., p. 29.
3 Ibid., pp. 29, 197, 98 and 210.
4 Halle, *Cold War as History*, pp. 412–13, 264; also see pp. 316–17 about the role of vested interests in particular foreign policies.
5 Owen Lattimore, *Solutions in Asia*, p. 106.
6 This section draws on several news analyses by Stratfor. (*http://www.stratfor.com*).
7 See the 'Guidelines for Japan–U.S. Defence Cooperation: Ministry of Foreign Affairs, of Japan'; 'The Japan-U.S. Defence Cooperation', Ministry of Foreign Affairs of Japan: and 'Treaty of Mutual Cooperation and Security Between Japan and the United States of America'.
8 Samuel P. Huntington, *The Clash of Civilizations and the Remaking of World Order*, New York: Simon & Schuster, 1996.
9 Stephen Walt, 'Testing Theories of Alliance Formations: The Case of Southwest Asia', *International Organization*, 42/2 (Spring 1988).
10 A. Kapur, and A.J. Wilson, *Foreign Policies of India and her Neighbours*, London: Macmillan and New York: St Martins Press, 1996, chs. 2 and 5.
11 Seyom Brown, *Causes and Prevention of War*, my emphasis.
12 For instance in the Indo-Pakistan Vajpayee-Musharraf Summit in Agra on 14–16 July 2001, China played an instrumental role in encouraging the failure by the two sides to agree to a joint statement. Clearly, Indo-Pakistani reconciliation is not in China's interest. Confidential interviews with Indian and Pakistani sources, Delhi and Agra, 10–15 July 2001.
13 Martin Wight, *Power Politics*, UK, 1979 edn, ch. 15.
14 A.B. Bozeman, *Politics and Culture in International History*, 2nd ed., London: Transaction Publishers, 1994.

6 Multipolarity in Asian regions 1940s–2000: an overview

1 Robert Gilpin, 'Hegemonic War and International Change', in L. Freedman, ed., *War*, New York: Oxford University Press, 1994, p. 94.
2 International Institute for Strategic Studies, *Strategic Survey, 2000–2001*, p. 1991.
3 Z.A. Brzezinski, *The Grand Chessboard*, p. 209.
4 Kissinger, Henry, *Diplomacy*, New York: Simon & Schuster, 1994, pp. 809–10, 23.

7 Multipolarity during the Cold War

1 *The Cold War in Asia*, Woodrow Wilson International Center for Scholars, Washington, DC (Winter issues 6–7, 1995/6).
2 Morris Jones, 'South Asia' in R.H. Jackson and A. James, eds., Oxford: Clarendon Press, 1993, p. 157.
3 Ibid., p. 170.
4 A. Buchan, *The End of the Post War Era*, London: Weidenfeld & Nicolson: 1974, p. 294.

8 Regional multipolarity after the end of the Cold War

The reader is referred to a number of useful sources.

1 **BBC (British Broadcasting Corporation) Website** <http:/news.bbc.co.uk/>
This website is an excellent source of current information about international politics. On specific country information go to 'Country Profile' section: <http://news.bbc.co.uk/2/shared/bsp/hi/country_profiles/html/default.stm> This section offers up-to-date description of all countries in the world. It provides the reader with a brief historic background of each country, information about its current leader and government, and chronology of key historic events that shaped the country. There are links to further in-depth stories and analysis of current developments.
2 **On-line CIA Factbook** <http://www.cia.gov/cia/publications/factbook/>
CIA Factbook provides information on geography, population, and a brief description of current political and economic problems of every country in the world.
3 **Human Rights Watch Website** <http://www.hrw.org>
This website contains news and relevant information about current international conflicts. It circulates articles on global issues such as the status of refugees, minorities and women; its publications also address the question of human rights in foreign policy and provide an independent review of a state's performance. The web site contains valuable profile information about most countries in the world.
4 **Far Easter Economic Review Website** <http://www.feer.com/>
The website is a good source of information on recent political and economic developments in Pakistan, India, China, Indonesia and other Asian countries of the Far East.
5 **Eurasia Net Website** <http://www.eurasianet.org/index.shtml>
This Internet site offers reliable information about Central Asian states (Afghanistan, Azerbaijan, Mongolia, Turkey and others). The articles published on this site provide analysis of current developments in individual countries and in the region.

9 The future of geo-politics

1 Martin Wight, *Power Politics*, pp. 255-7. His scepticism was rare and farsighted at a time when the vast majority of Western practitioners and scholars misled the world about the relationship between non-proliferation and world order. I have discussed the problem of Western overconfidence and smugness about Indian and Pakistani nuclear policies and behaviour, and the over-reaction to the Indo-Pakistan tests in A. Shastri and A.J. Wilson, eds., *The Post-Colonial States of South Asia*, London: Curzon Press, 2001, ch. 15.
2 Lattimore, *Situation in Asia*, p. 224.
3 See B.R. Barber, 'Jihad vs McWorld', in R.K. Betts, *Conflict after the Cold War*, 2nd ed., New York: Longman, 2002, pp. 558–67.
4 Bozeman, *Politics and Culture*, introduction to Transaction edn, 1994.
5 Huntington, Clash of Civilizations, pp. 209–18.
6 From Wight, *Power Politics*, 299.
7 Ibid., ch. 7.
8 M. Wight, *System of States*, Leicester: Leicester University Press, 1977, pp. 34–5.
9 Huntington, Clash of Civilizations, pp. 186–90.
10 A. Kapur, 'China and Proliferation: Implications for India', in P.R. Kumaraswamy, ed., *China and the Middle East*, Delhi: Sage, 1999, Ch. 10.
11 'Expediency' means what is politic and advantageous, rather than what is right or just..
12 Ahmed Rashid, *Taliban: Militant Islam, Oil and Fundamentalism in Central Asia*, New Haven: Yale University Press, 2001.
13 Brzezinski, *The Grand Chessboard*, ch. 3.
14 Aziz Haniffa, 'US may have Forced Pakistan to Prune ISI', India Abroad (1 March 2002), 6; also Mubashir Zaidi, 'Pakistan Purges ISI of External Elements', *India Abroad*, (1 March, 2002, 12.
15 Aziz Haniffa, 'After Rebuff, US Welcomes Indian Nuclear and Space Czars', *India Abroad*, (1 March 2002), 6, and Aziz Haniffa, 'US Arms Sales to India to Cross $1 Billion by Year End', India Abroad (1 March 2002), 1 and 6.
16 Huntington, *Clash of Civilizations*, ch. 8.

10 From conflict to conflict resolution: an outline of the process

1 M.L. Sondhi, ed., *How India and Pakistan Make Peace*, New Delhi: Manav Publication, 2001.
2 Tony Armstrong, *Breaking the Ice*, Washington, DC: United States Institute of Peace Press, 1993.

Index

Page references in **bold** type refer to figures, maps and tables